BY FATE OR
BY
FAITH

THE SAGA OF A SURVIVOR

ISAAC GOODFRIEND

EDITED BY PERRY B. GOODFRIEND

LONGSTREET PRESS

Atlanta

Published by
LONGSTREET PRESS, INC.
2974 Hardman Court
Atlanta, GA 30305

Printed in the United States of America

1st printing 2001

Library of Congress Catalog Card Number: 2001091248

ISBN: 1-56352-666-2

Jacket and book design by Burtch Bennett Hunter

BY FATE OR BY FAITH

This book is dedicated to my life companion, Betty,
and to the memories of our parents,
Szoel and Pesse Gutfraind
Mordechai and Beila Grossman
and their children, our brothers and sisters,
who perished in the Holocaust.

B'gan ayden t'hay minuchatam
In Paradise may they find comfort.

PREFACE
BY THE AUTHOR

"Poverty, sickness and terror are easier to bear with faith."

— Ibn Gabirol, from *Mivchar Hapininim*

"The road is predestined, but the way we walk it, the attitude with which we bear our fate, can be of great influence over events."

— Beer-Hoffmann, 1945

My main purpose in writing this book is to share with the reader my life story. I do not pretend that mine is a unique story of a survivor of the Holocaust. It is, rather, a recounting of the people and events that helped to shape my life from the days of my childhood to the present. It is neither a manual nor a survival guide for future generations that might (God forbid) suffer similar trials. I am trying to convey to the reader that, for me, a synthesis between fate and faith is always the solution to any problem. In order to dissolve all the troubles that I came across in my life — from childhood through adolescence to maturity — I tried to deal with any given situation in the only way I knew: as a strong believer in my faith. As the great nineteenth-century Hasid, Rebbe Nachman of Bratzlav, said in his text *Likutay Aytzot*, "Where reason ends, faith begins." Faith alone is sufficient to carry one over all obstacles that life has to offer. Faith can solve everything, can fulfill your dreams, your wishes.

The reader will find that my encounters with fate were just as important to my survival as my faith. Our tradition always taught us that we do not rely on miracles. But at times of distress, when a person is drowning, he would accept any definition of rescue, whether it is miracle, faith or fate. Now that I stand on the shore and look back at the episodes I relate here, where my life was hanging by a thin thread, I know that my being saved by an unknown, supernatural force could have involved any one of the three.

Another purpose in telling my story is to relate that through all the despair, one need not lose the drive, the will to achieve their goals, to reach all they aspire to. I have reached my goals not in spite of my circumstances, but because of them. The same fate that kept me alive provided me with the opportunities to fulfill my dreams. Indeed, I have lived a life beyond my dreams. I have been able to serve not only my community, but also my country.

INTRODUCTION
BY ELIE WIESEL

Translated by Harvey M. Mendelsohn

In our group we called him "the hazzen," the cantor.

It was in 1979. As directed by President Jimmy Carter, the Holocaust Commission inaugurated a tradition that was to take the forum of an annual event: the commemoration of the tragedy of European Jewry during the Third Reich by a solemn ceremony in the most prestigious space in the Capitol, the Rotunda. The nation's leaders and other important figures were present. The president himself participated in the ceremony, delivering a moving address that reflected his ethical commitment to the victims' right to be remembered. Six candles were lit for the Six Million. Then it was Isaac Goodfriend's turn to intone the funeral chant imploring God to finally grant them peace. Everyone's eyes were filled with tears.

Since then, every year, the speakers and the other participants have changed, but not the cantor. Goodfriend has remained the stable element in the ceremonies. And each time, when his deep and melodious voice rises as if to climb to the heavens in order to plead for the martyrs, the men and women who are listening to him are touched to the depths of their being.

This is because Goodfriend is not only a cantor; he is also a storyteller. More precisely, he is a witness. And this book proves it. One reads it from beginning to end with a growing emotion mixed with sadness but also with gratitude. That is what I myself felt while reading it. It always happens to me: I cannot hold in my hand a survivor's testimony without thanking the author.

I have always believed this, and I believe it more and more: the writings of the survivors are among the most precious and the most necessary for understanding an Event that, very often, because of the magnitude of its horror and the depth of suffering endured, defies and surpasses understanding. Whether one would admit it or not, Auschwitz rises up like a monument of ashes accessible only to those who have been there. Even with the best will in the world and the greatest talent, one cannot really describe it or explain it.

But Auschwitz, sometimes, encompasses more than a place. One could live and die in its shadow. This is the case of Isaac Goodfriend. The story of his survival is in this sense exemplary.

Like other survivors, he evokes first of all the pre-war period. The youth of a Jewish boy born in the shtetl of Piotrokov. Adolescence in a Chassidic milieu in Lodz, and the Yeshiva in Sosnowiecz. His shopkeeper father, whose wife helped out in the store. Financial troubles, the Jewish holidays, a musical debut as a member of the synagogue choir, the joys of the Sabbath, his Bar Mitzvah, his commitment to Zionism. In short, everyday life. The feeling that, in spite of what was happening in Hitler-led Germany, everything would continue as before.

Then came the occupation. Like many Polish Jews, Isaac thought that it would not last a long time. How could he foresee subsequent events? The burning of the synagogue, with the Grand Rabbi inside. The first anti-Semetic measures. Vexations and humiliations. The ghetto and its misery. The threats. The separation: Isaac returns to Piotrokov, while his family remains in Lodz. The feverish quest for ways of warding off a thousand dangers, of overcoming despair, of just staying alive.

The reader, of course, will find in this book events that occur in other memoirs, but, at one level, each author preserves his or her unique personality for the very simple reason that each being is unique even when the destiny of all of them remains the same.

When Isaac Goodfriend sings Yizkor for the deceased, his pain expresses that which dwells in all those who hear him.

It is that pain which is also borne by this book.

PROLOGUE

Out of the corner of my eye I could see a little girl of not quite ten. She was standing to my right, looking up through her thick eyeglasses at every note leaving my mouth. She smiled and applauded loudly when I finished. It was Amy Carter.

"What a voice," Nelson Rockefeller said gruffly as he jabbed me with a friendly elbow and reached for my hand. The man who up to moments ago had been the vice president of the United States gave me one of his broad grins. I thanked him and tried to pull away to greet and congratulate the new president of our country, Jimmy Carter. I really wanted to be the first, but the chief justice who swore him in beat me to it. I turned to move toward the president, but Rev. Martin Luther King Sr. also slid in front of me and got to him before I did. Daddy King was one of the other members of what one Atlanta journalist called "The God Team," a small group of clergy assembled by President Carter to help celebrate his inauguration on a cold Washington, D.C. morning in 1977.

January 20, 1977, was my fifty-third birthday. In my family we usually celebrate birthdays with a card and maybe a small present after a quiet meal at home. I had known for about a month that this was not going to be one of those kinds of birthdays. Mostly, it began to hit me the day before, when I stood on the steps of the Capitol to do a sound check with the U.S. Marine Corps Band.

"This is where you will sit," our official marine escort, Lieutenant Colonel Bowers, pointed out as we walked down the stairs. "Mrs. Goodfriend will sit here," he pointed, "where Bob Hope sat for the last two inaugurations." That night, the marine handed me my schedule of activities for Inauguration Day.

At 8:30 in the morning I was taken to the barber to get my hair touched up. At 9, I gathered with the new cabinet designates and other dignitaries in the Capitol Rotunda, and we waited to go to our places. To say that I had butterflies would be an understatement. I was working with my entire mind to remain calm in the face of what was going to happen in the next few hours. Then a CBS reporter asked me, "How does it feel to know that 150 million people are about to hear you sing?" That certainly did not make anything less tense. But a newspaper reporter standing nearby overheard the question and pushed his tape recorder toward my face. "Yes, tell us how you feel," he said, "and what does this mean to you in terms of your past?"

I thought about it a moment as I tried to regain my composure, and I told them, "I feel a certain awe and reverence. It is the same feeling of humility I usually experience before I approach the pulpit on Yom Kippur to intone the most solemn prayer *Kol Nidrei*." The thought moved me. Every Yom Kippur, when I stood before God on behalf of myself and the congregation, any thoughts of being saved for some special personal destiny were humbled to an unwavering faith. This was how I came before Him, and it was this feeling that was with me now.

I was still calming myself when I felt Lt. Col. Bowers slide a piece of paper into my hand. I looked down at it and saw that it was the text to "The Star Spangled Banner." It was time for me to take my place. As I sat waiting for my cue, when I would walk from my seat to the podium and stand before the world and sing the National Anthem, the questions of the reporters came back to me:

"Cantor, how do you feel?"

How did I feel? Well, there was the numbness, the feeling of euphoria that held my mind as if it were in a jar. I was exuberant and I was frightened. If this was about my success, then I was satiated by the honor, but scared by not knowing if I deserved it.

"Cantor, what does today mean to you in terms of your past?"

I knew I was a man with painful memories standing victorious over a difficult past, but I found it hard to recognize the stages of my achievement. How had I managed to receive this great honor, or accomplish anything in my life? I was like a man near the top of a ladder who has spent so much time just stepping up that he has never looked down. Here I was, reaching a pinnacle of personal success, having it in my hand, and then asking, "Why me?" I did not ask for it. I did not search for it. I never would have thought to. It was as if I chose that exact moment to look down the ladder at where I had come from, and to realize how precarious I felt. I had been so busy living my everyday life that I did not know how high I had climbed.

It was my birthday and I was standing on the steps of the Capitol in Washington for the inauguration of a president; the day I was born was not just a lifetime away — it was a world away.

PART I

A HASIDIC
CHILDHOOD

---

*"One must study how to pray properly, that even the melodies be sung
with quiet introspection and the outcries come out in whispers, in
order to attach oneself to the presence of God."*

— Baal Shem Tov

CHAPTER
I

HASIDIM

I will go back as far as I can remember. There are also stories that were told to me when I was growing up from the times that I cannot remember. My family — that is, my parents and grandparents — belonged to a Hasidic sect called the Alexander Hasidim: a Hasidic dynasty.

There were a few Hasidic dynasties in Poland at the time. This particular dynasty traced its roots to the founder of the Hasidic movement, the Baal Shem Tov. In the year 1750, or thereabouts, the movement founded by the Baal Shem Tov branched out into different dynasties, or Hasidic courts, as they were called in those days.

There was one group of Hasidim that were followers of Rabbi Mendel of Kotsk, and their descendants became known as the Gerre Hasidim. And then there were the descendants of those who followed Rabbi Isaac of Vorke, who became the Alexander Hasidim. (There has always been a little rivalry between the Gerre and Alexander Hasidim.) The reason we were called Alexander Hasidim was that the seat of the group, and its spiritual leader, its Rebbe, was in the town of Alexander, Poland, less than twenty kilometers from Lodz, where I was raised. My entire upbringing was in the framework of this particular Hasidic movement.

My mother's family and my father's family belonged to the same group of Hasidim. I gather that is how the match between them was made, because they used to go to the same rebbe. When my father married into the Lipschitz family, he was given, as was the custom in those days, a year's *kest* — that is, the couple was given one free year of food and lodging by the bride's parents. It was toward the end of that year, in my grandparents' house in Piotrokow, that I was born.

My father was a traveling salesman for his family's dry goods business in Lodz. His name was Szoel. I remember him to be extremely good natured and always young looking, his beard trimmed neatly and tucked under his chin, his small *peyes*, or earlocks, tucked behind his ears. Those close to him lovingly knew him as Szoelshi.

I was born during the severe Polish winter. There was a big snowstorm in 1924 and my father, taking the train from Lodz, nearly missed my bris because he could not reach Piotrokow in time. My mother always reminded him, "You almost missed the bris of your son."

My mother, Pesse, was shorter than my father, with beautiful blue eyes and a face that was the epitome of kindness. I remember her to be logical, rational, intelligent and full of common sense. She was the oldest of nine girls. Her parents never had any sons, so I was the first boy born into the family, the first male. Well, it's understood that this was the greatest "simcha," the greatest joy, and a cause for celebration. Of course, everybody tried to spoil me — and rightfully so! After the year of the kest we settled in Lodz where my father's parents lived, and where he and my grandfather had their business.

＋━ ━＋

Parents always have ideas from the time a child is born of a direction they would like to see his or her life go. As part of the Hasidic movement, the course for a boy was clear, and his parents made plans for him — where he should be when he is five and six and seven and ten. The goal was for him to study, become learned, study more, become a scholar, and study even more.

Certain rituals were practiced at home, as part of our daily life, so we did not have to wait to go to school to learn them. My father saw to it that I made a blessing as soon as I could talk: to recite the blessing for bread; to say the first prayer of the day, thanking God for returning the soul to the wakened body; to say the prayer after I washed my hands and nails in the morning in the *naygel vasser*, the bowl of water, left at my bedside the night before. In order to learn how to read and to study, however, it was necessary to go to school.

I remember the first day that my father brought me to the classroom where all young Hasidic boys start their education, my first *cheder*. He quietly wrapped me in a big woolen prayer shawl and carried me to the rebbe. Being carried like that was the ritual for all three-year-olds beginning their religious education. The *cheder* was in an apartment building on the second floor. There were about twelve or fourteen other boys, most approximately the same age, and a few who were maybe two or three years older, but there were no children older than six. My cousin, Mendel, who was about my age, was in the same *cheder*.

The rebbe's name was Wiatrak — a mean-looking man — and I reacted the same way any child of three would react being left in a room full of strangers for the first time without Mother or Father. I cried a lot, especially when I saw the four leather straps, the disciplinary *kanchik*, hanging on the teacher's side. I was horribly frightened. I remember most of the kids were crying. You cry for a while, and then you get used to it.

It was the beginning of our formal education. We studied the Hebrew alphabet, reading mostly from the prayer book. We did not start immediately reading entire words. First we learned the aleph-beis. Then we matched the letters to the vowels, and recited them, "*Komets aleph aw, komets beis baw...*" and so on. After that, we learned the syllables, what we used to call *halb-traf,* and finally the complete words. Within a year we were supposed to be able to read, not fluently, but fairly well.

By the time I was four, I was going with my father to the *shtiebel,* a small room where other Alexander Hasidim would come to pray. My father had a very pleasing voice and loved to sing and conduct the services, and he expected me — after all, I'm already half a scholar at four — to be able to follow the service and join in the singing as well. This was no problem of course, because at home we recited the prayers and sang the traditional table songs, the *z'miros,* for the Sabbath and the festivals. *Z'miros* and *orchim,* Sabbath guests, were part of the atmosphere of yiddishkeit that engulfed my mother's table every Shabbes. Even during the times when food was not too plentiful, when we could not afford a bottle of wine for *kiddush* and had to boil a handful of raisins or currants, the meal was always *Shabbesdig.*

After eating, there was usually a discussion about the weekly Bible portion, the *sedra* that would be read the following morning in the synagogue. But as I said, I was only half a scholar at four! Children began studying the *chumash,* the Five Books of Moses, at age five. In those days three- and four-year-old boys looked forward to the great event of their fifth birthday in the same way that boys nowadays anticipate their Bar Mitzvah. First, you know that you are going to have a big party and your friends and your family will be invited. I remember the small, bright red packages of goodies, with my name written in gold on each one, that I gave out to the kids who came to my *Chumash Seudah.*

Also, I had to give a speech, a discourse on some portion of the Torah. At the age of five, the rebbe prepared you to give your speech. I remember the first few words, starting in Hebrew and then going over to Yiddish. But I was never given the opportunity to finish because the adults interrupted me with loud wishes of "Mazel Tov." Why did they do this? They felt they should not allow the child to say everything he knows, because it might bring an evil eye, an *ein horeh.* Somebody might say the wrong thing, such as "How beautifully he did!" This was not the proper Jewish way, not without adding "*kaynan horeh* (without the evil eye)," or turning and spitting to chase away the evil eye, as was the custom when you praised somebody.

The emphasis was put more on custom and tradition in Hasidic circles than on the strict interpretation of the laws on which the traditions were based. In most instances, custom became stronger than law. We did not question it because it was a natural, normal thing. For example, it was only about a two-minute walk from where we lived in Lodz to my grandparents' house, but I was never permitted to cross the street by myself to go there because the streetcar ran on the road where they lived. Even when I was older, my father or my grandmother used to hold my hand, or at least watch, when I crossed the street. One of the first things I ever learned was that the word of a parent, or most certainly a grandparent, was the law, and if they wanted to hold my hand crossing the road, I could not protest. Well, I could have, but it would not have done me any good. In fact, it would only have made it worse. Talk back, or question my elders? Obeying one's elders was to me, at the age of five, a tradition that had gone on for thousands of years, just as important as the fringed *tzitzis* I wore beneath my coat, and the *tefillin* my father put on his arm and head every morning. It was our way of life.

Similarly, when we started learning *chumash*, it was customary not to start a child from the beginning, from Genesis, but from the first chapter of Leviticus, the third book. The reason given was that this chapter deals with a clean sacrifice, "*b'lee mum*," without blemish, and a child of five is as pure as a sacrifice.

Chumash was taught in a different *cheder*. This *cheder* was also close to my house, but this time I walked instead of being carried. Instead of being upstairs, it was downstairs. The kids were older and it was a different environment. I remember this rebbe's name also, his nickname, that is. We used to call him "Parech" because of the pink blotches of psoriasis on his scalp: Nossen Parech. He was mean, too. He used to put kids in the corner, facing the wall, with their hands around a broomstick and their trousers pulled down to their ankles. This was his way of punishment, not for any mischievous things, but simply for not paying attention.

Of course, there was always beating and hitting. It was part of the education. I could not even come home and tell my father that the rebbe hit me, because he would say, "There must have been a good reason for it. Where did he hit you?" If I said, "This side," he'd say, "I'll have to finish it. Come on, I'll do it on the other side."

Double punishment! And he would keep hitting me until I told him that I would not do it again. He only did it because he wanted me to do better; he did not do it because of any real anger or hatred, and I never hated him because of it, God forbid.

At school, I also had lessons in Polish history and geography, math, and nature. We learned about the Polish kings, the tributaries of the great Vistula River, and plants and animals. My sister, Hinde Braindl, and I were seven and eight, respectively, and very close. She would help me with my homework in secular studies and I did pretty well. Polish grammar is very difficult. At home, we did not speak Polish; Yiddish was the mother tongue. At school, all my friends came from the same background, so I seldom had the opportunity to use Polish. While my education was continuing, my father had a tutor come to the house to teach us conversational Hebrew, with proper Hebrew grammar, as opposed to the Hebrew that we read in the Torah and the prayer book. This came in handy later in my life. He also taught us Yiddish literature.

Meanwhile, my religious education moved on to the study of Talmud when I was nine, and later, at age eleven, I went to a Yeshiva where secular and Hebrew studies were given equal time. The Yeshiva, sponsored by the Alexander Hasidim, was located in Lodz. Every day, my mother saw to it that we did our homework when we returned from school; she was very strict about it. My father would help me with my homework in the Hebrew studies, and my mother and Hinde Braindl would help me with my secular homework. My sister was an "A" student in Polish because the girls went to a regular school, learning the language as would any other Polish child. I was a better student in the religious subjects.

At the same time, all this education was not developed in my mind as a means toward the goal of finding a career. "What can I become?" was a question that did not apply to my way of life. Of course, like many other young boys, I thought about what it would be like to be a policeman or a fireman or even a soldier marching with a rifle. As kids, we used to take broomsticks and pretend we were soldiers. But in our society, career plans would not and could not be made. We took certain things one day at a time. All the planning for our lives was really in God's hands, anyway, according to the way we believed. A person can only plan to fulfill whatever daily obligations he may have, and to study.

The idea was for children being brought up in a Hasidic home, a strictly Orthodox home, to become knowledgeable in Jewish studies, like the Talmud and rabbinical teachings. The goal was not necessarily to become a rabbi, but to be educated as a Jew who practiced Judaism the way it was supposed to be practiced, and to know why it was observed in that way. I certainly did not think along the lines of being a rabbi, even though there were rabbis in my family. I was thinking about money.

CHAPTER
2

CITY LIFE

Piotrokow, where my mother's parents lived, had the feeling of an ageless Eastern European town, a typical *shtetl* flavor. I remember a particular visit there when I was a child. One of my aunts met me at the train station and we rode back to my grandparents' house in a *droska*. Now they have taxicabs, but then it was a horse and buggy.

As the Jewish driver took us through town, people stopped to watch us go by. "Who could it be?" they asked, "Where are they going?" It was everybody's business to know. That was the flavor of the *shtetl*. I was a new person to them, a stranger. They looked at me and who I was with and realized, "Oh, this must be Reb Beirish Lipschitz's grandson," and before long, the whole *shtetl* knew that I came to visit.

This was not the case in Lodz. Lodz was the second largest city in Poland. Most of the memories I have of life before the Second World War are from there. Even though it was a big city, my world within it was not much different than the life I would have had in a small *shtetl*, because I was a part of the Hasidic community.

Cheder was always within walking distance of the house, even if it took a half-hour to get there. I would meet my friends along the way, and dressed in our gray *kapotes*, we would walk to school. The *kapotes* were long robes of shiny gabardine. They were very light weight, the sort of material that might be used for lining today. For the Sabbath and holidays, we wore *kapotes* made of black silk. On our heads we wore the distinctive round hats with the little peaks, called *Yiddish hittels* because this kind of dress was associated with being Jewish. Hasidic men and boys all dressed this way.

There was a clothing shop that catered especially to Hasidim. A regular two-piece suit this tailor did not have. Once a year, usually before Passover, my father would take all the boys there to get new *kapotes*. Mother would take care of getting the girls' clothes.

On the street, my friends and I probably looked strange to the people who did not dress as we did. They certainly looked strange to us. We used to call them *daitshn*, meaning German. They were not German. They were Polish Jews, but their clothes and behavior on the street were "not Jewish enough." We looked down on them. It could be they looked down on us as well. From our point of view, they were goyim. A non-observant Jew in our eyes was considered a goy. That was the characterization, albeit an unfair one, imparted to us by the adults.

Hasidim took the prerogative of minding the business of every Jew in town, observant or not. For instance, Fridays at twilight the streets were full of observant Jews making their way to the synagogue or the *shtiebel* to welcome the Sabbath. On the street corners, vendors sold roasted pumpkinseeds, hot dogs, candy, nuts and other goodies for Shabbes. It was already close to the time for lighting the Shabbes candles, but they still were trying to make some last-minute sales. My father could not watch another Jew desecrate the Sabbath by selling. He would walk over and argue with them. "My God," he would say, "it's Shabbes already. Why do you still stand here? Go home already."

They were young boys, and full of spunk. "I didn't make enough money to buy a little bread for my mother," they answered my father, "I can't even buy a herring for Shabbes. You probably already have food in your house."

My father did not hesitate, "You're hungry? If you're hungry, come to my house and I'll feed you." None of the boys ever accepted this invitation, even though my father meant what he said. They stayed on the street perhaps ten minutes more, because they knew that once people started coming back from *shul*, they would not get any business. Even the Jews who were not religious would not buy because they did not want to antagonize the observant Jews returning from the twenty-five or thirty places of worship that were scattered around the neighborhood. As we walked home, we could see hundreds of people coming and going in all directions. We greeted each other, wishing even those who were strangers a good Shabbes.

After a while, the streets emptied and the sounds of families singing *zmiros* and making *kiddush* poured out of homes and into the night. Sabbath candles flickered from windows all over town, like fireflies caught in a jar. It was the time of the week for family gatherings. My father's sister would visit often, with a knock on the door as her only announcement. We did not have a telephone, and besides, if you were family or a close friend, you just had to show up: "Good Shabbes. I'm here," is all you would have to say to be welcomed to our home for a *shabbesdig* dinner.

After the meal, everyone remained around the table as a bowl of fruit and a plate of cookies and cake were spread out in front of them. The men would go over the Sedra twice, and then read Rashi and the other commentaries. The children would sing and play. Later everybody would read and discuss what was in the newspaper. In the wintertime, we would all sit around the oven chewing on roasted pumpkinseeds and spitting out the shells.

Among our own we lived the way it was proscribed. This was the whole idea of the Hasidic upbringing. Regardless of who you were or where you lived, there was a certain way of life that you observed. It is what we were taught and what we believed.

In Lodz, some Jewish people sent their children to the modern gymnasium, or secondary school. These Jews also dressed differently than we did, wearing more contemporary clothes, and of course, their heads were not covered. We did not ask, "Why can he walk like this when I can't?" We would not dare raise such questions. He was not I; we were different. Still, I had friends among the less observant boys, and there was a sort of envy on my part when I would be invited to one of their houses. I thought that I might want to be like them. It is normal for a boy to think that way. After all, they lived in a nicer area, in an apartment that had more than one room. My friend having his own bed, to me, was already a luxury. I had to share a bed with my father or my brothers.

Our apartment was in a block-shaped house that surrounded a small courtyard. You did not have to know the street number to find the building. It was sort of a landmark. People knew the place because for a long time, it had its own *mikvah*, a ritual bath, downstairs. The house had four entrances, but the main access was through a big gate in the front. At eleven o'clock at night the gate was closed. To get in after eleven we had to ring the bell, and Jozefier the superintendent — who was the only non-Jew living in the building — would come down and unlock the door. We used to give him something small, like ten groszyn, for letting us in. If we did not tip him, he would be mad at us, and besides, he had a big dog that I was afraid of.

Our apartment was directly opposite the main entrance on the second floor. The house had four stories altogether. There was no elevator, of course. That gave us kids stairs to race up and banisters to roll down. After all, children never walk when they can run. You entered our apartment through the kitchen; there was no entry hall or foyer. From the kitchen, we walked into the bedroom. On the left, as you entered the bedroom, was a large, chromium frame bed; on the right, there were two large beds for my parents, separated, of course. Hasidim did not put beds together. My mother's bed was the one closest to the warm tiles of the huge oven that heated the whole apartment from the kitchen. Against the wall across from the doorway loomed a large armoire that held all our clothes and books, and in the center of the room stood a table and some chairs. From the windows, we could look across the stone courtyard and see the big front gate. That was our apartment: a kitchen and a room that was the dining room and living room and bedroom and salon, all in one. Seven of us slept in that room, and we had a maid who slept in the kitchen.

Because my mother helped in the business, we needed a maid to take care of the small children. As I was the oldest, to me it seemed that we always had little ones, so we usually had maids. Most of them were Jewish, from other small towns, and usually they had references. They worked for room and board, and a little extra pay. After a year or two (or three) they would move on, so they never really had a chance to become part of the family.

With the seven of us and the maid living in such a small space, you might think that it would be crowded, but there was always room. For my

Bar Mitzvah, for instance, my father made a little *kiddush* in the apartment and somehow we fit forty people in the place. For Passover, we always had guests. We would move the table over to the children's bed, and the bed became a bench. We piled pillows on it so those sitting there could reach the table, with an extra pillow in one spot so the man who conducted the seder could sit like a king.

We never had a meal on a Friday night without guests. It was part of the Shabbes ritual. When you went home from the synagogue or *shtiebel* where you prayed, there were always about half-a-dozen people, students and strangers mostly, who had no place to go. My father knew without asking that if he saw a man standing and waiting at the door, this man had nowhere to spend Shabbes. My father would beckon the stranger to follow him home, knowing that it was not necessary to tell my mother to set another plate because such a guest was always welcomed. Whatever there was, we shared. Nobody went away from the table hungry.

During the week, I helped with household chores like chopping wood and going to buy something at the store. A chore like washing dishes was not heard of; by tradition, it was beyond a man's dignity to wash dishes. To me it was a great surprise to come to America and see a man putting on an apron and doing the dishes. It opened my eyes and I was shocked. A man washing dishes? But the girls did not chop wood, either. They helped my mother, whom I think was a superb homemaker, a great *baale-bussteh*, with the cooking and cleaning. When I was small, I used to watch my mother in the kitchen, and I would nosh from the pot cooking on the stove — a habit that, my wife will tell you, is still with me today.

CHAPTER
3

FAMILY

When I was ten or eleven, I worked in my father's dry goods store. Like my friends, I was expected to go into my father's business when I grew up. He had learned the business from my grandfather, whose store had a great reputation before the Depression, especially if you were looking to assemble a trousseau for your wedding. My grandmother, who was known as the "kupka" because of the garnet brooch she wore in the turban on her head, was the person a bride's family would come to, to *koifen dem oys-shteier*, to buy all one needs for a young couple starting a new life. Both my parents were involved in the operation in my father's store as well. I would try to help by measuring material, serving customers, or going to the trucking company with my father to ship out parcels that I had wrapped. I still tie packages today the same way my father taught me.

There were wonderful days at the store, and terrible days, and like many enterprises during the Depression, ours went broke. I remember closing down the shop and re-opening a short time later in a different place. I remember the creditors coming to our house. I could feel when there was money at home, and when there was not, and whether there was plenty of food, or just enough. I could sense it by looking at my parents' faces. When they would speak to each other about the hardships, I would overhear and want to say something, but I knew that I could not because a child did not meddle in the affairs of adults.

I remember one Passover, around that time. It was a bad season and the store was not doing well. Usually, before the holiday, my father would rent an oven at the local bakery and we would bake matzohs. The whole family would bring flour and pillowcases and after three hours, everybody would carry the pillowcases home filled with enough matzohs for the entire holiday. Likewise, there would usually be eggs in the house. But here it was, the day before Pesach, and there was nothing.

That evening, my father was getting ready to say the prayers before performing the traditional search of the house for *chometz*, crumbs of leavened bread and other food not approved for Passover. I usually prayed with him, just to sit next to him. I took my prayer book, even though I already knew the service by heart, and we began to pray together.

He sobbed as the words went from his heart to heaven. It was the first time I heard him cry, really cry, like a baby. He cried, and of course, I started to cry. My mother was in the kitchen, but I am sure that she heard it too. I knew why my father cried. With just a look, a squeeze of the hand, I could feel his distress.

"God will help," I told him. Of course, I did not know this for certain, but it is what a Jew says in times of trouble. "God will help."

At 7:30 the next morning, my father stood in the little mall, in front of the door to his shop, turned the key, and opened for business. He did not expect many patrons on this troubling Erev Pesach, so when a customer entered the store a short time later, my father's heart lit up. It was one of his regular customers who happened to be in town. A cash customer! And he bought quite a bit of merchandise. My father came running home immediately and told my mother. Oh, it was *yontif*! Happiness was in every corner of the house. I was jumping for joy.

In my father's mind, his prayers were heard in heaven. There was no other way. He would not attribute it to the fact that the customer just happened to be in Lodz at the time and happened to be looking for merchandise. God sent this man. There was no other way. This was how strongly he believed and, of course, I believed exactly the same thing. You should never lose faith, never lose faith.

I often wondered why my two aunts, my father's sisters, did not come forward to help during that time. They lived nearby, with their husbands, in my grandparents' house. For a couple of years already my father and his sister Toba had not been talking. I did not understand why a brother and sister would not talk, why they were enemies. When I was told that I should not play with their son, I said, "But he's my cousin." I could not understand why I should act the same way the grown-ups were acting, but I also could not ask any questions. Had I asked, I would not have gotten an answer anyhow.

Sometimes, I would walk over to my grandfather's house to study. He used to get up at five o'clock to learn. I would spend the night so I would be there when he woke up. He would wake me, and together we would sit and learn until it came time for the morning prayers. He was pious and observant, of course, but he was also a great scholar.

My grandfather also was a kind man who would not let his daughters and their husbands struggle alone, so two of his daughters, Chanale and Toba, lived in his apartment with their husbands. It gave me sort of an unpleasant feeling when I visited my grandfather's house, because not only were my Aunt Toba and her husband not speaking to my parents, but they were not talking to my grandfather either, and they lived in the same apartment! A daughter should not talk to her mother and father? Are they really enemies? You have an argument, and then you make up.

Eventually I was told what it was my aunt and uncle had done to cause this rift. When the collapse of the world's economy hit Europe in 1930, Toba, her husband Itche Stern, my father and grandfather were all partners in my grandfather's business. Late one night, they took a truck to the store below my grandfather's apartment at Nowomjenska 26 and carried out every piece of merchandise, goods that belonged to my father and grandfather, and they opened a store of their own. My father and Toba never spoke again, even to the day of his funeral. And though my grandfather was deeply hurt by the actions of my aunt, he still let her stay in his home.

My grandfather's name was Reb Fishel Gutfraind. Because of his unique relationship with people, and his inner refinement, he was known within the community as a "*scheiner yid*," what we might call today a dignified person. When I went to the synagogue with him, he was always greeted warmly. I was proud to be there when the people would come over to show him their respect.

My grandfather had the unique honor of being a *tish zitser*, which means he sat at the rebbe's table. Only great scholars and dignitaries were given such an honor. To me, this achievement made me feel as if I had great *yichus*, or honored lineage. *Yichus* was of great importance in those days. If you came from a wealthy family, that was a different kind of status. We did not have money. We had our roots, our family tree, and our reputation. This was *yichus*.

Hannale, my father's oldest sister, was considered the crown of all the daughters that his parents had. Unlike the sister with whom my father had problems, Hannale's deeds and actions made her the true *aishes chayil*, the "Woman of Valor," that we read about in Proverbs. Her husband was the confidante of two Hasidic rabbis. If he were alive today, I would call him a Kissinger.

His name was Avram Kubets [ז״ל (of blessed memory)], but everybody called him *der kleiner Avramele* because he was very short. Years later, I received a letter from the Alexander Yeshiva in Israel from someone who remembered my uncle. He had given him an even more descriptive title: "The unforgettable dynamo of the Alexander Dynasty."

I never remember seeing Avramele walking; he was always running. He was an arbitrator and a sort of troubleshooter. His connections reached all the way to deputies of the Polish Seym, and he was able to use his influence to keep religious boys out of the draft. He also helped people get out of jail, not for remuneration, but just to do a good deed.

Within the community, his devotion was so strong that he became a policy maker for the Hasidic movement. Whenever I visited the court of the Alexandera rebbe, no matter how busy Avramele was — and he was always busy — when he saw me, he stopped what he was doing, took my hand, and dragged me wherever he wanted. I went along without saying a word, because I knew that wherever he was taking me was a good place to be. Sometimes he would take me directly to the rebbe just so I could be in his presence. When he was not with the rebbe, my uncle was with the family. He and my aunt were not blessed with children, and because he was so busy, my aunt usually took care of the business. Hannale knew that at any time he might pick up his tallis bag and tefillin not to go pray in the synagogue, but to catch the streetcar to Alexander and see the rebbe.

My father always looked up to Hannale. He was the youngest and she was the oldest. My father was the little boy that everybody took care of, the one they always protected. I was proud of his vivaciousness. He was always smiling, always happy, always singing. My father loved to sing, and he had a pretty good voice, even though he had never studied voice or music. Although he was not a professional cantor, he was the *ba'al tefila* in the *shtiebel*, singing and conducting services, and I loved to help him by singing along.

On Saturday afternoons, I would get together with a few kids and, wearing towels as prayer shawls instead of *tallesim*, we pretended to have a service and one of us acted as cantor. Being that I was blessed with a voice, I would sometimes conduct the mock service that was complete with a small choir.

Some of my friends sang in the choir at the Workers' Synagogue, which was only two blocks from where we lived. My father never permitted me to sing in this choir because, he said, the synagogue was too free, too progressive. It was the synagogue of the tailors and the cobblers, the very poor families. There was only one boy in the choir who wore Hasidic dress. Still, when I went there to watch my friends and hear them sing, my eyes opened wide enough to swallow them up in awe.

When I was six years old, I became a *meshorer* in the choir that was singing with the rebbe of Alexander. They needed a boy's voice, and my uncle, who also had a tremendous voice and sang in the rebbe's choir, asked me to be his *tsu halter*, his helper. Like every Hasidic movement, we had our own *nigunim*, our own melodies. Because of the privilege of being in the rebbe's choir, I was able to learn the songs before anybody else. I had a good memory for music, even though I did not know how to write it down, and I only had to hear a song once to pick it up.

Every Shabbes afternoon before the High Holiday season, my father and I would meet with one of the Hasidim who used to compose the new music for the holidays. These songs were a closely guarded secret. The older men used to try to get me to sing the new compositions for them, and I would say, "No, I have sworn not to sing them until after the holidays. I don't give out any secrets."

Sukkoth was my big debut. The neighbors would come to the community *sukkah* in the courtyard of our building, and my father would ask me to chant a *nigun*. I sang for the pure enjoyment of carrying a tune, to be sure, but I also sang because of the thrill of being the center of attention. After all, when I was at a party and sang, all the goodies on the table were mine for the taking! If my father were taking me somewhere, I knew that at any time he might want me to sing so he could show me off. He took me around with him all the time, so much so, it seems that when I was not at *cheder* or doing my homework, I was off somewhere with him.

From the time I was five years old, I went with my father to the rebbe for the holidays and festivals. I do not remember exactly how Rosh Hashana, Yom Kippur, Pesach or Shavuos were observed at home because we spent those days with the rebbe and slept at my uncle's house, nearby. Spending that much time together made my father and me very close. When things were difficult for him, I could feel his pain, and when things were going well, I could feel his happiness.

My father raised me and my brothers and sisters as was customary in those days. In other words, when he thought we deserved spanking, he did not hesitate to discipline us. He used to say that he spanked us so that we would learn not do it, whatever it was, again. We may not have agreed that we deserved to be punished, but we knew not to resist. In his eyes, we committed great sins that deserved a firm hand across the behind.

I remember one pleasant Saturday afternoon in the summertime, I went to the park with some friends instead of going to the rebbe to study *Pirke Avos*, a portion of Mishna known as "Ethics of our Fathers." It was customary to study the *Perek*, as it was called, on Shabbes afternoons during the summer. The park was far from my house and by the time we returned home, it was pitch dark. I walked through the door with my hands covering my backside because I knew what was coming. Today, I would not spank my children for the kinds of transgressions that raised my father's anger.

I regret not living with my father long enough to get to know him better. I was only seventeen when he died. Just as I was becoming mature and needing him to help me understand a little more about life, he was no longer there. In my heart I hold only loving memories of the brief time that he was part of my life.

Although we lived closer to my father's family, we saw a lot of my mother's relatives, who visited from Piotrokow quite frequently. Of course, they stayed with us. To me, and my brothers and sisters, it was like a holiday when our grandmother, or grandfather, or any of our mother's eight sisters would visit. I am not sure why, but we always felt closer to my mother's side of the family. It was more than the goodies that they brought for us; I know they felt close to us as well.

I was proud of belonging to this side of the family — not that I was less proud of my father's family (a boy always looks up to his father) but the *yichus* of my mother's family was one of unbelievable character. For example, my grandfather's brother, who moved to Lodz when I was twelve, was a recognized rabbi among the six ruling rabbis of the city. He was also the son-in-law of one of the first rebbes of Alexander. "You know who my uncle is?" I boasted, "Rabbi Elazar Lipschitz."

If I were ever to picture the face of the Prophet Elijah, it would be my Uncle Elazar [ז״ל]. He was tall, with a face like an angel's, and a snow-white beard to his waist that was so fine, you could count every hair. He had tremendously long eyebrows; I have never seen anyone with eyebrows the size this man had. From behind his warm smile, he would teasingly test me on what Torah I had learned.

When he recited the *kiddush*, I was afraid to look at his face because of the way he completely divorced himself from the earthly existence. He was "up there," somewhere on high. His eyes would turn and it was like looking into the face of God or a saint. When I talked with him, it was with a certain awe and a great reverence.

I was afraid to call him Uncle Elazar, because then I would have to say his name. That is not the way things were done in our circles. Even when I was talking to my father or mother, I never addressed them in the second person. I always said, "Let my father do..." or, "Let my mother do..." out of respect.

I had the greatest respect for my grandfather, Reb Berish Lipschitz [ר״י]. I still have not met a man as virtuous as he. I would classify him among religious people as very saintly. Besides observing the laws of the Torah and the rabbis, he would do more. He practiced Hasidism the way it was meant to be practiced, going beyond the requirements of the law.

For example, an observant Jew had to do something in order to follow the commandment of preparing for the Sabbath. A religious Jew thought about *shabbes kodesh*, the Holy Sabbath, all week. In our tradition we hold that the three days after a Sabbath belong to the Sabbath that has passed, and the next three days are part of the Sabbath to come. In the Talmud it is written that certain rabbis did something for the Sabbath: one prepared the fish; another prepared by shopping for the Sabbath. Being that my grandfather had nine daughters, there was no place for him in the kitchen, so he used to put the knives to a whetstone and sharpen them. Then he would cut the toilet paper into pieces for the whole family so they would not violate the law against tearing on Shabbes. Then he would go to the *mikvah*, the ritual bath, and purify himself for the Sabbath.

I always looked forward to visiting my grandparents in Piotrokow. Even though it was only forty-four kilometers away, it was like taking a big journey for us children, spending a few hours on the train or the bus. I was there one Shabbes, and I went to my grandfather to get some toilet paper before I walked down the steps and through the long courtyard to the outhouse. He said to me, "What do you mean, you didn't prepare? A Jew prepares for Shabbes."

To him, it was a great catastrophe that I did not cut up paper for myself. I was only a child at the time. He was trying to impart to me, especially because I was his grandson, the value of custom and tradition, even to the minute detail of preparing toilet paper. It annoyed him that one would attempt to be observant, and yet would forget to do certain things that by law or tradition were obligatory.

The same thing went on with the white yarmulkes we wore when we slept. When I was little, I loved to sleep in my grandfather's bed and cuddle beside him. We would pray before going to sleep. When I got up, I could never find my yarmulke; it would always fall off. "I don't understand," my grandfather used to say, "I too wear a yarmulke; my yarmulke never falls off." It was in a friendly manner that he spoke, not in anger. He never raised his voice to anyone; he controlled his anger and did not express his emotions. Still, he meant every word he said. There was no joking around when it came to these things. He used to admonish me for a simple thing like laughing. To him, laughter was mundane.

Simply to laugh was not Jewish to him, and neither was the Polish language, especially on Shabbes. Many times he would exhort my aunts, his daughters, when they would speak Polish to each other on Friday nights. "Do you have to speak the language of the superintendent?" he would ask. To him, our superintendent was the caretaker and, like the man who cleaned the streets, to speak as he did was a degradation of the Sabbath. The superintendent was the one who was used as a *shabbes goy*, the non-Jew who would light the oven, turn the electricity on and off, and would do other things that a Jew was forbidden to do, or could not prepare for, on the Sabbath. For example, Jozefier, our superintendent in Lodz, was also our *shabbes goy* there. His hands were always so black from coal that he could not touch the fresh, white pieces of challah we gave him when he helped us on the Sabbath. Instead, the bread went from our hands into the pocket inside his coat that opened into a sack-like lining, so that by the end of his duties in the building on Friday night, his coat was inflated like a dough-filled mattress. To speak the language of such a man as this, my grandfather felt, was sacrilegious and a desecration of the day.

Still, there was a special warmth between my grandfather and his nine daughters. I remember how, one by one, they kissed him on the forehead in greeting. He had a dowry prepared for each of them, despite the economic difficulties of the time.

My grandmother was stricter with my aunts than he was. She ran the household. I remember her being angry with my grandfather because of how much water he used. There was a man in Piotrokow we called Avram the water carrier, who carried buckets of water to the house. We had running water, but most of the time, especially in winter when the pipes froze, it did not work. With girls, you need a lot of water. My grandfather used a lot because, being that he was so observant, he would fulfill the commandment of reciting one hundred blessings a day, and in order to recite a blessing, he had to wash his hands. Before an observant Jew eats fruit, there is a blessing; when he finishes eating, there is a blessing; after coming out of the bathroom, there is a blessing. My grandmother used to argue with him: "Why do you use so much water to wash your hands and recite your blessings all day long?" she would ask. "Think of that poor man carrying those pails of water...."

My grandfather was busy day and night with a twofold purpose: to serve God and his family. By day, he was a businessman. He dealt in men's and ladies' hosiery. Sometimes he visited Lodz to buy merchandise, and he would stop by to visit us. As the years went by, his children would make the buying trips, but he usually went along. He was held in the highest respect by his business associates because of his integrity.

At his house, as long as his eyes were open, as long as he was awake, I rarely saw him without a book. He did not go to movies or the theater. There was neither a record player nor a radio in the house. This man would not sit down for a minute without something to read. He only got up to visit with his brothers, who came by often, or to go to the synagogue and pray. He was unusual; even among his own family, his brothers, he was considered the most saintly and highly respected.

CHAPTER
4

MY BAR MITZVAH YEAR

When I was thirteen, I was called to the Torah for an *aliya* for the first time and this was my Bar Mitzvah. There was no big party. My father had a *kiddush* for me in our small apartment, and to mark the occasion of my being counted as part of a minyan for the first time, I was given the opportunity to lead the Grace After Meals. My father had *tefillin* ordered from a scribe in Warsaw, written especially for me. This was not commonly done. In those days it cost a small fortune. Chaim Ben-Tzion was one of the finest scribes in Poland. Not only was he a great scribe, but he had a beautiful voice and would conduct the *Shacharis*, the morning services, at the rebbe's house during the High Holidays.

I kept those *tefillin* with me until I escaped the Nazi labor camp in 1943 and went into hiding. I could not take them with me because of the danger in case I was caught. It pains me to this day that I had to leave them behind.

My Bar Mitzvah was in 1937. That year, I was sent away to Yeshiva in Sosnowiec, a small town in the Polish coal mining region of Silesia, at the western edge of the Carpathian Mountains. Just like the Yeshiva in Lodz that I had gone to the previous year when I lived at home, this one was run by the Hasidic Movement to which we belonged. To this day, I don't know why my parents sent me away for that particular year. There was a belief, though, that you study better when you are living away from home.

There was a great rabbi in this particular city. He was the richest rabbi of the Hasidic Movement in all of Poland. One might say, his wealth was twofold. His family owned a large textile plant, so he had money, and he was a rebbe, with a dedicated group of disciples. I visited him when I was in the town, so I could hear and learn his *nigunim*, his melodies. I was too shy to sing. Even when I was among my own, I always had a lump in my throat when I had to sing. It did not matter that I was used to being around the same sort of people at home. Being out in the world, my behavior was no different.

The whole experience of being so far away from home, however, was very exciting to me. Besides meeting other boys from all over the country, I had my first taste of independence, without my parents or grandparents around to check on everything that I was doing. Still, because we were such a close family, it was a funny feeling to be suddenly away from them. My parents wanted me to write a letter every week. This was a great ordeal for a couple of reasons: first, I was not very good at writing letters, and especially lazy when it came to answering them; and second, I wasn't sure exactly what I should tell them. If I said that I was studying every waking moment, that would have been a lie; if I said that I was not studying all day, then what was I doing there? The only answer was to study as often as I could, and when I was not at my books, to do other things that my parents would believe were good for my religious experience.

I slept in the same house as some other boys, not at the Yeshiva itself. There were four kids in one room, five kids in another. My host was the watchmaker. The Yeshiva paid him a certain amount each month or week for housing the students. My parents did not have the means to send me money so that I could afford to feed myself. When it came to meals, *Ich hob gegessen teg* — I ate days, as we used to say. In other words, everyday, I would eat at somebody else's house. For the hosts, helping out a Yeshiva *bocher*, giving him one less thing to worry about so he could concentrate on his studies, was a form of charity.

There was one day of the week when I would eat with a certain family that had two girls. Their names were Esther and Bracha, and I remember that they were good looking, at least, by the way I judged looks in those days. As the weeks would roll around to the day I was to eat at this particular house, the other boys would tease me. "Yeshiva *bocher*," they would say, "Oh! There's Bracha. Look! There's Esther." I still remember the tingling in my face when I blushed.

On Saturdays I ate at the house of the richest man in the community. I was very lucky to have a day to eat with him. His house occupied the entire first floor of a building. It had two entrances from the outside leading to twelve rooms on the inside. The dining room was as huge as any you would find in a palace, and it was normal for there to be thirty people for a meal. Family, strangers and friends sat around a lavish table with real silver settings and food that was as varied as it was plentiful. He had servants and a large family for them to serve.

That year, Purim fell on a Sunday, and one Shabbes, the rich *balehbus* invited me to return the next day for the Purim Seudah that he was hosting. I knew it would be a big celebration and I would be asked to sing. I also knew that Sundays I ate with another family, and they too were looking forward to having me over for a Purim Seudah of their own. I had a dilemma, which the rich *balehbus* solved for me. "You'll come and be with us here," he said (sounding like Tevye from "Fiddler on the Roof"), "and then you'll go to your place where you go Sundays. You'll eat twice!" What could I do? I could not insult the richest man in town.

I not only ate twice as much; I drank twice as much. On Purim a Jew drinks until he is so *shicker*, he doesn't know the difference between praising Mordecai, the hero of Purim, or cursing the villainous Haman. One family made me drunk, and then another made me drunker. How much beer could I drink at the age of thirteen? I was sick for a week.

At some of the other houses where I ate, it was not unusual for me to be tested by the *balehbus*. There was one in particular, a dignified man with a beautiful beard, who was always studying. I did not feel very comfortable going there because I knew that he was going to ask me what I learned, so I actually had to study before coming to his house.

On the other hand, I always looked forward to Fridays. That was the day that I ate at the leather man's house. The smell of freshly tanned leather drove me crazy! There were other smells in the house that were nearly as intoxicating: the fatty, but rich, aroma of fried *gribbenes*, the warm, fresh cornbread and a cake so special I can still taste it. I felt that after eating there on Friday, even if I had no other place to eat the rest of the week, I would be satisfied.

One day, while at this Yeshiva, word reached me of a tour being organized to visit the grave of a great rabbi. His name was Dovid of Leluv. For short, they called him Reb Dovidel. He was considered to be a miracle worker by many Hasidim. The stories and legends surrounding this rebbe were fascinating. For instance, religious boys did all they could to keep from being drafted into the anti-Semitic, Polish army. It was believed that if a boy who was about to be drafted visited Reb Dovidel's grave on the anniversary of the rabbi's death, his *yartzeit*, and the boy prayed very hard, then somehow he would be able to avoid conscription.

The older boys at the Yeshiva all told me that the yearly journey to Reb Dovidel's grave was the most fascinating trip that I would ever take. They told me that by tradition, you had to get lost on your way there. In his book, the story went, Reb Dovidel had written, "...when you come to my grave, on my *yartzeit*, and you find your way, without getting lost, in that year the Messiah will come." Losing your way was not a difficult thing to do, since the village was not on the map, and was tucked in among ten other similar towns.

The whole thing sounded like a fairy tale to me. It seemed that it was a mystical way to observe the *yartzeit*. If you believed these stories, then you had to believe and follow the way of life of this miracle man. If you had to question the stories, then you did not really believe them. I was intrigued. It cost me about a dollar for the bus ride and some food, to join the tour and find out for myself what it was really like. Although it was a lot of money for a Yeshiva *bocher* away from home, I had managed to put away the few zloty that my parents had sent. There was also a local merchant who had owed my father some money for a couple of years, and, with my father's encouragement, I was able to collect it from him. So, getting a few zloty from one, a few more from the other, I had enough for a rainy day and enough for the trip to Reb Dovidel's grave.

I went with a friend, being afraid to travel alone. We had a deal. "If you go, I'll go," he said, so we went together. We started out around seven in the evening from Krakow. It was toward the end of February, when the winter nights in Poland are long and cold. The roads were covered in snow, and in some places the snow had begun to melt. Along the way, we listened to more stories about the miracle man, especially the one about getting lost. Sure enough, we lost our way and the bus got stuck in the mud. It was certain that the Messiah was not coming that year.

By the time we reached the village, it was not quite dawn, but in the fading darkness, the little town was wide awake. The shops and restaurants in the square were opening for the thousands of pilgrims that were expected. The square, in fact, was the whole town. As we used to say, if the horse's harness was past the town, the wagon was in town! The pilgrims came by bus, by wagon, and even by foot from nearby *shtetls*. Most were Hasidim, but there were others in common clothes. We went from the bus to the *mikvah*, which had already been prepared, and, as was the tradition before visiting a cemetery, we bathed. The little mausoleum that marked Reb Dovidel's grave was in the cemetery, next to the *mikvah*.

Once inside, I saw mountains of bits of paper that people had dropped there. People gave me a lot of little notes to intercede on their behalf, to pray for them. Some notes had a few passages of Psalms, or a simple plea for whatever it was the person who authored the note wanted. I remember thinking, "Is he going to read all these notes?" But just leaving the prayer made you feel as if you had done the right thing.

I had been told about how crowded the tiny structure around the grave became at this annual ritual. Reb Dovidel was a man of small physical stature, and his grave was built to match his size. There was not enough room in the mausoleum for the thousands who were streaming through it that day. There was only one doorway, and once inside, it was impossible to push against the flow of people to leave the way you came in. The only way out was through a window at the other side of the mausoleum. It was a small opening, and two big men waited outside to pull each petitioner through it. Once I was out, I was relieved. "Mission accomplished," I thought.

Afterwards, we went to a restaurant for warm rolls and milk, and whatever other food they served us, and then we boarded the bus for the trip back to the city. We traveled through the most beautiful areas of Poland, past mountain forests more lush than any I had ever seen. The bus stopped, and we went to a cool river and splashed some water on our faces. Some who had been on this trip before brought empty bottles to fill with the fresh, spring water that rolled down the hill. I cupped my hands and drew some water from the spring to my lips. It tasted heavenly.

Of all the stories I had from my year away at Yeshiva, the tale of the visit to Reb Dovid of Leluv's grave was my favorite. I told it often when I returned to Alexander the next year to study at the Yeshiva there. My grandfather was tired of hearing it. "Never mind the stories," he told me, "How much did you learn?"

CHAPTER
5

THE YESHIVA *BOCHER*

I returned home from the Sosnowiec Yeshiva in 1938, and was then sent to study in the Alexandera Yeshiva, where the rebbe was. Although the school was only a streetcar ride away from my parents' house in nearby Lodz, I spent the year living with my mother's sister and her husband in Alexander. I had been going to their house for all the holidays and festivals since I was five years old because they lived so close to the rebbe. In the mornings, I walked from there to the Yeshiva; it was not far. In a small town like Alexander, nothing is far.

At the Yeshiva, I was considered to be a *bocher* who had been around. After all, I had come from the Yeshiva in Sosnowiec. I was here and I was there, and because of my Uncle Avramele's close relationship with the rebbe, I was considered privileged.

The teachers at the school guided our learning, but because we were older, we were given more time to study on our own. The headmaster gave one lesson of Talmud a day, and afterwards, we formed ourselves into study groups of two or three or four. If we were studying something that I liked, of course I paid closer attention to it and wanted to know more about it. There were always some older boys, and even scholars, walking around the Beis Midrash, in case I had a problem understanding the tract of Talmud I was studying. If I had a dilemma, I walked over, and asked them a question pertinent to the text. "How do you solve this passage?" I would ask, "I don't understand it."

They explained it to me, telling me its meaning, why this rabbi said that or that rabbi said this. We were encouraged to ask and to challenge. That is the whole idea of studying the Talmud: asking questions so you can learn. It was put into our minds that we were not studying just to show the world that we could read Talmud; for the sake of knowledge and understanding, we had to study, as it is written: "you shall dwell on the Torah day and night."

Sometimes I had to study extra hard because I knew that I would be having Shabbes dinner at the home of this or that rabbi, some great scholar. I was invited for dinner, but I lived in fear of what came after dessert. They were always testing me to see how much I knew — although "test" may not be the proper word. It was more like an inquisition! I would study and memorize, but no matter how prepared I thought I was, they would ask me something else. They tried to catch me on just a little nothing of a mistake, just to show that they knew more than I did. They had a way of twisting and messing you up so they would come out the winners. Sometimes I came across a decent man who was not too cruel, but mostly, they were relentless.

There were some that I learned to stay away from. When I saw them on the street, I quickly crossed to the other side because I was afraid they would ask me something. I might have known the answer, but I did not want to be asked.

Looking back on it, I think that this tactic of scholarly intimidation was counterproductive for me personally, and for the other boys as well. It made me wonder, "Why should I bother knocking my brains out studying? Because I have to please this guy? I might as well give it up, not study at all and play a little...run on the ice, throw snowballs...."

Playing is something we did not do at Yeshiva. We knew nothing of television, and had no radio. Books, such as novels, were taboo, because the feeling was that if you have to read anything besides the *Chumash* and the Talmud and anything related to Torah, you do not belong at the Yeshiva.

The only time I saw a newspaper was at my uncle's house when I came home to sleep. My father used to get the newspaper also, and I remember there was a serialized novel about Chicago gangsters, like Al Capone, running in it everyday. It was fascinating, but I could not be caught reading that when my father or grandfather was in the house. Secular novels were strictly underground reading material, even if they appeared in a newspaper.

Because of our limited view of the outside world, we often came into conflict with other observant Jews who were not Hasidim. I will never forget one episode, while I was at the Yeshiva in Alexander. After *mincha*, the afternoon service, on the eve of Yom Kippur, it was traditional to put out plates for different charities. The people would throw a few coins on the plates as they left for their final meal before the Yom Kippur fast began. I was put in charge of watching the plates. Some young people came around who were clean — and wearing regular suits. They were not Hasidim; they were non-religious Zionists, members of Betar. They brought a plate to put out for Keren Kayemet, the Jewish National Fund. I did not see anything wrong with it because charity is charity, *tzedakah* is *tzedakah*. But the older *bocherim* — they were supervisors already — almost started a fistfight. "This is not the place for Keren Kayemet," they screamed, "this is the place for charities for our Yeshivas and our movement."

Others said, "They are Jews, and charity is charity. It's for *Eretz Yisroel*, the land of Israel." But the older boys had already chased the Betar out. I was an innocent bystander and just had to make sure that no one took money from the plates.

I always looked forward to the Sabbath. Every Shabbes I was at the rebbe's *tish*, his table. The rebbe did not eat with his family; he ate with his Hasidim. A meal at the rebbe's table was more than just a meal. Hasidim surrounded the table to get just a taste from the *shirayim* of the rebbe, the leftovers from his plate. An amount the size of an olive, from whatever food was blessed by the rebbe, was enough to protect you from thieves, murderers, mad dogs — from any and every evil in the world. Privileged people were given a place to sit around the table. My grandfather was given the great honor of being a *tish zitser*. I was not that lucky, but when I was a child, my privilege was getting to go under the table. I took some friends with me and we poked at someone's knees, and down came a piece of challah, meat or fish. I knew whose pant legs I had to pull on to get something, usually my Uncle Avram's.

One Pesach, I remember, Avramele passed me the rebbe's gilded soup bowl. For Passover seder, the rebbe's *tish* was covered with silver dishes, special for the holiday. The spoon was still in the bowl as it came at me from between my uncle's knees; usually, the rebbe's spoon was lost in the tumult of a hundred hands scooping up the hot soup right from the bowl. Avramele got away with it because he could do anything he wanted. After all, he had carried this rebbe when the sage was just a baby.

After crawling around under the table with all those boots and legs, my fine, black *kapote* was covered in dirt. When I came home, my mother asked, "Where have you been, to get so filthy? Look what you did to yourself!" But I did not care; I got to eat the rebbe's *shirayim*.

When I was a Yeshiva *bocher* already, and too old to crawl under the rebbe's *tish*, I stood around the table and was shoved and jostled by the one hundred other black robed Hasidim pressing against me. They also wanted the blessings that came from being and eating with the rebbe on Shabbes. I was given the honor of singing *z'miros*. This was a great thing. I was scared to death, because to sing before the rebbe was like singing before kings, queens and presidents.

+— —+

One morning, Avramele, my uncle, telephoned the rebbe, and I was summoned home from the Yeshiva. My grandfather, Reb Fishel Gutfraind [ז״ל], had died.

My grandfather had been very ill for nearly a year before he passed. He was so well thought of by the Alexander rebbe that he received a visit from him when he was ill. The rebbe did not pay calls on just anybody. It was an exceptional honor that he came to visit. Word of the rebbe's visit spread so fast that Hasidim by the thousands lined the streets of Lodz simply to get a look at him on his way to and from our house.

I remember my grandfather telling me about the discussion he had with the rebbe. In a portion of the Talmud, there is a story of one rabbi visiting another who is sick. The sick person stretched out his hand and said, "He gave him his hand and he got up," and so my grandfather reached out his hand to the rebbe and quoted in Aramaic from the

Talmud, "*Yawhiv lo yawday v'ukmay*" (Ber. 5b).

The rebbe took his hand and replied, "Your hand is fourteen, and my hand is fourteen, and that is twenty-eight, the numerical value of strength." *Yad*, the Hebrew word for hand, because of the letters in it, has a value of fourteen, and two hands add up to twenty-eight, which makes the word *koach*, the Hebrew word for strength.

When I returned home for the funeral, I heard my father crying, wailing loudly, and that was all I needed. I was more overwhelmed by his pain and suffering, I think, than I was by the loss of my grandfather. This was my first experience with the death of a close family member. I did not know what to say. We were not taught how to deal with death, and there were no words that my parents could find to explain it to us. Explanations were considered unnecessary. We were taught about the laws and customs regarding death, of course, but that was it. The rest we learned from experience.

Earlier in the year, when the rebbe's nineteen-year-old son died of a misdiagnosed appendicitis, it was my responsibility to wake the *chevra kadisha*, the volunteers from the community who were responsible for preparing the body for burial. I ran from Jewish home to Jewish home knocking on the shutters of the windows in order not to disturb the entire household. "Get up! Get up," I said in a firm but subdued tone. "*Der rebbez zun is niftar*. The rebbe's son has passed away." When talking about the passing of great men, we always used the word *niftar*, which is closer in meaning to "passed away," rather than *geshtorben*, which was the word we used for "died." I also woke up the group that would guard the body through the night.

The year before, in Sosnowiec, I had the experience of being a *shomer*, or guardian, for a deceased person. Some other boys from the Yeshiva and I were called to sit by the body as our law dictates. There were no funeral parlors, so everything was done in the family's house. The body was lying on the floor covered with a sheet. Two candles burned by the corpse's head. We sat and studied the Mishna all night long and helped prepare the body for burial. It was customary to study certain chapters of the Mishna for a dead person before the funeral for his soul, because the Hebrew word for soul, *neshama*, has exactly the same letters as the word

Mishna. Afterward, the body was taken to the cemetery where the *tahara*, or purification, was performed.

The *shiva*, or week of mourning, for my grandfather was held at his house. Kaddish was recited in the *shiva* house, along with the regular prayers, for seven days. Some people would come by and stay for a while, others would just recite the phrase, "May God comfort you among the mourners of Zion and Jerusalem," and then leave. There was no need for them to say anything else.

In the beginning of my life in modern America, it was strange for me to watch people come to a *shiva* house and make it a social event. I have more or less become accustomed to it now, but it is still a bit annoying to me. According to our laws, you do not come to a house of mourning and discuss sports or politics. It is not soothing to the family, and does not help comfort them in their time of pain. You simply come to express your sympathy, and you do not have to justify it. Even by justifying it you are doing the wrong thing.

The *shiva* for my grandfather was done according to the proper ritual, and at the end of the seven days, I returned to the Yeshiva.

CHAPTER
6

A YOUNG MAN'S FAITH

The first time that I saw a piano was when I was in *cheder*. It was an old piano, and I had a thought that I would like to learn how to play it. It was a wish that began and ended in my mind. We did not have the money for piano lessons, and besides, it occurred to me that in the framework of my daily life, there was no place for piano. Who teaches piano, or plays it? I had never seen a Hasid play the piano. A Hasid with a clarinet or violin I had seen, of course; it was part of the lore — *yiddle mit dem fiddle*, you know? But then, I always imagined these musicians, the klezemer, to be a different breed. A voice is God-given, but instruments such as piano were outside the realm of our movement.

I would not dare bring my desire to play the piano from its secret place in my head to my lips and ask my father. "Piano?" he would have said. "Are you crazy? Talmud! There's something you should know: Talmud, *Chumash*, commentaries, but piano? This is for goyim."

Not that the instrument was evil, but to take piano lessons you have to have a teacher, and maybe the teacher is less observant, and then maybe because of your passion for playing, you will be influenced to stray from the path of the Hasidic movement. Like the Hasidim who went off the track by cutting their *peyes* and shaving their beards, you would become *farblunjet*, lost in the darkness outside the movement.

I never tested my father on such issues. Even when I went to the park with my friends on Shabbes only to watch them play football, I had to be careful that I was out of sight of not only my father, but friends of my father as well. Had they seen me, they might have denounced me. I was afraid.

Mostly, I enjoyed going to the parks across the street and playing harmless children's games, like Hide-and-Go-Seek. I was the sort of child who feared doing things that could result in physical injury. I was a ten-year-old afraid to go bicycle riding with my friends after school. I might get hurt, and then how would I explain to my parents if I were injured doing a certain thing that I was forbidden to do? It was a sin to ride a bicycle without their permission, but that did not keep my friend from taking me for a ride on his jump seat. Fortunately, nothing ever happened, so I never had to tell them that I was on a bicycle. I sometimes looked at my friends with envy, wishing that, in this at least, his father would be my father. "It would all be so much easier," I would think to myself, "if I had been born in his house."

During the severe winters, the townspeople took pieces of plywood and a little bit of metal, and fashioned ice skates for themselves. But they usually preferred to push themselves along on only one skate. This, to me, was like taking your life in your hands, so I abandoned the skate and sledded on the soles of my shoes until they were worn away. When I came home with my feet damp and my soles gone, my mother knew exactly what I had been up to. She did not miss the opportunity to tell me that I could catch a cold with the soles of my shoes worn to the soles of my feet. This was more than just over-protection on her part; she was reminding me that I could not do what the other kids did.

The development of a child's mind in that environment was hampered in certain ways by his upbringing. A child did not meddle in the affairs of adults. Similarly, if I was asked by anyone outside the family how my family was doing or how the business was going, I was taught to answer, "I don't know." The idea, of course, was that I should not bring an evil eye on the family by getting unknowingly caught up in gossip. But to me, as a child, it seemed that my mind was limited to that three-word response, regardless of the nature of the social questions that were asked of me.

I was boxed in, living within the narrow bounds of my faith, restricted by invisible walls of laws and ethics that dictated the proper way of life for a Hasidic Jew. I was not supposed to feel the winds of temptation blowing outside of the movement, but they were there. Certain freedoms I wanted to scoop up in my arms and run away with. Still, I hesitated, wondering if my parents were right, if I really was getting ready to make a mistake. I began to think that maybe they look down on these activities because these are things that God wants us not to do. In that case, I would have to answer to God, and that would be going too far. You do not play with God. Something might happen to you. It was the guilt and the fear that stems from the biblical belief that if you do something wrong, God will punish you for it. If you do what God commands, the Bible says, you will have it good: the rain will come and there will be enough food; God will provide. If you do not follow God's commandments, well, the Bible is full of examples of what happens to those who go up against God.

But it did not end there. When I returned to Lodz in late 1938 after finishing my studies at the Yeshiva in the tiny village of Alexander, I was again tempted as cosmopolitan winds tried to penetrate the walls of my box. After all, we were not truly isolated and I was increasingly aware of the other side; we had neighbors who were not Hasidic. Theirs was another world, one that existed beyond the four-cubit radius wherein a Hasidic Jew is supposed to live and walk. They were not observant: they played ball on Shabbes; they roller-skated and ice-skated; they walked, boys with girls together; they went here and they went there, going everywhere I was not allowed to go doing everything I was not allowed to do. Sometimes I looked down on them, not because they were evil, but because they represented the evil inclination, the *yetzer ha-ra*, that I prayed every morning to be guarded against. Yet every day my eyes were opened a little more. After all, the girls in my neighborhood were turning into young women. The time of playing like three-year-olds in the backyard was gone. Now that we were fourteen-year-olds, when the girl who was my downstairs neighbor came up to me in the hall, in that moment I felt the walls of conflict surround me. She wanted me to talk with her and did not let me pass. I was not conflicted by having the desire, but for the first time I noticed how important it was to me to fight the *yetzer ha-ra*. I could not ignore the man I had been raised to be. I turned away from her. I did not engage her and did not give in to the temptation to talk to her. Allowing the good inclination to overcome the evil was a personal victory.

Embracing my faith like that brought me closer and closer to the center of the movement. I went to the *shtiebel* together with some older Hasidic boys to study every day. We went there in the mornings to pray, and sat until noon and learned. After going home and eating lunch, we went back to the *shtiebel* and studied the rest of the day. At one point, Menachem Domb, an older boy who was a leader among the teenagers of the Alexander Hasidim, approached me to see if I wanted to become a leader. Watching me study, watching the way I lived, he saw in me the *midos*, the innate qualities and virtues that go with a person who lives what is relevant to the framework of Hasidism. I looked up to him for the examples he set of devotion and faith. It was because of my respect for him and the deference to the virtues I was taught that I sincerely felt I could not be as strong a leader as he was. I told him I wanted to remain a follower. I quoted to him from Pirke Avoth, "It is better to be the tail of a lion than the head of foxes," and I went back to my studying with even greater fervor. I picked up the Gemorrah, "*shuckled*" my body back and forth as I considered and analyzed each page, and my *peyes* grew longer.

At the same time, I began to notice a change in some of the boys with whom I had been to Yeshiva. What was the change? Their *peyes* were getting shorter and shorter, until there was nothing left. Of course, if I were to be seen talking to these boys, my father would break all the bones in my body. But I went to school with them, so I had to ask, "What's happening with you?"

"I just joined Betar," one answered. Many of them were part of Zionist revisionist organizations, like the Betar. "Why do you sit learning all day long and *kvetching de bankh* (squeezing the study bench)? You should come to a meeting."

I went to one of their meetings and heard somebody speak in a way that was unfamiliar, yet moving. It was adventurous. It was something new. But I did not belong there. I felt like a stranger. I was afraid of losing my way in a life that was not mine. The Betar Movement was a little less religious than the Zionist organizations my father had belonged to when he was younger, like the Mizrachi Movement and Agudath Movement. I remember we had pictures of the dedication of the Hebrew University in Jerusalem in our house, and hidden in a dresser drawer, my father kept a shekel that was used for casting votes in the Zionist Congress.

At the Betar meeting, I saw boys and girls together, talking. By nature, I was very shy. I did not know about girls. There was a distant cousin I remember who was a beautiful girl. One Shabbes, a few years before, I was walking home from the *shtiebel* with my grandfather, and she ran from across the street to kiss me. I never knew why. They said that I was good looking. I was so embarrassed.

In our circles, a match was usually made between a boy and girl, a *shiddach*, sometimes years in advance. I never found out if my father had already arranged a match for me, but he probably had talked to somebody who had a girl. I had no hand in the decision, other than to tell him if I met a man who I would like as a father-in-law. I could say, "I would like to have him as my *mahuten*. He's a fine man and his daughter is a fine girl." But, really, how did I know? I never talked to her. I only saw her.

I was not supposed to look at a woman on the street, or pass two women by walking between them. I was not supposed to look at a woman's naked elbow, or her empty dress hanging on a wall. This was tempting, according to Hasidim. I saw girls on the street, and my eyes popped out! I was fourteen and very naive. "What do you do when you get together?" I would ask the boys in Betar, "What do you do with the girls?" My thoughts were maturing, in a way, and I had strange feelings. My mind was going in a hundred directions. I was not thinking about love; I was thinking about sexual satisfaction.

I was tempted, and it was confusing me. "Remember who you are," I told myself. "Temptation is a bad thing. How can I recite my morning prayers knowing that I have temptation?" I was having typical, adolescent sexual urges, but to pursue them would have violated the code by which I was raised. The only way I knew how to control my feelings was to get deeper involved in self-education, self-control and self-discipline. I tried to chase them away by reading certain books on aesthetics and virtues, formulas that I was taught as part of the Hasidic movement for chasing away the evil eye.

To live as a Hasid, one has to be familiar with the esoteric texts, writings that deal with the higher levels of virtue. The eighteenth century religious philosopher Moishe Chayim Luzzato wrote a text called *M'silas Yeshorim*, or *The Path of the Righteous*, an aesthetic's guide to living like a Jew. It was like a medicine for avoiding evil inclination. If your symptom was being in a room alone, thinking about forbidden things such as sex and wondering, "Why can't I be like the others?" then the remedy is in the writing. It tells you to recite the biblical verse, "And I shall be sanctified among the people of Israel." The moment you say the word "sanctified" you are uplifting yourself to a degree of sanctity and you include yourself as part of a holy people. Suddenly, you are transformed. It worked — but the effect only lasted until I was out on the street again. After all, I had eyes and I looked!

Another text I often had with me was called *Tzetl Katan*, or *The Little List*, by Rabbi Elimelech of Lizensk. It contains sixteen virtues for practicing to become a more ethical person, and the filters to find the virtue in every deed. For example, humility is a virtue. The point of having a degree of humility was drilled into us as children. We were taught that it is impossible for a person to be as humble as he thinks he is, for any weighing of our own humility is bragging, the opposite of humility. Only God has the right to brag, as it says in Psalm 93, "*Adoshem melech gayoos lawvesh*, God is king, clothed in majesty."

The continued study of those writings brings a Hasid to a plane of mysticism. From there, he may pick up the Zohar, and from there, a righteous man might get involved in certain rituals, like meditating at midnight, the hour of mystery, when the time is ripe for prayers to be heard by God.

I studied until I sincerely felt God inside me. Everything a Jew does is guided by His hand. "I am part of a holy people," I said to myself. "How can I defile that holiness by my temptation?" It was as if I were defiling all of Judaism by my thoughts. I felt guilty, and I was unable to have a frank or any other sort of discussion with my parents about the changes I was going through. That would have been playing with fire. I could only deal with it myself, with my own power and my own knowledge. Once I had my Bar Mitzvah, handling questions like devotion versus temptation became my responsibility, and I searched for answers within the guidelines of my faith.

As a Hasid I did not need to start with challenging my own people —
I had enough problems with the goyim. I did not understand the term
anti-Semitism in the classic sense, but I did know we were hated by our
non-Jewish neighbors. Because I was dressed as a Hasidic boy should be,
with my *peyes* dangling from below my broad hat, I was an easy target. I
often heard remarks like, "Dirty Jew," "Jew go to Palestine." I was, like
many of my friends, afraid of the harassment. Our clothes, our manner,
were not done for fashion — they were symbols of our way of life. When
a group of young Yeshiva students had their hats grabbed from them on
the street it was more than teasing. It was an insult to what was important to us.

There were of course times where we dealt with non-Jews in my
father's business, but in our community we were the exception. In fact,
we dealt mostly with non-Jews, specifically the Polish-Germans. They
were heavily involved in the textile industry. With most of them we
had good business relationships, but we were never invited to their
house socially nor were they invited to our home. It was strictly business. Still, we had to be careful because even the people my father did
business with had sometimes made anti-Semitic remarks. It was hard
to give our trust because of that. Even when one of the Polish-German
women who wove bath towels for the store spoke Yiddish to us we
could never be sure whether she was making an effort to communicate
or just making fun.

It was almost innate for the Jews and non-Jews not to trust each
other, especially around Easter and Passover. Lodz was a religious town
in a Catholic country. If you were Catholic, you celebrated Easter, and
if you were Jewish you celebrated Passover. At these holidays we were
told not to walk by a church and not to go on the streets, especially in
the Christian neighborhoods. This was the time when they blamed the
Jews for killing Jesus, and when the lies about using the blood of
Christian children in matzoh abounded. Historically, it was the time of
year when many European communities experienced pogroms. Of
course there did not have to be a holiday for the streets to be dangerous. I was often frightened when I would have to go by myself to the
weavers' homes in the strictly Polish-German neighborhoods. I felt it.

I could not close my eyes. It was treacherous.

We could not escape anti-Semitism in our daily life. We were resigned to the pain and the fear. As long as there are Jews, we knew there was no end to it. We live in this world, a world of Jews in the Diaspora. People do not like us and, as we read in the Passover Hagaddah, in every generation someone rises to destroy us. In Poland there were many Hamans and Amalekites who wanted to destroy our way of life. There was a Polish priest by the name of Czeczak who wanted to do away with the kosher animal slaughter. Another anti-Semite, a woman named Priesterova, also wanted to end kosher slaughter. It would have been a catastrophe for us. All of a sudden, there were a huge number of animal lovers who were also Jew haters. We combatted it the only way we knew how: we declared a fast day and gathered in the synagogue to recite prayers of penitence. We repent always as a nation as well as individually. There was even a sect of Hasidim that would lock themselves in booths in their synagogues at midnight and confess their daily sins to God. They believed that at that mystical hour the ears of the angels are the most receptive, that God will hear their repentance and forgive them. Penitence is a Jew's way of perfecting himself. Once we become perfect, all our ills will go away and the Messiah will come. According to the Kabalists it was part of each Jew's responsibility to perfect himself in this world, for this is only the foyer of the palace we may enter in the World to Come. That is the way I was brought up.

That is one reason we never left, never fled this tyranny that was so prevalent in Eastern Europe. To uproot oneself, to go because you want to go and not because of some forced exile, was not our way. Very seldom did people like us move, because it was important to stay close to family. We did not move for anything except perhaps business, and only when the business had moved — not because we wanted to move. If we wanted to move for safety, where could we go? There may have been some acceptance in Palestine but even there they had problems with their neighbors. My father at one time very early in his marriage had planned to move to Palestine, but once the family began to grow it became impossible. We stayed because it was our responsibility to do so.

In early 1939 we began to hear rumors of war. There was talk of mobilization and the situation in Sudetenland. Soldiers were marching in the streets. At home, we talked about Hitler and Czechoslovakia, how the Czechs and Germans have an old account to settle, and once he gets Czechoslovakia, he will leave the rest of Europe alone. We thought that there would be a peaceful separation of the Polish Corridor from the rest of the country. But it was soon afterward that my father's business began to suffer because German-Polish Nazi sympathizers, the *Endekes*, stood in front of his shop in their brown shirts and turned non-Jewish customers away. Within weeks we did not have enough money to buy a loaf of bread. It was then that my father arranged that I apprentice with a man who made socks on a machine. I was the oldest son, practically a man at fifteen, and whether or not he did it because he needed my help, he felt I should learn the work according to the Talmudic dictum that a man should teach his son a trade.

The first few days I hated it because it was so strange to me to sit with a machine and learn how to thread yarn to make socks. Even though there were girls also working on the machines, my preoccupation was with learning to work. I think my father paid him so that he would teach me. As an apprentice I learned everything from scratch — how to oil the machine, how it works, how to fix the machine, how to fix the needle — everything. I wasted a lot of time sitting at a machine that would have been more productive with someone more experienced running it. I am sure I ruined a lot of merchandise in the weeks it took for me to make my first sock.

The whole ordeal made me a little resentful. "Why do I have to learn a trade?" I said to myself. "Why couldn't I have been born into a richer home? My friends that I went to school with sit around all day and don't do anything." But I did it because that is what I was told. To do otherwise would have been a violation of the laws that I was brought up with, and I was not as afraid of displeasing my father as I was afraid of God. I was afraid something would happen to me, because once in a while I did test the waters by playing hooky and going to the park with my friends.

Being in this new surrounding once again played on my feelings of wanting to be part of a different world. I wondered whether I was in the right world, or whether the world these people lived in was the right world for me. That confusion and doubt about whether or not I belonged in *peyes* was with me often. By the time the German army rolled into Lodz in September, certain things were beginning to pop into my mind about the way I needed to be and they stuck.

PART II

AN INESCAPABLE WAR, A SLOW DISINTEGRATION

"Be not far from me, for trouble is near and there is no help."

— Psalm 22:12

CHAPTER
7

MY FATE IS THE FATE
OF MY PEOPLE

When the occupation began, my *peyes* were the first things to go. Unlike the yellow stars which we were forced to wear, I cut my *peyes* by choice. I did it not so much to defy the Nazis as to protect myself from them by not flaunting my "Jewish-ness." In no way was I preparing for a long occupation. This was just my time to begin to test my upbringing. *Peyes* were part of my life, like the clothes I wore, and I was a little ashamed at removing them. The barber, a Jewish man who was actually an atheist, had a shop in our apartment building. During normal times, my father would not take me there for a haircut. After all, the man kept his shop open not only on Shabbes, but even on Yom Kippur. He despised Hasidim, and of course my father would not even speak with him. When the time came, he triumphantly snipped my *peyes* from my head. For him, this was victory!

My father said I did not have to do it and he was critical, but not nearly as critical as my grandfather was. For him, it was a bitter pill. His grandson was without earlocks. To him, without *peyes* I was already a goy. "Did you have to cut it all off at once?" he asked.

I was ashamed because I knew it hurt him. My shame was automatic because I knew that to him this was a sign of disrespect and a breakdown of tradition. We were losing our link to our Hasidic lineage, a label to our Jewish identity. Later that week, our label became a pair of yellow stars and my grandfather's criticism waned, for he saw how irrational the times were.

When I noticed that nothing happened to me, that no lightning bolts came down, it was like Adam and Eve's eyes being opened after eating from the Tree of Knowledge. Slowly I began to do other things that were certainly against the proscribed way of life. Once I let go of one thing, it was easier to let the others go. I did not give up on my religion; I just expanded my horizons a little. I picked up political material that was forbidden to us, like books about the Russian Revolution. I was especially fascinated by stories about the fall of the czar.

I was not permitted to read anything that did not have to do directly with Judaism or Jewish education. The only secular thing allowed in the house was the newspaper. My father used to get week-old papers that had been smuggled in and he would read it out loud to us. Of course, because we had the paper we all read it. Our minds were now preoccupied with the war and seeing when it would end. It was only just beginning and we really did not know what we were preparing ourselves for. We thought this was going to be a short-lived war. Once the suffering started, each day brought bigger blows than the previous day.

For us the first blow came when they dragged my father out on Rosh Hashanah. We were eating whatever meager food we could find since the occupation had begun a few weeks before. There was a banging on our door, and when it flew open there was the Gestapo with two uniformed Germans. Behind them was one of our suppliers, an old Volksgerman weaver named Schmidt. With a mock bravado enabled by the armed soldiers, Schmidt demanded my father go with them. "And bring the keys to your store," he said.

They took my father out and when they got to the store, they made him fill up a truck they had brought. Under their vigilant eyes, my father emptied every piece of the material from the store by himself. I wanted to go, to help him. They did not take me and my father insisted I stay. He did not come home until midnight. He had been beaten and could hardly walk up the stairs. There was no way we could find words to comfort him under the weight of this big blow. He just kept repeating the same question, "What can we do? What can we do?"

Some of the neighbors had a plan. They were picking up and leaving, heading to the Russian border. They approached my father. "So what will you do?" they asked. They wanted to get everybody packed up together and walk to the border.

"How can we go and leave my mother?" he told the neighbors and us. He was her only son. "And the rest of the family, picking up and running where? We don't have a place to go."

"We'll go where everyone goes," our neighbor said.

My father pointed to his family. "I have a little boy who is barely two years old, a little baby. Will we walk all that way with him only to get shot? It's too dangerous. The Germans are still fighting in Warsaw and a stray bullet could kill us." Besides, we were not used to moving and leaving all we knew behind. We decided not to go.

After the incident at my father's store on Rosh Hashanah, our shelves were empty. Still, there were German soldiers who had just come into town in the second wave of the occupying force who needed things. There was an interim period after the holidays where we were able to organize a little business. I went to someone who manufactured socks — since I had become such a sock expert — and I said, "Sell me two dozen men's socks." Suddenly we had merchandise, and whatever we asked the Germans paid in marks or zloty. The socks went quickly, so I immediately got five dozen more. Those were sold in two minutes, so we bought ten dozen more and sold them. My father and I split up and went looking for more merchandise while my mother stayed in the store. For the next six weeks we gathered merchandise to sell and used what little money there was to buy food from the dwindling supplies in the stores. People were hoarding, especially flour and sugar, and we wanted to have a few kilos to feed the little ones.

The search for merchandise we could sell, such as socks and towels, became increasingly difficult. I ran every backroad and alleyway in Lodz to find a supply. Before the war, businessmen would gather at a hotel on Piotrokower Gass to trade at a wholesale merchandise market. At this point in the war, the trading was still going on. But after the incident with Schmidt and the Gestapo, my father wanted to keep a low profile and did not want the sellers to know that he was still in business. After I exhausted all my back-alley connections, we had no choice but to visit the wholesalers. Since they knew my father, he would not go in to the hotel but decided to wait in the shadows of the alley, just inside the hotel gates, and watch for the Gestapo or other German Poles like Schmidt. The hotel was in the center of the Volksgerman neighborhood that was naturally enjoying a heyday under German occupation. They made up a full third of Lodz's population, the other two-thirds being made of roughly equal numbers of Poles and Jews.

I picked up two big parcels and made my way out to the gate. As I passed my father he started to emerge from the shadows, but before he could join me, two Gestapo men saw him moving in the shadows and grabbed him. They beat him and kicked him, then dragged him away. I followed from a distance so I could see where they were taking him, my blood boiling all the while as I contemplated tearing the Germans to pieces. It was getting dark by the time they reached Poznanski's Palace, a mansion on Zachodnia Street that used to belong to a wealthy Jewish textile manufacturer. The Nazis has made it their headquarters. I stood outside, bundled up against the November cold, waiting for him to come out. I waited for hours, reciting Psalm 83 as night fell:

> "O God, do not keep silent; do not hold Thy peace and be still, Almighty God, for Thy enemies make a tumult, and those who hate You have risen up....They have said 'Come let us cut them off from being a nation, that the name of Israel will be no longer remembered.'...O, my God...As the fire burns the wood, and as the flame sets the mountains on fire, so pursue them with Thy tempest and terrify them with Thy storm...."

It was the only weapon I had. "This is the only remedy I know," I thought with each repetition. "There is no other way I know to fight these tremendous beasts."

In the darkness, my yellow star left me more exposed and I had to get home to let my mother know what happened. It was after curfew and I ran up the alleys until I got home. When I told my mother, she cried. We did not know what to do. Finally, in the middle of the night, my father returned, black and blue from his beating. Both his eyes were blackened and his back was so bruised he could hardly walk.

"Father, what did they do to you? What did they do?" I asked him.

"They took me to Poznanski's Palace and laughed at me. They made me dance for them, the animals. Then they took me and some others and made us move stones from one end of the courtyard to the other, for no reason except to make us work." My father was tall and strong, but he could not resist them.

My father was not alone. The same thing happened every day, neighbor after neighbor being dragged away to work and be tortured. Every morning around seven o'clock the Germans came to the courtyard of the building where we lived. Except for the superintendent, Jews occupied every one of the seventy-six units. The Germans brought young Polish boys with them to help ferret out any Jews who may have been hiding from them so they could take them to do work. There was no actual work yet, of course, so the Germans just did with everyone as they did with my father — a lot of useless labor moving big rocks around.

This was something that had been going on since the occupying force arrived. We were forced to hide our Jewish practices from them, lest we make it easier for them to single us out for labor and torture. Rosh Hashanah morning, before the Gestapo dragged my father away to his store, we had services at our house. My father led services as the ba'al tefilah and one of the neighbors brought a Torah to the house to read. We began services very early — around 5:30 in the morning — so the Germans would not be suspicious of a group of Jews gathering in one place. We sounded the shofar under a bed in case the Germans came for one of their daily roundups and harassments. On Sukkoth, the Festival of Booths, we were not allowed to build a booth out in the yard like we always did, so we built our Sukkah in a shaft between two parts of the building. It was too tiny to do anything but say a blessing, and it was not a kosher Sukkah by rabbinical law, but at least we were able to find a few branches to cover it and have some observance.

We also had daily services so people could say Kaddish when they had to. These observances were dangerous, of course, and we had a relay of six lookouts making sure no Germans were approaching. If the person on the street saw Germans coming he would signal by saying "Zex!" to the next person on the chain until it got back to us during services. "Zex" was short for "zexamay," an expression we used to describe policemen. It came from the Hebrew word *maylitz*, which means protector, but in this case these men were anything but protectors.

One night at the end of November my father awoke in the middle of the night because of a bright light bouncing off the wall opposite his bed. As he rubbed his eyes awake he saw the huge light was flickering. "Oy!" he shouted as he turned to look out the window, "Oy! *De shul brent!*" The Alte-shtayteshe Shul, our beautiful old synagogue, was burning. Its flames danced in shadows on the walls.

The next day we went to look at what was left of the *shul* we used to call the Workers' Synagogue because it was where all the tradespeople — the tailors, the cobblers, the weavers — used to go. As the neighbors looked over the smoldering ruin of the synagogue, someone explained that the *shul's* chief rabbi had been taken from his bed in the middle of the night and dragged to the synagogue. There the Germans made him wrap himself in the scrolls of a Torah and they lit him and the synagogue on fire.

This was a catastrophe for us as a community, of course. We had only heard rumors of Kristalnacht, the so-called "Night of Broken Glass" that had taken place in Germany and Austria in November 1937. It was a Nazi-led pogrom that resulted in the vandalizing and looting of Jewish-owned shops and businesses, and the burning of synagogues throughout both countries. We had only heard about it through German refugees who had come into Poland in the time since, but few of us paid attention to such rumors. Who could fathom such a large-scale pogrom?

"This is the end," some of the neighbors said as they looked over the synagogue's debris. My father and I walked silently back to the apartment. We stopped at the entrance to the building and I asked him, "How could it be? A house of God, and God let this happen?"

"Shah," my father said, lest the angels hear my blasphemes. "You shouldn't say that. This is God's will."

I could not believe it. "Maybe," I said, but inside I was wondering why nothing came down from heaven to strike the animals that burned a house of God. I thought God would make something happen, but there was nothing. We were only beginning to see how lawless the world was becoming. The president of the Jewish community in Lodz, Laibel Minzberg, who was also a member of the Sejm (Poland's parliament), was taken away one night with sixteen other community leaders. Another Jew, a wealthy Alexander Hasid named Asher Cohen who made his fortune as a weaver of Polish linen, was thrown from his house and made to sweep the streets before he bought his way out and escaped to Mexico. Meanwhile the laws against Jews owning a business were being strictly enforced and my father could not work anymore. As each suffered we all suffered, and the travails we were enduring brought us closer to each other as Jews than we had ever been. Everyone had adopted an attitude of unity that we had not experienced in our diverse Jewish community. We needed each other, and began to lean on each other for support. As we used to say, "*Vos vet zein mit k'lal yisroel, vet zein mit reb yisroel.* My fate is the fate of my people."

CHAPTER
8

RESETTLEMENT

It was the winter of 1940 and nearly six months after the German army had rolled its tanks into Poland. I had just turned sixteen, and my family was sending me and my cousin, along with some family belongings, to my mother's parents in Piotrokow. Lodz was beginning to change and it was time to leave.

Across the street from our apartment, we had watched German soldiers and Polish workers dig a row of holes, each a few meters from the other, and thought that they were preparing trenches.

It was the time of the first resettlement. Jews were being moved from one part of the city to another — from the wealthier Geyers Mark section of the city to our working class neighborhood. With only an hour or two of notice, they packed what they could and left their homes. Their belongings filled tall wagons and spilled from tiny children's buggies. No transport company could be hired to move their possessions because the Jews had no permanent destination. They did not know where they were going.

Like a plant pulled from its native soil, the unexpected uprooting sent a shock through the community. The people were scrambling around, trying to make sense of the chaos their ordered lives had suddenly become. Most looked for an empty place where they and their families could lay down their heads and sleep. My uncle, who lived on the other side of town, brought his entire family — with children and grandchildren it was nearly twenty people — over to our apartment to spend the night. There was not an empty space, of course. Since the bed was longer than wide, we slept across its width with our feet sticking out from the covers.

Soon, we realized the trenches we had seen the others digging in front of our building were really post-holes, and it was not long before a fence started winding its way around the old *balut* section of the city. When we were told that it was to be a ghetto for the Jews, we were puzzled. We already lived in a Jewish neighborhood, a ghetto of sorts, but it was not surrounded by long stretches of fence, brick walls and barricades of piled debris; the Germans' idea of a Jewish ghetto was.

Our house was just outside the fence. Within a few days Rumkowski, the head of the Judenrat, came to our building, and before he could make it across the courtyard we surrounded him and bombarded him with questions. "Mr. Rumkowski, will this building be part of the ghetto?" I asked him. It was what we all wanted to know. The man quickly tired of our persistent queries, and being mean and ill tempered, he kicked me in the shin. If he had any answers, he did not tell us.

It was not long afterward that we stood in front of our building with our neighbors and watched the people coming by the thousands in one continuous stream and entering the enclosure. Old people and people not so old crowded the sidewalk and the middle of the road, some carrying knapsacks. Mothers held their children; children clutched their toys; young boys held their baby sisters' hands.

From out of the crowd, we heard someone shouting. Down among the hundreds of feet plodding by, a legless man was rolling himself along the ground on a flat cart. As he pushed the wooden blocks in his hands against the road and moved himself forward, he screamed, "*Yiden! Zeit zich nisht meyaesh!* Jews, don't give up! Don't despair!"

With all his *tsoris*, he had the strength and the spirit to yell at the top of his lungs so that we would listen. There was a look in his eyes and in the eyes of all who heard him. He made us feel that no matter what may befall us, it is still good to be a Jew. Just as you praise God for the good things that happen to you, the Talmud says, you must also praise Him for the unhappiness, the misfortunes, of life.

This man's shouting was an act of defiance, of passive resistance, and it gave him the courage to face an uncertain future. No matter what, he was saying, we are Jews: we survived before, and we will survive again. For a moment, an expression of hope crossed everyone's faces, and we smiled — but slowly making its way down every cheek was a tear, and from deep within came the perennial sigh of Jews in despair.

It was this despair that had led my family to decide to send me and my cousin, a girl about my age, to Piotrokow. My mother did not want to be separated from her parents, so my father, of course, agreed to move everyone, including his mother and his sister, to Piotrokow. My cousin and I were sent ahead, to wait for the rest of the family there.

And there were other reasons to leave Lodz for Piotrokow. Because of its size, its large German population and its proximity to the German border, the invaders made Lodz part of the Third Reich. Piotrokow was not under the same jurisdiction. Like most of Poland, it was under a protectorate run by a governor. In 1940 and 1941, the occupation in the protectorate was relatively lenient, compared to the way things were run in the Reich. For instance, Piotrokow was an open city: Jews were still allowed to own stores and do business in town, a privilege withheld from the Jews in the Reich.

Also, in Lodz, as in other parts of the Reich, Jews were required to have a yellow Star of David stitched to their clothing. But in Piotrokow, in the protectorate, we wore blue and white armbands so we would be seen if we left the "Jewish Zones" and entered areas that were forbidden to us. I knew people who regularly removed their armbands in order to go places where they would not otherwise have been allowed. It was risky. Despite the difference in jurisdictions, the SS and Gestapo were in the protectorate as well as the Reich, and the consequences of getting caught not wearing an armband or the yellow star were exactly the same: certain death.

Moving to Piotrokow was a family decision. Only two of my uncles, on my father's side, had chosen to remain in the ghetto in Lodz. They were both well known and had connections with the leaders of the Jewish community. That same man who kicked me had great respect for my uncle, the rabbi, and my aunt. He visited my aunt personally. "I'm going to see to it that you and the rabbi get the nicest apartment," he told her. And that is what he did.

Jews in Poland were no longer allowed to take the trains from city to city, so for our journey my family hired a Polish coachman and his wagon — a common means of traveling the short distances from village to village — to take us the less than fifty kilometers to Piotrokow.

At around eleven o'clock on a cold Saturday night in early March, my cousin and I climbed into the wagon that had rags for a canopy and nine loose planks of wood to accommodate the behinds of nine narrow rows of passengers. The unfastened boards jumped with every bump of the wagon's wheels on the rutty dirt roads. We did not have enough cord to tie our belongings down and had to shove our pile of linen and clothing under our seats to keep it from spilling on to the muddy, snow-sloshed road. The driver gently coaxed his one poor old horse to go, and as the wagon rocked and creaked away from Lodz, we bundled ourselves up against the long winter night.

Despite our heavy clothes, we were both freezing. The driver exhorted us to stay awake, "Don't fall asleep! Do anything you can to keep awake, but don't fall asleep!" There was danger in going to sleep in weather that cold.

In a way the danger and the mystery of fleeing into the night by horse and buggy was intriguing for us. Whatever obstacles lay ahead, perhaps because of the naiveté of my youth, did not concern me. Although every moment of this risky adventure brought new perils, it did not feel like we were running away from anything; that is, it seemed that the hatred that was unleashed at the beginning of the war, like my father being taken and beaten, could not be avoided. We were just relocating, moving within the war, not away from it. For the moment, we had a destination. We did not see the real obstacles of pain and trouble that were already with us, and would be until the end. We did not see.

CHAPTER
9

OBSTACLES

After ten kilometers or so, we came to the town of Brzezin. Before the war, it was known as "The City of Tailors," a place where nearly everyone, especially the Jewish households, had a sewing machine in the window. Sewing was the trade of the community, very few houses had electric power, and the machines were in the windows so the tailors could work in the daylight.

There were many villages like Brzezin before the war.

As we rolled into town on our packed wagon, three Polish hooligans, German sympathizers, met us. They wore swastikas.

"Dirty Jews," they swore at us. "We've got to get rid of you." It was my first exposure to anti-Semitism since the war began. They could have done anything. We were afraid they would try to stop us and beat us, but they simply satisfied themselves by calling us names, and without a word the driver gave the reins an extra shake. The horse sped up and soon we were through town and on our way.

We were only two or three kilometers past Brzezin when we came upon a roadblock. By the roadblock was a booth, and in the booth were two German soldiers. They stopped the wagon and ordered us inside. Of course, right away, we went in. There was an old one and a young one. Despite a wood-burning stove that kept the little station warm, there was a chill in the room.

"You are Jews," the older one said as he opened my coat. Coming from Lodz, we still wore yellow stars on our clothes. "Where are you going in the middle of the night?" he demanded.

"We are going to visit our family in Piotrokow," I answered them in German. I had learned a little German in my father's business. "I was born there and my cousin and I are going for a visit."

"No," they said, "we will not let you go."

I began to shake and shiver. My cousin and I both started crying. We begged and pleaded. "We have not harmed anyone; please let us go."

"Please let us go," the younger soldier mimicked, and they both laughed.

"We've harmed no one," I repeated through my tears. They just kept mocking us and laughing. The more we begged, the more the Germans taunted us.

Maybe because of how pitiful we looked, they did not harm us physically. After all, we were frozen from the ride. Whatever the reason, after a while the older one said, "Alright. Go. Get out."

We hurried from the booth and back to the wagon, so relieved at having been released that for a few moments, we did not notice the cold. Without a word, we climbed to our seats on the rig. Even to my own cousin, even with this excitement, I was too shy to speak to a girl. There was nothing to say anyway. The fear was loud enough, and the obstacles were just beginning. As we pulled away from the roadblock, the snowfall became heavy. The farther we rode, the thicker it came down. It was unbelievable, to the point where we could not see the road ahead of us.

About twenty kilometers out of Brzezin, the tired horse stopped moving, unable to pull the wagon through the thick snow. We had to get off and push, but it was physically impossible to move through the three-foot-high snow that was still coming down. The wagon was old and probably more tired than the horse, and soon the axle broke. Now we needed a sled to get through it!

We were on the other side of the city of Koluszki, a railroad hub where freight trains coming in were switched to different parts of Poland. There was a depot there for locomotives. Tuszyn lay just ahead, but we could not go there because my relatives and all the other Jews were already gone from that town. The Nazis had come in one Friday night and rousted all the Jews from Tuszyn. They all went to Piotrokow. All we had, as we stood among the white drifts between the two towns, was a stuck vehicle and a name scribbled on a small piece of paper: Rubenstein. We waited in a field, with a tired horse and a broken carriage, until morning.

Fortunately, my family in Lodz had given the driver Rubenstein's name just in case we should need something on our way through here. He was family, one of four or five brothers, some of whom I knew, although this one I had never met. The cousin I was traveling with and her family, though, knew them well. When it was just becoming light, we bundled ourselves up, unhitched the horse and went to his house.

By the time we got to Rubenstein's door, it was already Sunday night. The driver walked the horse to the barn and fed him, covered him with blankets to keep him warm and let him rest a little bit. We had been traveling for nearly twenty-four hours and had only gone thirty kilometers. We stood like frozen bundles at the front of the house, our knee-high Russian cloth volenky boots soaked right through to their leather soles.

"Take off your clothes. Come. Sit next to the stove," Rubenstein invited. "Take off your volenkys and warm yourselves."

Inside the old-fashioned farmhouse, the air soon thickened with the rich smell of warm, fresh milk and cooking potatoes and large winter mushrooms that hung from long strings by the stove. A *krupnik* was put on the table. A *krupnik* is a hearty soup made from beans, barley and gribbenes. What a *mechaye*, a real pleasure, it was! Whatever they had, we ate. Oh, God, did it taste good!

Rubenstein was a kind man, and after we ate we stayed the night. As we were going to bed, Rubenstein promised he would help us get to Piotrokow. "Don't worry," he said. "I'll arrange everything."

And he did. The next morning, he had arranged for a new horse and a sled. He had also transferred our belongings from the wagon to the sled and he then drove us to Piotrokow himself. The wagon driver took his horse and went back to his family in Lodz.

We finally arrived in Piotrokow on Monday afternoon. My grandparents were looking out the window and they ran to greet us. "Oy! *Got-su danken*! Thank God you're alive," they screamed as they hugged us and showered us with kisses.

They were worried, naturally. After all, how long should it take to travel forty-four kilometers? Ten hours? Twelve? They expected us Sunday morning and this was Monday afternoon. We could not telephone; we had no phones. There was no way of sending a telegram about what had happened to us, so they worried. Of course, we told them all about our adventures. It took me a week to remember it all.

A month later, my parents and brothers and sisters arrived. They teamed up with other families either going to Piotrokow or other places in the protectorate. They had to take side roads to avoid the guards. The drivers had learned the way around the army posts. Sometimes, the travelers would leave the wagon and walk through the woods, and the driver would pick them up on the other side of a guard shack. The drivers put themselves at risk, even though they were not Jewish, and of course anyone making the journey was at risk. It was a risk from the first day the Germans came into Poland.

PIOTROKOW

It was a relief to be in Piotrokow again, especially because at this time it was less tense. The occupation was not felt as much. I was surprised to see my grandparents still operating the dry goods business from their house, just as they had before the war began. People still came to buy. They could not get much new merchandise, of course, but whatever my grandparents had, they sold. They still had inventory from the First World War, and that they sold also because there was nothing else. Underwear. Stockings. People did not care that it was out of style. It was something to put on your legs, to cover your feet. It was something to keep you warm in Poland in the winter of 1940.

There were also ways to smuggle in merchandise from nearby cities, textile towns. Everybody was trying to make a small living. With a few zloty, you could still buy things from the farmers. They still took money.

The Germans who occupied Piotrokow then were not the same group of SS that the Nazis would bring in to liquidate the ghettos. That did not happen here until 1942. The soldiers who held our town were all on their way to the Eastern Front. All the army, every tank, every soldier, went through Piotrokow because it was on the road from Germany to Russia. There were SS on the streets in 1940. We already knew to look for the insignia on the lapels. We knew to stay away from them and from the "brown shirts" too. These were the tough guys. They probably belonged to the Nazi Party or to Hitler Youth. They were mean. Those who worked for the Gestapo were a different story. But most of the men were regular soldiers, infantry. Some of them were human beings and treated us well. Still, nothing was normal, despite outward appearances.

Everyone in our house was jittery, not only because of the occupation, but at the inconvenience of having all those extra people in that tiny apartment. It was a bedroom, a dining room, a kitchen and a store. Not just food, but space had to be shared as well. When my mother, father, sisters and brothers came down a month later, we added seven people to the already crowded house. Everything had to be split seven more times, dwindling the portions of about forty people.

We slept on the floors, on the chairs, on the bed and on the sofas. If neighbors had an empty space, some of us would go sleep there. You could not even rent space. Luckily, my grandfather's family was large, and there were uncles and cousins in the community we would go to from time to time in order not to have to crowd in. One uncle had a one-room apartment nearby, with a little baby. Some nights I would sleep there, sometimes my sister or my brother would go there.

Naturally, with all those people in my grandparents' house, it was impossible to keep up all the Hasidic customs and traditions. There was no way for us to sleep separately, men from women, for example. It was a time of war, and certain things were let go as *pikuach nefesh*, as a matter of survival.

There was a lot of friction because of the situation. You put that many people in a small area, and naturally they become jittery. Something is said that is not meant to be said, or something said is misinterpreted. Even between the closest sisters in that situation, steam has to be let off, and afterward, you feel better. The same situation that caused the strife brought us together. It is difficult to stay angry with someone when the next day they may disappear, taken away by the Germans, or killed. From day to day and hour to hour, every moment was a question of not only personal survival, but also the survival of everyone in the family.

Anything we could do to survive we did. We could not sit around the house all day and do nothing. Everybody felt they had to be responsible, so my father started to deal on the street, buying and selling what he could. I did the same thing. We traded yarn, clothes, and even dollars. We even traded American money, the old long notes, gold certificates and gold dollars. I became a connoisseur in detecting the real gold from the counterfeit.

There was a particular man in the Piotrokow ghetto at the time — not very nice, but also from Lodz — who was rich, and he supplied the different foreign currency that we dealt. I used to go into his house and I had no money to pay him, so he would give me, say, a ten-dollar gold piece with the promise, "Sell it and bring me the money and I will give you something else."

I learned to buy from Moishe and sell to Yankel, and sometimes I would sell the same money back to Moishe. There was a market that fluctuated so everyone was buying and selling. There was nothing dishonest about such wheeling and dealing. A word was a sacred pledge, as good as any signed contract. It had to be. A broken promise meant that no one would trust you. You had to be 100 percent honest.

Some sold to the Polish people or to others outside the ghetto. One had to have connections, and this rich man from Lodz would send his daughter to Warsaw and other parts of the country to buy the currency; she even bought from the Germans, until she was caught and they killed her. But that did not stop him from dealing. It had the whole town talking.

"He killed his daughter," the people would say, "and now he sends his son to do the same thing."

It was all part of the ghetto mentality, to look for a way to get a little extra food by buying from the Polish farmers. The rations that the Germans gave us, some frozen potatoes and a bit of bread, were not enough. Those with fast hands, who hurried up to the potato trucks, were able to stuff their paper bags and sacks with more, sometimes as much as they could carry. We all had coupons, but the quick ones were able to finagle to get more than they were allowed.

Even within my immediate family, there was envy when it came to a piece of bread. If my sister or brother got a larger piece of bread, even though I did not say anything, it hurt; I felt it. We looked at everybody else's plate — you know, maybe they have a milligram more of food than you do. "Why wasn't I the lucky one," I would think, "to get that piece?"

We were forced to adopt a ghetto mentality, a way of coping with the abnormal by making it seem normal. It was not real; it was a make-believe life. The business, the wheeling and dealing, was there a future there? Was this a normal way of doing business affairs? Of course not. It was survival.

Eventually, I bought a machine that made men's stockings. I needed yarn, so once I bought some from a man who cheated me with material that looked good on the outside but was rotten on the inside. Even with that rotten yarn, I tried to make socks. Whether or not I produced anything, at least it kept me busy. Everything we did was an adventure that kept us preoccupied, and any benefit it may have brought to the family, in terms of a little money, almost became secondary.

One of our neighbors had an illegal bakery in his house. They built an oven by themselves, and ground the cornmeal by hand from ears bought from Polish farmers and smuggled into the ghetto in false-bottomed wagons. The hand grinding left the flour coarse and unpurified, but however the dough came out, we used it to make bread. It was terrible work, very hard. It took at least sixteen hours a day and put the whole family at risk, and for what? For a loaf of bread that tasted like clay. Still, at least it was something to eat.

We always hoped that our situation would be temporary, that one day soon the war was going to end. How long, we thought, could it drag on? We did what we could to keep track of the battles on the fronts. Even though it was illegal, we had ways of finding out what was written in the German papers, and Polish people would share information with us at their own risk. We were prohibited from having radios, not permitted to have newspapers or to gather, but in 1940 and 1941 Piotrokow was not a closed ghetto, and Poles who lived in our building were just as eager for the war to end as we were, so they would tell us what was happening. Still, the penalty for either Jew or Pole caught defying even these minor laws was death.

We occasionally received smuggled copies of *Das Reich*, Himmler's propaganda newspaper of the German war effort. I read the paper voraciously whenever I could get it. It was the only news we had. In such a paper you read even in the white spaces; like the Talmud, there is as much to learn from interpreting what is between the lines as there is from reading the words. By reading and listening, even though I had no geography lessons after the fifth grade, I suddenly became an expert on the globe. I knew where Grodno was, and Bengazi and Tripoli; then, as the war continued I learned the names of other cities and towns on the front lines.

"If I were the general...," I would say, frustrated by what I read in the papers, having ideas of what I knew was *the* way to end the war. This was something common, second-guessing the war. We called it "*mikvah* politics."

What is *mikvah* politics? It is politics decided between two Jews in the *mikvah*, the ritual bath where Hasidic and Orthodox Jews go on Friday afternoon to be clean for the Sabbath. These men talk about how many more days the war will last. They turn the palm of one hand toward you and point with the other at the lines in their hands as if they were the Vistula River and her tributaries, and the fleshy parts were the Caucuses. The German army, according to these hands, was on one side of the river, the Russians on the other. With a finger leading the Russian army like a general, they skillfully drew a circle around the unsuspecting Germans. "Ah!" they shouted as they pulled their fingers into a fist, "with this move, the Germans are crushed and the war is over!"

While we strove to hear the news of the world, my grandfather still studied Talmud with me from the books that were, for now, in his library. I could see his face shining, see the way it pleased him to see me going to the bookshelves and taking out a volume of Talmud or the Bible. He was always happy when I sat down to read, and the louder I read, the better it was. He felt, and I did too, that just because there is a war does not mean a Jew stops studying. You still have to know. You still have to learn something.

So at night we sat around the table and learned, and although I knew I should be studious, my mind was often somewhere else. I was interested in the outside world, to see what was denied me in the cloister of Hasidic life. I wanted to read novels and revolutionary pamphlets. We had an exchange called a *groszen bibliotek*, a penny library, where for five groszens you could buy a chapter of a book about the size of a pamphlet. It was barely more than a couple of hours worth of reading. When we finished one, we traded for another.

This was not open trading. The SS guards did not allow us any reading. I read books about the Russian revolution, the fall of the czar. It impressed me, people of strong will and courage overthrowing a government because of the strength of their beliefs, to make the world a better place to live. I wondered why there had to be a ruling class, where one has everything and the rest have nothing, why there had to be corruption and killing. Others in the ghetto found this revolutionary material fascinating as well.

Once, while walking on the Stara Warszawska — a road in the old Jewish neighborhood even we used to call the Yidden Gass — I saw a familiar figure, about my father's age, coming toward me. It was Reb Getzel Zeide, a dear friend of my father, and a rather liberal Alexander Hasid from Lodz who never wore a full beard or earlocks. He had instead a little goatee. In Lodz, he sold life insurance for the company Reunione Adriatica di Sciutra, and had sold some to my father. He was also a fine composer of *nigunim* for the Alexander Hasidim. This was the first I had seen of him since Lodz. Still, it was the middle of the day and our greeting was subdued. There was never any reason to call unnecessary attention to yourself in the ghetto.

As he approached me, he glanced cautiously from side to side. Putting one hand up to hide his face from the crowd slowly going by on the street, he brought his other hand up and pointed to his mouth. "Itchele," he said, "*Du host eppes tsu nemen en moil arein?* Do you have something I could feed myself with?"

He may indeed have been hungry, but he was not asking for food. This was a code we used around the ghetto for reading material. He wanted to know if I had anything that he could use to feed his mind. With the same caution as Reb Getzel, I reached inside my jacket and slowly removed a pamphlet I had only just received from a boy up the street. "Thank you. *A sheinem dank,*" said Reb Getzel with a little nod, and he continued walking. In this way, we made trades with our pamphlets, and we were able to have something different to read.

My aunts were able to get Polish books that they read to me on the balcony during the summertime. Although I read some Polish, I could not understand all that I read, so I sat and listened to their stories. Sometimes, when I was not quite sure of a word, I asked its meaning, and the aunt that was reading turned red. She never explained certain words, so I was left to guess.

My cousin from Tuszyn, Aharon Dovid Krieger, who got stuck in Poland as a military conscript when his family emigrated to Colombia in 1937, was another entertaining source of information. A walking encyclopedia, there was not a thing this man did not know. Not only did he know Jewish history, but he also remembered facts from world history, philosophy, and languages. He was even teaching me Spanish, because he promised that he would take me to his family in Bogotá when the war was over. We got a hold of some Spanish/Yiddish books, and English/Yiddish as well, and this is how we learned.

It was a surprise when Aharon Dovid found a copy of *Mein Kampf* in the ghetto. He read it many times. While I read German easily, the Nazis printed their material in *gottesschrift*, old-style German lettering that was difficult to read. I listened carefully as Aharon Dovid explained his understanding of the German ruler's politics. We always did this away from the Germans, for all these books were forbidden to us.

My father left all of his books, his religious books, in the water tank of our apartment in Lodz. The water tank was above the attic and was designed to supply water to the entire complex, only the plumbing was bad and it never worked. Everybody drew their water from a well in the yard. The tank was dry. So before we left for Piotrokow, my father gave me his books and I climbed the ladder in the attic that led to the tank (when it came to climbing, I was always the first one up), and I opened the tank and put all our books inside it.

My father did not want to leave the religious books where the Germans could find them, and some other neighbors did the same as we. After the war, the first thing I did when I got back to Lodz was to look for that house, for that dry water tank. I wanted to climb up the ladder in the attic and retrieve those books. There was no house. The house was gone because the Germans had cleaned up the entire section of the city so they could watch the ghetto fence from miles away. All the houses along the fence were torn down. There was an empty space where our home had been. Fifty years later, I met a man who had actually taken part in the dismantling of that house. "I never saw so many religious books in one place," he told me. He was there when the Germans opened the water tank and found all the books.

It was amazing that my grandfather still had his books. At my grandfather's home in Piotrokow, while the Germans were destroying the books they found in Lodz, my father, grandfather and I would study from the *chumash* and *nach*, the book of Prophets and other writings. I hid my little chapter pamphlets I had gotten on the street inside the pages of the holy books, so I could turn the pages and they would not see what I was doing. It was taboo, after all, from a Hasidic point of view to be reading those things.

Real schooling happened only privately. Four or five students met with a teacher in a designated place, the location always changing because of the danger of being discovered. After all, we were forbidden to learn not only Judaic studies, but secular as well. Among those who attended religious study groups was my cousin Henry. Although already quite religious, he became fanatically Hasidic, even growing little *peyes* that he hid behind his ears. In the ghetto, none of the Hasidim had visible earlocks, or even beards.

Henry managed to keep the small earlocks he grew hidden. For him, and for others like him, this was passive resistance. Even in the cramped living conditions of the ghetto, he was driven to the strict practice of genuine Hasidism. In the small room that he shared with his mother, he put up a *mechitsa*, a dividing curtain to separate himself from her while they slept.

This was what learning under such circumstances produced. We learned what we could and took away what we could. There was no regular curriculum. We learned from whatever text was available. One textbook in the ghetto could have been used by more than twenty children. It did not matter. We could not graduate. There was nothing to graduate to. We did it just to have something to learn, something to know. Something to keep our faith.

In many ways, we managed to keep some of our traditions even while the Germans were trying to take them from us. We still learned *chumash* every Friday night, studied Talmud on Shabbes, as though it were a normal thing. We observed Shabbes as if nothing unusual were going on. We did not have all the ingredients to make a traditional Shabbes dinner, so we used eggs to make the gefilte fish. We made fish out of eggs.

It had all become a sad routine for us, being in a house with so many people, standing in a small room, warming ourselves beside the ceramic tiled oven, but at least it was a routine. It gave us what we were used to — a structured way to live — in a way that we were not used to living.

In the morning, we awoke and said our prayers, then we ate what was available and tried to organize food for the evening. Forty people ate a lot of potatoes, when we could get potatoes. We would peel huge kohlrabi, scrub them out and pass them around raw for each person to take a bite. "It's good. It's healthy," my great-grandmother used to say, and at the time, it was good; it was delicious.

We did the same thing with sugar beets, when we could get a hold of them, because in order to get any vegetables, we had to go outside the city and trade our dwindling merchandise with the farmers. Far from adventurous, we did what we had to out of necessity — the necessity of day-to-day survival.

The mystery for us as Jews was not in the compromising of our observances because of the circumstances. For us, the mystery was whether we had been observant enough. There was talk that maybe we did not observe fully to begin with, and that was why we were here. As time went on, we started to see what the Nazis were doing to our people, how they were really clamping down on us. Every day there were new edicts, new problems. We began to question whether we did it, whether we were responsible for what was happening to us. I too questioned, though not openly, not in front of the family.

I also worried and fantasized about the future. Would I ever get married? Would I be at my sister Hinda's wedding? I visualized my four-year-old brother Yechiel Yaakov's Bar Mitzvah. Maybe the day will come when my father will be a rich man. I was looking forward to things I wanted to see happen, that I would love to see, and it kept my mind from dwelling on what was going on around us.

We passed the time studying, praying, reading, dreaming and wondering. It was like that every day, until nighttime when the Germans came around to catch people for forced labor. In the middle of the night, they rousted people out of bed for the next day's work. They took people to work in the brick factories, in the lumberyards, in the glass factories. Some were taken to clean the Nazis' barracks and sweep the floors, and they looked forward to going because there they would be fed. Everyone who was taken worked late into the night before they were sent home. Those who did not want to be taken hid where they could.

Because I was young and able, my family hid me when the Germans came. Sometimes it would be in a bed, beneath the blankets, with somebody else sleeping, sometimes on a windowsill behind the drapes, even under a bed, which was really no hiding place. Still, they never caught me.

The Germans usually took the youngest and most fit laborers they could find. Sometimes they would take one of my uncles. Most of my uncles were in their forties, and looked much older, so they were rarely rounded up. My grandfather was in his sixties, and they did not even bother with him. They were looking for people to work — hard labor.

When my Uncle Nachum, a man in his late thirties, was taken, he came back late at night, tired and beaten. I was frustrated and hurt. He told us how it was out there, how the Germans treated them and how grateful he was that he was not as badly beaten as the man next to him. I felt sorry for all of them, and I was relieved that I was not among them.

As these labor roundups continued into 1941, my family bribed a doctor to provide false papers for me that said I had a terrible, contagious disease and I was not to be touched or exposed to others. Together with my Aunt Perl, we rode to this doctor and presented two pairs of stockings and whatever else had been arranged in exchange for the documents. Even though the transaction had been set up beforehand, I was scared. Having such papers, they would not grab me for work, but if the Nazis were to find out I had false papers, or if the doctor were an anti-Semite or changed his mind, the results would have been disastrous.

In early spring, before Pesach, a person brought us the news that the Nazis were going to round up two thousand healthy young men and send them to Belzec, a town on the Russian border near Lublin, to dig trenches. Among them was my cousin, Aharon Dovid. Though I had the doctor's papers, with such a big roundup we did not want to take any chances.

My great uncle, Hershel Pacanowski, had owned a roofing factory that the Germans had nationalized. He still ran the production, but only under the supervision of a *treuhander*, a trustee who was German and was put in place by the Nazis. Coincidentally, my uncle told us they were about to deliver a load of roofing paper to a nearby town. Tomaszow, which is less than forty kilometers from Piotrokow, was on the way to that town, and we had distant cousins there. I could hide with these relatives, whom I had never met, until the roundup was over, so they built a place in the load where I would have enough air to breath, and they covered me with roofing paper.

A year and a half into the war, hiding like this was a normal way of life. We learned to live with it. We adapted without thinking. "Maybe tomorrow it will change." Hiding was part of it; eating was part of it; sleeping was part of it. We did not get used to the suffering — we became immune to it. That way, the most terrible, the most horrible expectations were removed from our minds.

"As long as we are alive," we thought, "as long as they do not kill us, we can cope with it." We lived that way because otherwise we would die. Being buried under a pile of roofing paper and being transported to avoid something, as odd as it may seem, was a way to live another moment, another hour, another day. We did not know what to expect, and that is how we lived. It is not as if we went around expecting the unexpected. We assumed it, just as one assumes their next breath.

The wagon of roofing paper came to our house around five in the morning, I climbed in and we drove off. I was able to vaguely look out the narrow cracks in the pile of paper and see the driver and what was happening around us. It was only the two of us. The Germans stopped us in a forest on the outskirts of Tomaszow. I peeked out of the paper and my heart started going a mile a minute. I thought, "Uh-oh. Here it is."

The Germans had set up a roadblock, and they were checking everyone. "Are you transporting any people or other illegal materials?" the soldier asked.

"Of course not," the Polish wagon driver answered sternly. "I know better than that," and he handed the guard his papers and waited. From my hiding place, I watched the Nazi guard circle the load. It was probably roofing material for one of the German barracks in the next town, since private citizens could not get things like roofing paper at the time.

He was not interested in searching it. "*Dummkopf*," he shouted at the driver as he threw back the papers. "Move! Move along!" and we went on to my relatives in Tomaszow.

My cousins fed me what they could and kept me hidden, for there was a ghetto in Tomaszow as well, and I could not move around freely without someone wondering who I was and what I was doing there. I stayed in their house for two days, until the wagon driver came to take me back to Piotrokow. Since he no longer had the roofing paper, the driver covered me up with different material, some rags, some junk, whatever he had in the wagon.

When I returned, Aharon Dovid had been the only one from the family taken. We did not expect to hear from him at all. No one had ever come back from hard labor on the Russian Front. On the last day of Pesach, we had just finished saying *kiddush* for the afternoon meal, when the door opened and he limped into the house. Sunburned, dragging his right leg, the first words out of my cousin Aharon Dovid's mouth were," *Gut yontif!* Happy Holiday," and then he began to tell us of his two-week ordeal.

We wanted to hear every detail, and at the same time we were overwhelmed with relief at having him with us again. He brought us news that we could not know, for even the German newspapers we had smuggled in did not tell these stories. These were stories from the Russian Front, only months before the Germans attacked Russia.

My cousin said that he and the other workers were clearing forests and digging trenches for the Nazis. Some of the Jewish laborers, he told us, used the opportunity to escape to the Russian side, but for most, the freedom was short lived. The Russians shipped them right back to the German lines. There were a few, however, that managed to remain with the Soviets.

Aharon Dovid told us that when the Russians captured the escapees, they interrogated them. If, when asked why they wanted to enter the Soviet Union, the distraught Jews answered, "To escape the Germans," they were sent right back. If, however, they said, "I am Communist. My father is a Communist. I embrace Communism," the Russians would say, "Alright. We will send you to where communism begins," and they were sent to Siberia. To some, even at that time, being in Siberia was better than being with the Nazis.

My cousin said that he too thought about going to the Russian side. After all, it was a way out. But he thought of his sister, Bela, who was in the ghetto with us, and he thought of his family in South America, and how he hoped to one day be reunited with them.

He also told us of the labor, made even more difficult by the terrible beatings from the Nazis. One German, Obersturmbandfuhrer Kolff, a short, most vicious beast, with his black uniform, his merciless expression and hateful eyes, had taken his hard whip to my cousin. I remember watching him limp around the room as he showed us how they beat him.

In pain, and unable to take the torture any longer, Aharon Dovid saw a tree coming down close by and in a flash he was underneath it, letting it fall on his leg. He was taken to an infirmary, and he escaped from there. He was able to hitch rides with Polish farmers all the way back to Piotrokow. Despite the severity of his injuries and his obvious pain, I was especially delighted to see him. He was my teacher, my mentor, my friend and my hope. His courage inspired me not to despair.

Beyond the risk of being taken to work, there was an episode, around Purim in 1941, when we really felt the oppression and fear for the first time. It was nighttime when we heard horses and wagons pulling up to the house. Within a few seconds there was a really "German" knock at the door. "*Aufmachen!*" they screamed. "*Aufmachen! Polizei!*" When we opened the door, four men came into the room: a Polish policeman, a tremendously huge German civilian with a gun, a German in uniform and a man from the Gestapo.

I was standing in the room with everybody else when these men began yelling, and we did not know what it was they wanted. They came into the store, which was part of the apartment and they started packing things away, throwing things on the floor, tearing the whole thing to pieces. They looked over shelves and in books. The civilian kept his gun leveled and we were scared. They came to frighten us, to harass us and to molest us. They may have wanted to take some of my aunts, who were still quite young, with them.

I wished I had a knife so I could go over to the German civilian and take his gun. He had his back turned to me and there was no one between us. "I think I'll kill him," I thought, "but what about the others?" The

Polish policeman was unarmed — they would not let the Poles keep guns — but there were still more of them than me. What could the girls, or my grandfather, do to put a stop to this?

One of my aunts yelled out the window to a neighbor crossing the courtyard below, "Go call Tennenberg." Zalman Tennenberg was the head of the Judenrat for Piotrokow and a friend of our family.

"These people are respected in the community," Tennenberg told the Gestapo man when he arrived ten minutes later. "It does no good to harass them," he pleaded. Whatever else he said, the group of men took what they had stuffed away and left us. We were grateful for his intervention and relieved when they left, and I remember how we looked at each other and for the first time we talked about what might come next.

"We were lucky," someone said.

"They didn't hurt anybody," another agreed.

"What if they come back?" someone else asked.

The next day, I went down the street to see some people, to wheel and deal a little for some money. As I got back to the house, I saw horses in front. There was a Jewish man holding the horses so they would not run off. The wagon, a luxury coach, was on the sidewalk. "Who is this?" I asked the man. He told me who it was. It was the same group from the night before. They had come back.

I thought about staying downstairs, but I knew that I needed to be with my family, so I walked up. The first person I saw was this big civilian again. Again they were shlepping the store. Again somebody sent for Tennenberg, and again Tennenberg came and straightened it out, and they left and never returned. But from that time on, we were always on the lookout; there was always someone keeping watch.

We never knew why they had come to begin with. We thought that it might be money. We thought that two young boys, brothers, who were collaborating with the Nazis, had turned us in for something. These two were well-known collaborators in the ghetto.

We had other *tsoris* to deal with as well, such as the typhoid epidemic that quarantined my whole family. Someone in this house of forty people caught typhoid and everyone in the apartment was quarantined, except me because I was staying at a friend's house at the time. When a house was quarantined, you had to move out. They locked up the house and took you to isolation, a special place, a fenced-in field on the outskirts of the ghetto, for a week or two until they let you back in to your home.

I realized I was seeing what it must have been like in biblical times, when those plagued with leprosy and other contagious diseases were sent "*michutz la-machaneh*," outside of the camp [of the Israelites]. What I could only imagine as a youngster studying the text, I now saw with my own eyes. Only it was not the high priest who sent us outside the camp. In one of many ironies, it was a German with a hammer, a nail and a skull-and-cross-boned sign marked "*Gefahr! Fleck Tyfus*" posted on the door.

The family had only been back from the quarantine about a week when my father became ill. This was three weeks before Shavuos, 1941. When he became sick, we were afraid to take him to the hospital. The hospital was part of the ghetto, but it was managed by Poles who were supervised by the Germans. Jews were afraid to go to this hospital because those who went in never came out. We also did not want to send everyone into quarantine again. I was in the apartment this time and would have had to go as well. Everybody was there, and we tried to avoid being exposed to my father's illness, to keep the house open.

One of my mother's cousins said, "There is a doctor who heals by remedies," meaning he was not a real doctor, but a man versed in the uses of herbs and potions. This healer, a Hasidic man with a little beard, had helped one or two of my mother's cousins, so he was allowed in the house. He cooked roots and vinegars. It smelled awful. He locked himself in the room with my father and would not let anybody in. Maybe a real doctor would have saved my father. Maybe he would have lived. By the time his condition worsened and we finally hospitalized him, it was already too late.

The last time I talked to my father, I did not know what to say. He could not make himself clear, and did not even recognize me. His eyes were glazed like a veil, open and looking but not seeing. His body was burning with fever. All the while, my brother and I, in separate corners of the house, were praying and reciting Psalms for my father's recovery. We continued to study, continued to learn, for that is all we knew how to do.

About four days before my father died, his temperature was high and he was deteriorating. We had no choice but to call a doctor. We called Dr. Jacobowitz, a Jewish doctor, and he took my father to the hospital in the ghetto.

My mother did not allow me to go to the hospital. In fact, two days before my father died, my mother, my sister and another friend of the family split us up, sending me to stay with a distant cousin in the ghetto. I did not understand why, but I was told so I went. All I knew was that it was too much for my mother to have to see everybody in the house, especially around a holiday, so we were sent away.

Every day I stood in front of the hospital and waited for someone to come out and tell me what was happening. Every day I went. "God will help," we said. "God is the only one who can help." This was our belief, that doctors could not do what God could do, and that everything was according to His will.

We did not tell my father's mother, who now lived on the other side of the same ghetto with my aunt, just how sick my father was. He was the only son of my grandmother's four children. We did not want her to know. But my grandmother was very smart, beneath her *sheitl* and *kupka*, her wig and her turban. She was sort of a landmark, even when we were in Lodz. She would dress up in old lace, traditional in Eastern Europe, especially among Hasidim. Being that she was in the dry goods business, like my father and grandfather, wedding families came to her for the linen, tablecloth and towels for the trousseaus.

She was a short little lady, and nothing could be hidden from her. On the first day of Shavuos my aunt told her my father was very sick. I had not seen my grandmother since my father went into the hospital. As soon as she saw me that day, she asked, "*Vos macht de Tate?* How is your father doing?"

"*Gezundt*," I answered. "He'll be well."

"*Oy, 'ch bet bei dir Goteniu!* My God, I'm pleading with you," she cried, "*Ich vil zein zein ois-leizer.* I want to be his redemption. *Nem ich tsum ersht!* Take me instead of him!" Over and over she wailed and repeated, "*Nem ich tsum ersht!*"

The next day, the second day of Shavuos, one day before my father died, the Kupka, my old and sickly grandmother, passed away. She was buried the same day, as is the custom for those who die on holidays. There was no way to tell my father. He had been in a coma for days.

One day later, the day after Shavuos, my father died. I was at my family's home the night before, only a two- or three-minute walk from the cousin I had been sent to, and there was whispering. The soft voices and the thoughts of the imminent passing of my father kept me awake. Around six o'clock in the morning, before I left for my vigil outside the hospital, my aunt came in and told us he was gone.

I screamed and I cried at having lost him. Even though surrounded by my distraught family, I was still alone with my thoughts, alone in my sadness. Never again would it be like it was before the war. Never again would I walk with my father to prayer services; never again would I accompany him to the rebbe's house; never again would we be together for joyous *simchas*. These thoughts and these memories are all I have left of the father whom I honored and respected, the man I was always with, the man I admired and loved.

My father was buried in the Jewish cemetery, in the ghetto in Piotrokow. Aharon Dovid delivered the eulogy. He was very eloquent. Drawing on my father's name, Shaul or Saul, and my cousin's name Dovid or David, he cited David's eulogy to Saul from the Book of Samuel. "...*Mi-nesharim kalu, may-arayos gavayru.* Swifter than eagles, stronger than lions," he quoted. "*Aych naflu giborim, va-yovdu k'lay milchama.* How the mighty have fallen and the weapons of war have perished."

There was no rabbi for the funeral, no *tahara* (purification ritual) before the funeral. It was a funeral of circumstances. I was told later that the *chevra kadisha*, the group responsible for guarding and preparing the body for burial, secretly went to the cemetery that night, took my father's body out of the ground, performed the *tahara* and buried him in a shroud, according to our law.

There was pain when we prayed during the *shiva*, and there was *tsoris*, and it all seemed to pile on the pain and the suffering of our everyday lives in the ghetto. It was everything together. The prayers of mourning took on a focus beyond my father's death. It was then that I began to notice the words, when the prayers stopped being automatic and there was meaning in every phrase. The sound of every word I prayed became important. It was as if there was a soul in each pronouncement, a tone coming home to its proper interpretation. It was when I learned to pray, how to conduct the services and give the prayers proper *kavana*, their spiritually unique expression. To this day, every time I conduct a weekly service, I have to control myself, because with each verse of the *Ashrei* (Psalm 133), each response in the *Kedusha* ("Holy, Holy Holy is the Lord of Hosts. The whole world is filled with His honor") of the morning and afternoon prayers I am back there, at this *shiva* for my father.

I was seventeen years old and I grew into a man overnight. I was the oldest son with four little ones — my two sisters and two brothers were much younger — and suddenly I was responsible for the family.

A GHETTO WEDDING

It was in 1941, after the *shloshim* for my father, that we had a wedding at my grandparents' house in the Piotrokow ghetto. My cousin, Aharon Dovid, was marrying my mother's sister Rikel. They were first cousins, but that is permissible by Jewish law. Aharon Dovid was a handsome young man, in his twenties, well learned and knowledgeable in Jewish and world literature and philosophy. He had a beautiful voice and would read the *gemorrah* like a song, though he was not 100 percent observant. I felt very close to him. Rikel was the sixth of the nine girls my grandparents had. She had big, dark eyes, good business sense and a voracious sweet tooth.

I was surprised at the match. I knew Aharon Dovid had his eyes on my Aunt Perl, my mother's youngest sister. Even under the unreasonable conditions of ghetto living, and maybe because of them, my grandparents followed tradition and did not permit the younger to be married before the elder.

I remember sitting around Shabbes afternoon and kibitzing with Aharon Dovid as we teased his grandmother, my great-grandmother. She was well over a hundred, but with all her senses.

"Bubba Chava," we used to say, "how many grandchildren and great-grandchildren do you have?"

"Fifty-seven," she answered, and she would name them all, every single one.

"And what about *yichus*," we kept teasing. "You talk about heritage and standing in the community? I know what your father did! He was a firefighter!"

Sometimes she would play along. "No. He was a volunteer. It was a small town and when there was a fire, they called him to put it out. He did a *mitzvah*."

We did not let up. "No. He was a real firefighter. He drove the horses...."

We knew we won when she would call over my grandfather. "Berish, *nem de poshim avec*. Get these sinners away!" She called us "sinners" because, of course, it is not proper to make fun of an older person, but we did not care. We were in stitches. We wanted her to call over my grandfather and complain, create a bit of mischief.

Bubba Chava kept her crochet and sewing, all her possessions really, in a little straw suitcase on a high shelf. Every day, she would get on a stepladder and check the suitcase, making sure everything was arranged neatly. This was her little area in a house of forty people. We teased her about that too.

"You just fixed that yesterday. Nobody touched it," we chided.

"You can't trust anybody here," she said, knowing that sadly, under the circumstances, she was right.

Yet it was the circumstances that made humor as important to our family as the small ration of bread we received every day. It was a staple for our survival. We joked and teased, laughed at stories of others and ourselves. Sometimes, I came up with things I thought were cute. Maybe they were stupid. Like the way I asked my grandfather, "Zeydishi, don't you have a pipe?"

This was Saturday night, after *havdalla*, and I remembered that when I was in Yeshiva, visiting the rebbe's home, he would light up his treasured *lulke* when Shabbes was over.

My grandfather turned to me with a smile as understated as his gentle character and said, "Why should I have a pipe? I never smoked in my life!"

"Usually old people have pipes," I said. Although he played along with me and laughed at my pretentiousness, I was ashamed that I had disrespected him by calling him "old." The others laughed with him, while shaking their heads at me as if to say, "You stupid boy. What are you saying?"

We found other ways of entertaining each other, like the old rope trick.

We folded a rope a certain way, cut it, tied knots in it, and when we let it go, voila! It was a whole rope again! These are the ways we found to amuse one another. Like the wedding of Rikel and Aharon Dovid, it was how we brought a little taste of happiness to the bitterness of life in the ghetto.

Of course the circumstances created a necessity for secrecy. The wedding was decided only the week before, and my grandparents did not divulge their plan until a few days after that. Even then, there was no joy, no excitement, no singing and no dancing. Only whispered blessings, quiet meditations and prayers, and the belief in the holy *mitzvah* of betrothal. The words were spoken *sotto voce*, for the ears of God and those assembled, and not for those outside the walls of our home. Only two neighbors who were there as the witnesses, the *eydim*, were allowed to take part in the ceremony. The wedding was simple. The *chupa* was a *tallis*, held at the corners by four of my uncles. My aunt wore my grandmother's wedding dress. My grandfather's brother performed the rites. The wine was cooked from raisins. You could see in the faces, the thinness of the faces, sad eyes instead of smiles.

I thought about my father [ז״ל], about how much he loved Aharon Dovid and was not there to see him married. Nor would he be at my wedding, or those of my brothers and sisters. I watched, and in my heart I saw my dreams, my hopes, that someday, if and when we survive, the family weddings would be celebrated as they were before the war — with music, dancing and of course the great wedding feast.

For this modest event, some special food was prepared. When I say special, I mean there was a fresh-baked white bread, instead of the black bread we were usually rationed; there was an egg, or powdered eggs for an omelet. There was no meat available, of course. Everything had to be prepared fresh to keep from either spoiling or being stolen from a windowsill where sometimes food was left to cool. Whatever we had, it was just for the sake of partaking in the ceremonial meal, the *seudas mitzvah*, which was part of every wedding.

After the wedding, Aharon Dovid and Rikel moved into a little apartment around the corner. My grandmother gave them some bedding and whatever else she could that they needed. Soon afterward, they had a baby girl.

Eventually, Aharon Dovid had to do something to provide for his family, so my aunt told him how I made socks and stockings and sold them. Soon, he was doing the same thing. Suddenly, I had a competitor because he sold to the same people I did. We were competing for customers, and even though we were family, it was natural that there was a little resentment. I was frustrated and unhappy, and even a little jealous. But as conditions in the ghetto continued to worsen, all the pettiness over business and money seemed less important than being together as a family and trying to survive.

It was during the *shloshim* for my father that we heard that the Russians had entered the war. That was June 21, 1941. The news was smuggled in from the outside. I remember getting a hold of a month-old copy of *Das Reich*. Himmler's propaganda paper was obviously one-sided, but at least we knew what was going on and how the Wehrmacht was progressing on the Eastern Front.

In the meantime, I had to grow up in a hurry. Being the oldest, it became my responsibility to provide for my mother, brothers and sisters. I continued to wheel and deal in whatever I could, this time on my own, using my father's connection to the money dealer, buying and selling goods as we did before, just trying to get by with the few zloty that we made.

It is hard to imagine a boy in the Piotrokow ghetto, not even eighteen, carrying diamonds, gold, and American gold certificates, but people trusted me; when people trust you, especially under those circumstances, they watch out for your safety and you do the same for them. After all, there was real danger in the kind of dealing that I did. Being trustworthy was just another way to survive.

Still, being honest in business did not keep me from going to the place where my grandmother hid the family ration of bread, and in the dark, while everyone was sleeping, stealing a small slice. I knew my grandmother made a mark on the outside of the loaf after the last piece had been cut so she would know if someone had been secretly helping himself. So after I cut my little piece, I made a similar mark with the knife.

We were only given a certain amount of bread per week, but when you know that it is rationed, you always want more. Was there a difference between cheating in business and stealing bread? No, of course not.

But in such a situation, action is beyond rationalization.

In the ghetto there were people who selfishly cheated others for not only food, but money as well. There were thieves and there were squealers. The thieves stole to survive, so perhaps that could be forgiven. The squealers, the ones who worked for the Gestapo, would kill you, or in their collaboration with the Nazis, cause you to be killed, thinking that they could save themselves.

No matter who they were, word got out among the people. "Watch out for him," they would say. We knew who they were. They were those who placed themselves above everybody, although to us, they were of the lowest moral character. We looked at them and said, "These are not human beings."

Of course, the Germans had the same feelings about us. To them, we were the lowest. One early spring day, I was walking down the main street of the ghetto with my friend, Label Sanik, whom I had known since early childhood. We grew up together and went to the same *cheder* in Lodz. Rounding a corner on our way to visit Label's grandfather, Reb Mendel Weinacht, we heard the noise of a motorcycle engine pulling up behind us. The brakes squealed as it stopped.

"*Jude! Komm doch mahl her!* Hey, Jew," one of the Nazi soldiers shouted (he was talking to both of us, but they never used proper grammar when referring to us; it was another way of treating us without dignity).

We turned and saw the motorcycle and sidecar with two soldiers, regular German army, not brown shirt or SS. "*Lauf doch!* Run, run!" they shouted at us. Of course we ran. We thought they might be taking us to do some work. This was, after all, the way they often rounded up workers, like dogs rounding up cattle. Label and I looked at each other. The soldiers were laughing as their motorcycle throttled at our heels, and it was the kind of laughter from an enemy that makes your heart jump from your chest in fear.

About a mile farther down this road, which led to Warsaw, was the German headquarters building. At the entrance was a big archway that opened to a courtyard. They parked the motorcycle out front and the two soldiers kicked us to the ground from behind. If there were any other Germans around, I did not see them. All I was aware of was my fear. They shoved us into the passageway beneath the arch, and screamed, "Against the wall! Hands up, Pig-dogs! *Schweinenhundt! De Juden haben den Krieg gewollt!* It's the Jews' fault that there is a war."

We stood with our faces to the cold, shaded white wall, hearing the epithets, the familiar piercing sound of the German *herrenvolk* — the commanding tone of a lord race over its weakened subjects — echoing through the passageway. I flinched at the rough click of a bullet being loaded into the chamber of a pistol. My mind was bursting with flying thoughts of whether I should pray or I should cry. Sometime in the middle of this noisy inner struggle, I started to do both. It was not until I felt the cold steel of the gun barrel against my right temple that I suddenly stopped thinking. In that brief moment, I heard only silence. The next moment was pain. The soldier behind me kicked my behind hard with his long boot and the gun came away.

"*Maches lose du arsch loch!* Get out of here, asshole!" he shouted and Label and I ran as fast as we could back to our families.

Meanwhile, the chill of early spring 1942 was not any different than the ghetto's cold winter. The change of seasons did not awaken in us the customary hope a warmer time brings. It did not matter to us whether the flowers would grow to full bloom or the sun would shine from day to day. The flowers did not grow in the ghetto, nor did the sun shine for us. All that is natural in a normal life did not exist for us in that place. It seemed, rather, that behind the walls that held us in, life was in a permanent twilight.

At the Sabbath services we had at my grandparents' home it was announced to the small minyan that the month of Nisan was about to begin. Rather than fill us with the joy the beginning of the Passover season brings, we were more gloomy than ever. We had hoped until then that our prayers would somehow be heard by the Almighty. The month of Nisan is the month of freedom, of liberation from bondage, according to the words of our rabbis in the Talmud: "In the month of Nisan Israel was redeemed and in the same month they will be redeemed." There would be no redemption this Nisan.

Still, we made plans for the Passover celebration, keeping in mind that it was a commandment, a *mitzvah*, to retell the story of the Exodus from Egypt. Somehow we managed to bake a few matzohs for the seder. We tried to follow the Hagaddah, reciting the story in the proper order, but we stumbled. At every passage we read, we found ourselves confronted by contradiction after contradiction. We had more questions to ask than the usual four. Our main question was, why? Why do we celebrate liberation when we are not redeemed? Why do we celebrate freedom when we are not free? The answers in the Hagaddah were unsatisfactory. We had no answers.

I fell ill with typhoid in the early summer of 1942. I was taken to a hospital in the ghetto on Pilsudski Street where there were doctors we knew. I stayed there a week or two and then returned home.

After I was really sick, I needed new papers from that same doctor that said I was healthy, had a strong heart and was a good worker, because by that time, if you were not working, you were worthless and would be shipped out. Young people knew that to stay healthy was to stay alive, because if you could work in the German factories, you were necessary and would be protected. Trading socks was not going to keep me alive. The Germans did not need sock traders. With my certificates of health, I went to the factory where fine glass objects and crystal were blown, called the *Hortensia*. The *Hortensia* was also the main office for the industrial glass factory called the *Kara*. Both were part of the same company. I walked into the office, showed them my papers and told them, "I'm ready to work."

"Fine," said Kuchhammer, the factory's director. "You can start tomorrow."

The next morning I reported to the *Hortensia*. It was hard. I carried sacks of soda as big as one hundred kilos on my back. With my bare and bruised hands, I unloaded chunks of black, dusty coal weighing ten kilos or more, and carried them from the railroad freight cars to the glass factory furnaces. I shoveled the sand for making the glass from the train into huge piles beside the tracks, jumping off the cars just long enough for the train to move forward to the next carload of sand, and the next, and the next.

For a few days, when I showed up at the *Hortensia*, I was put on a detail at the *Kara*, which was not unusual since workers were needed at both factories. The detail cleaned bricks from the factory, rubble from older, demolished furnaces and chimneys. It took two people to carry a box with twenty bricks in it. I was still young, barely eighteen, and my muscles still were growing. It was heavy, but I managed. I was assigned an older man, a man in his forties, to be my partner. His name was Ferenkranz, and he was from a well-known family in Lodz, people in the textile business. He knew my whole family. Unfortunately, he could hardly lift the load. To make it worse, he was much taller than I was and he was assigned to lift the back of the box so all the weight shifted toward me. We would pile the rocks high in the carrier to make it look like more than twenty bricks so we would be able to lift it. The foreman, a racist Pole named Wojdela, who saw us struggling, yelled, "Stop! Put down your load."

Thinking that perhaps he was taking pity on us, we sighed and set the carrier on the ground. Just as we were ready to rest, he screamed, "Lazy Jews! Put in twice again more," and we were loaded down with sixty bricks. With both of us struggling to lift the heavier load, Wojdela continued to yell names and throw bricks and stones at us.

In the rush of thoughts that crossed my mind under this oppression was the toil of our ancestors under the whips of the Egyptian taskmasters, the collecting of bricks, the burden of slavery. Wojdela also carried a whip, and he railed against us, as the taskmasters railed at the Children of Israel, "...*Nirpim atem nirpim....* Lazy you are, lazy. *V'ata, lechu ivdu.* Now go work."

Sometimes I wanted to cry. If I cried, he would be more vicious. The stinging words made me want to work, not to please Wojdela or the Germans, but to live above those epithets, to prove to myself that I am a man who can work.

If anyone took to the labor with relish, they were considered a "good worker," and they were rewarded, so to speak, with "easier" work. That meant that if four carloads of coal were unloaded quickly, the "privileged" workers were given a rest for the remainder of the day. What was the rest? They were given brooms and shovels and "allowed" to sweep the grounds.

The labor carried with it rage and frustration. In my mind I fantasized about how I could strike a blow against the Germans. I had what I thought were opportunities. When coming into the *Hortensia* for the start of our shifts, the guards frisked us. The entrance to this factory was right next to the gasoline depot. With one match, somebody could blow the whole thing up. Thousands of barrels of oil and gasoline were there, piled next to the rail depot. These were the tracks that took German soldiers to the Russian Front. What a disruption this would cause!

There had been other opportunities, too, earlier that year. Before I came to work at the factory, I was caught by the Germans and put on a special detail to unload trucks at Gestapo headquarters. The detail was comprised of about ten young men, all around seventeen years old. The trucks were piled with wooden crates, quite heavy, but light enough for each boy to be able to carry one at a time. As I lifted the boxes from the back of the truck, I could see something through the wooden slats — handguns. We were carrying boxes and boxes of handguns into the German warehouse.

While we were not allowed to talk with each other, from the glances of the others, it was obvious that we all had the same thought. We all thought about stealing a gun. I pictured myself with a pistol in my hand. And then what?

We were constantly watched, from the moment we picked up a case from the truck until we set it down on the warehouse floor. Soldiers were walking behind us, their bayonets and rifles leveled at our backs. There may even have been someone watching us from a window in the head-quarters building. It also occurred to me that the whole thing might be a setup of some kind, just to see if we would steal the weapons.

A month or so later, after coming to work full-time at the factory, I was put on a demolition detail in the nearby Rakow Forest. We filled up bags with gunpowder to blow out tree stumps. Supervised by Wojdela, we would fill the bags and place them by the trees and the German demolition unit would blow them up. If there were armed guards we did not see them, but they could have been hiding in the forest. It was only fear that kept us from pocketing some gunpowder.

But what would I, or any of us, have done with one pistol or a handful of gunpowder? Fight the whole German army? It was the same feeling of helplessness I had in my grandfather's apartment when the Gestapo and the three other men came in and I wanted to take a knife to them. It is good to take revenge if you know you are going to accomplish something, but then you have all the other ramifications. What could be accomplished by killing one German soldier? The army would be on you in no time. What would the consequences be for my family?

It was like a test. Like Abraham being tested by God when he was asked to sacrifice Isaac, or Samson when he brought the temple down on the Philistines: "'...*Ta-mot nafshi im p'lishtim*. Let me die with the Philistines....'" Was I being called upon to make the ultimate sacrifice?

A match. A pistol. Gunpowder. A knife. I could have acted with any one of those, and others, to be sure, but I did not. In fact, up to that time, my family was still relatively intact, except for my father who died of natural causes, so I had no real reason to act in revenge.

By late August 1942, word reached us from surrounding towns such as Czestochowa that ghettos were being evacuated. The few who managed to smuggle themselves into our ghetto before they too were taken told us how the Ukrainians and the Germans came into their ghettos, rounded up the people and took them away on trains. We did not believe that they would reach Piotrokow. "Well, Czestochowa is two hundred kilometers away. By the time they reach here, the war will be over. They will never get here. *Got vet helf'n*, God will help."

During the High Holidays, we heard that Radomsko, a town only eighty kilometers away, met the same fate. Still, we had faith that we would be spared. By *Sukkos* word came about Kaminsk, a farm town barely forty kilometers from Piotrokow. Although we still did not want to believe they would come to our city, despair slowly began to creep into our hearts. "It is too late," people said. "Let's try to do something. Get out. Run away. Go into the woods and hide."

Within our family, there were those who said, "*Vos vet paseer'n mit kol Yisroel, vet paseer'n mit reb Yisroel*. Whatever fate awaits all Jews befalls the individual Jew." This was an acceptance of fate, a surrendering to providence. I was not ready to surrender.

Eventually I was assigned to work in the *Kara* glass factory only, where I was mixing mortar. It was a privileged job, because I was a sort of errand boy for a group of engineers the Reich had brought in to build a new chimney for a new glass-making furnace. The Germans imported four Polish specialists from Lodz, a foreman and three others. The Polish chimney builders taught me a trade, how to mix the mortar. It had to have a certain consistency and required constant stirring or it would not be able to withstand the intense heat of the oven. I was lucky to be able to work unsupervised. The commandant of the factory complex, Mr. Kristman Sr., always nodded his approval at me as he passed.

The Polish engineers took a liking to me, and I soon was put to work cleaning their apartment, washing their dishes and preparing their food. To me, this was advancement, because this way I had plenty of food myself. It was non-kosher food, and I hesitated a lot before I ate it. It was cheating, it was wrong, but it was a way to satisfy my hunger.

Because it was not kosher, I could not bring the food into my grandfather's house. Instead, I managed to barter some of it with Polish factory workers for a loaf of bread or some fresh eggs. We were always searched as we left the glass factory, and if they found any food on you it was confiscated.

Once, while smuggling out a loaf of bread, it appeared to me that the guards were searching everybody. I wanted to get through cleanly and not get in trouble. The only thing I could think of was to start eating. Piece by piece, I broke the bread from the loaf and discreetly shoveled it in my mouth. "Better to be sick than to get caught," I thought. I even gave some to the person next to me. As I got closer to the front, the bread shrank, but I had to keep moving farther back in the line until it was completely gone.

Another time, I had traded for ten fresh eggs, and the only way to get them out without dropping them was to carry them in the hollow of my windbreaker, above the elastic, with my hands guarding them gingerly from inside my pockets. When I got to the front, I removed my hands from my pockets to show I have nothing and I prayed the loose eggs would not fall or be crushed inside my windbreaker if the guards decided to pat me down. I walked slowly away until I could get my hands back in my pockets, then with the eggs slightly more secure, I headed home.

Meanwhile, the evacuations of other ghettos continued to get closer. Every day, when I returned from my work at the factory, we heard of more ghettos closing. We could not run — not all of us. My grandparents were too old and there were small children. Talk went around our family that we must build a hiding place. "When they come, maybe they won't find us. We don't know how long we can hide there, but let's do something."

Building a hiding place took a lot of preparation. We had to be able to hide not only ourselves, but our resources as well. We took bars of soap, and with a small knife, scraped a little slot in the top of the bars, just big enough to drop in one or two gold coins. The coins we had were Czarist Russian gold pieces, British sovereigns and French Louis. Part of the collection was my grandfather's, from before the war, to use for his daughters' dowries. Once the coins were in the soap, we filled the hole with the shavings and smoothed out the bars. We did not know if anyone had done something like that. It seemed like an original idea. It was something that just came to mind. Soap made the most sense to us because it was the least likely to be confiscated by the Germans.

I remember sitting with my grandfather in the corner of the main room of the apartment as my aunts and cousins brought him the coins to be hidden. Although almost everyone in the house knew what we were doing, there was still a concern for privacy, a lingering sense of possession. For us, as Hasidim, counting money in front of someone, even family, brought on the "evil eye." We wanted to guard against that. Knowing how much gold or how many coins another had brought pettiness and envy. If one person sees that another has more, then an evil eye will enter the picture and the whole endeavor of hiding the coins would be jeopardized. Something might very well happen to these bars of soap if the evil eye was brought into the process.

People should not look. I remember when my father had to give someone on the street money for a charity, or even to pay some of his employees, he would not just peel off a ten-zloty note and hand it to the person. He used to turn around and, with his back to the person, take the bill from his wallet.

This superstition dates back to biblical times. In the Jewish tradition, people were not counted numerically. When Moses was commanded by God to take a census of the Children of Israel, he was told that each person should bring a half-shekel coin, and it was the coins that were counted. The rabbis tell us that the reason the coins were counted is that human beings are precious, and "...in numbers there is an evil eye" (Rashi, Ex. 30:12).

That is why I found myself sitting in secret, in the night, hiding pieces of gold in bars of soap. Because we were a huge family, everyone had a little something they wanted to hide. We had linens, pictures, a few pieces of jewelry and traditional Judaic pieces. We agreed the best possible place to hide these things would be in the storage room that was across the entrance from my grandparents' apartment.

One night, together with my cousin Aharon Dovid and my Aunt Perl, I walked into the little room and closed the door. Perl had a candle and in the dark, she struck a match and lit it. Walking over to the right-hand wall, we looked for a spot in the middle from which to remove some of the old bricks from the crumbling mortar. The walls of the building were thick, perhaps half a meter, and there was enough room to place some of the jewelry, some of the special bars of soap, and family photographs inside it. With a small bucket of mortar and the trowel I had brought with me, I began to shore up the wall. The closet was old and dirty, having been the room where we stored the coal in the winter. After I finished bricking the wall, we took some of the coal dust from the floor and smeared it over the new mortar.

Now it came time to prepare a hiding place for ourselves. With the help of my Uncle Nachum Naidat, who owned a lumberyard in Alexander before the war, we went to a wing of the apartment building that had a high attic. Next to the entrance to this attic lived a family of Seventh-day Adventists, the Makowskis. We knew they could be trusted. They had helped us to hide the merchandise from my grandfather's store. On several occasions, they risked their lives to bring us food from outside the ghetto. More significantly, while other Gentile families had fled the ghetto, they chose to remain. If we confided in them, we knew it was sacred.

The attic was actually part of the Makowskis' apartment. They hung their laundry in there. In order for my uncle and me to get into the attic, we had to go through their house. We were grateful that we could trust in their honesty. If we had gone to the attic on the other side of the building, we would have gone through a Jewish house. That would have meant accommodating them in our hiding place, and we had a big enough family as it was.

Once inside the attic, we looked over the space and decided where would be the best place to put a false wall. We also estimated the amount of material we would have to organize to build the wall. In the ceiling of the room there were two skylights. By placing the wall between the two, we would have access to the hiding place by climbing onto the roof from one skylight and entering the false room from the other.

We decided on a cement wall for many reasons. First, from my work at the factory I had become an expert at mixing mortar. Second, it required almost no nailing, since that would cause too much noise. Third, it would look more like the end of the room, preserving the illusion of a real wall, and lastly, if the Germans were to knock on the wall, the mortar would not give a hollow sound.

We went to work organizing materials everywhere we could without attracting any attention. Everyday I would smuggle a little mortar mix from the factory in a small paper bag. Makowski got us more cement, sand and lime. We picked up scraps of wood and pieces of screen for the frame of the wall wherever we could find them.

We could not hammer at night, and only with someone watching for Germans during the day. Makowski sometimes nailed board for us. Still, to keep the noise to a minimum, we cut most of the wood so it would join without nailing. We worked at night by candlelight. I had to mix the mortar quickly, before it could harden, and apply it to the frame of wood and wire. I was careful to mix so the texture would resemble the rest of the room as closely as possible. When the cement was dry, we painted the wall white with lime. As soon as we could, we stocked the hiding place with potatoes and water, and that is the way we left it. We still did not know if we would ever have to use it.

About two weeks after we completed building our hiding place, word had gotten out about another quota of Jews that were about to be sent away. We took these things seriously. It was also known by this time that if one were to bribe the right official, they would be saved for the factory and not sent away. When I arrived at the house I told everyone what I had heard. I did not know if I was on the list of those to stay with the factory or not, but we did not want to take any chances. Time was of the essence and Aunt Perl took it upon herself to go speak to the *Hortensia* director,

Herford. I do not know what Perl said to him or gave him, or even if she just smiled at him when she met him at his house, but she told me she talked to him. The rest was up to Herford.

The next day I was finishing up another shift in the glass factory. An hour or so before the end of our shift, the *Kara* factory director, a Polish German named Vogel, gathered all the Jewish workers in the yard by the front gate. As two hundred of us stood in the October air, Vogel, a short, unimpressive man whose dress alternated between German uniform, brown shirts and civilian clothes, moved by us in his familiar jackboots and swastika and bow-leggedly stepped in front. We all became quiet. Though he was always trying to make himself seem impressive, the only evidence of Vogel's limited authority was his loud, shrill voice.

As we all listened, he began to read names from a few pages of paper he held in his hand. The names were read in alphabetical order, and for all we knew, this could have been a list of men who were being sent away, maybe on to the trains that we had heard about from the people who fled from the other communities. When I heard my name, I prayed that this was a "good" list, that the risk Perl took was not in vain and that somehow it would be a turn in my favor.

After reading about one hundred names, he looked up from his papers and into our faces. "You have one hour to go home and pack a knapsack with whatever you can carry," he announced. "Be back at the gathering point (Plac Trybunalski, where we gathered every morning to be taken to work) at seven o'clock. Do not be late."

As quickly as I could, I ran home from the *Kara*. I knew that if I was even one minute after seven, the consequences would be harsh. Before I even walked into my grandfather's house, I sensed something. I opened the door and went inside. The faces of my family were not the regular faces I was used to. They were not smiling faces, looking at me with that kindness that was always there. Instead, fear was in their eyes. I was waiting for words to be said. A word of courage, anything. Maybe they knew more already than I did. It was a silent conversation between my grandfather and my mother, between me and my mother, between my aunts and uncles, between my cousins, my brothers and my sisters.

I opened my mouth to speak, to break the silence. "I have to go back to the gathering place at seven," I told them. "They told me to pack and be back at the marketplace." I wanted to know if I should stay with them, if I should not return to Plac Trybunalski and stay with them.

Someone picked my knapsack up from the floor and began to pack it. Soon others were helping. They did not want me to be late. All the while I was questioning them, wanting them to tell me that I should stay with them. They did not answer right away. Little by little, they kept packing my bag. My *tefillin*, my *siddur*, a few pieces of clothing. My grandfather gave me some paper money, maybe a few hundred zloty and some Reichsmarks. Then he turned to his bookcase and pulled out a tiny, thin book. It was *Milin D'Rabonnon*, "Words of the Rabbis," a collection of rabbinic wisdom. With watery eyes he held it out to me and as I took it he said, "Let this be *tsedo ladorech*, food for the journey."

"But I don't want to go," I protested. "You are my family. I want to stay with you."

In one voice they all began to shout, "Go! Go! You'll be late!"

I opened my mouth to say good bye. No words came. I could not hug anyone or kiss anyone. Before I turned to the door, I looked at their faces for the last time and we embraced with our eyes. With a very heavy heart, I reached up to kiss the mezuzah before I closed the apartment door behind me.

CHAPTER

12

IS A SON WHO IS SEPARATED FROM HIS LIVING FAMILY AN ORPHAN?

Out of breath from running, I made it back to the gathering place with a few minutes to spare. The square was packed with fifteen hundred Jewish men who worked in the different factories around Piotrokow. Some worked at Bugai, a furniture and woodworking factory, and the others worked at the *Kara* or *Hortensia* glass factories with me, though not all from the same shift.

As we were marched off to our factories, our group was buzzing with the different stories we all had heard when we went home. There was a lot of speculation. One heard that the Ukrainians were already in the town, and that they were worse than the Germans. They kill Jews mercilessly, we were told. Others heard how, in other cities, the Jews were dragged from their homes as Ukrainians stood in the apartment courtyards firing in the air. The Jews in those places were ordered to take their belongings and gather in the town centers, and from there they were taken to the train station and sent away. Those who were telling these stories as we neared the glass factory did not hear where the trains had gone. They did not know because those who told them these stories did not know.

When we arrived at the factories, we were divided into two groups. We were each given a jute, an empty burlap sack, and directed to the heaps of straw piled in the factory yard. I carried my jute over to the straw and began filling the bag. Like many of my neighbors before the war, I had never had to sleep on what we called in Polish a *sienik*. Still, I remember them being a big seller in my father's store. They were so popular that there was actually a government-controlled cartel that limited the supply of this much-sought-after commodity. Those who could not afford regular beds used jutes filled with straw. Once a year, at Passover, they would change out the old straw and refill it. After all, straw was cheap and plentiful. In the center of our apartment courtyard in Lodz, we collected the old stuffing and used it to build a big fire to incinerate the *chometz* of all seventy-two tenants in our building.

I stood in the factory yard with my *sienik* in my hands and acquiescence in my heart. While going from a padded mattress to a straw one was not the worst we had yet endured, it symbolized another sacrifice. Once again, I surrendered to fate. This time it was a bag of straw. What of the next time?

There was not enough room for all of us to sleep at one place, so one group went to the *Kara*, and one to the *Hortensia*. I was sent to the latter. Sleeping next to the furnaces would be warm on the cold nights of late October. I went in and found a space among the other mattresses on the stone floor. As I lay there with my eyes open, I tried not to think of the operators who would steal from you while you slept or bribe the foreman to move you so they could have your spot.

My thoughts were with my family. In my head, I was still there, where they were. Separated only a few hours, I was not detached. In my thoughts I planned a way to meet them again, to find them in the hiding place. I was at once certain that the Germans would not find the secret room, since it was done so well, and at the same time, I pictured huge cracks developing in the plaster. I wondered if my family even made it to the hiding place. Did they have enough time? Are they still together? I thought back on the stories we heard and I was afraid.

By the next evening, we found just how true those rumors we had been hearing were. Around six o'clock, a train went by the siding adjacent to the factory. Those who were working by the rails described how thousands of scraps of paper floated from the train as it passed. They were notes, and the non-Jewish workers who were standing at the tracks brought them inside to us.

Someone brought me a brown scrap of paper covered with Yiddish writing scrawled in pencil. It was from my aunts Sara-Chana and Hinde

Rochel. "We are going to Treblinka," the note read. "There is no point in continuing to work. Throw away your shovels. Your fate will be the same as ours." Besides my two aunts, the note said my cousin Aharon Dovid was there with his wife Rikel and their baby.

It would have been easy then to throw away our shovels, as my aunts suggested. But what good would it have done? Were we going to start a rebellion with shovels against bullets? My mind focused on the attic room I had helped prepare for my family. "If these people are on the train, my mother's sisters, my cousin, who managed to make it to the hiding place?" I asked myself. My aunts were supposed to be there with my grandparents, my mother, my brothers and sisters.

Every single one of us in the factory was afraid. Those with the courage to speak their thoughts asked one another, "What's the use? They will come for us tomorrow or the day after or two days after or a week after. They will get rid of the ghetto and then come for us."

"But the Germans need us," many said. "They need our labor. They're building a new oven. They're building new additions to the glass factory." That is, after all, what we had been told by the supervisors. I felt secure because I knew I was on the special list of needed workers. Under the circumstances, I thought I was going to be okay. The Germans were keeping us there to finish work for the German army.

Two days after the train to Treblinka passed by, I was sweeping the grounds around the factory, when suddenly I heard people yelling all around me. "A hundred-fifty people," they shouted as they ran by. "They need 150 more people for Treblinka!"

People were running everywhere, in all different directions. All of a sudden, the security I thought I had meant nothing. They had a quota. They would take anyone, so I was running also. Out of the corner of my eye, I saw my mother's cousin, Eliezer Rappaport, run by. I followed him because even before the war he used to do business at the factory, and he knew the place like a cat. There was not a hole or tunnel or brick he did not know.

He ran into one of the underground tunnels, where the gas used to run to an oven that had not been in operation for years. Into the channel he went, and I followed him. It was like crawling through a chimney, the fireproof bricks black with soot, the old gas fumes reeking from the charred walls. It was dangerous, to be sure, but I was too frightened to notice. All I could do was hope the Germans would make their quota before I got out of there again.

Finally, I called out to him, "Cousin! It's Itche. I'm right behind you." Until then, he did not even know I was there.

"You!" he turned to me in disbelief. "What are you doing? It's me they're after. Herford hates me."

Herford was the German director of the Jewish inmates. He supervised our work. He was *volksdeutsch*, a German who lived in Poland. He had some sort of grievance against my cousin Rappaport from before the war. I never found out what it was, but my cousin was sure Herford wanted him to be among the 150.

While we waited in the tunnel, we could hear Herford yelling out, "Rappaport! Where is Rappaport?"

We waited there for an hour, and when it had quieted down, we crawled out an end quite far from where we had entered. Inmates greeted us with laughter at the way we looked. We emerged black as chimneysweepers, but safe. The Germans had gotten their quota and gone. I washed my clothes well (they were the only set I brought with me) with the soda we used at the factory. Still, it took two or three days for the smell of gas to go away. Days later, Rappaport was taken. In the less than two weeks I was at the factory, the Germans had transported twenty-five thousand Jews from Piotrokow.

The Germans consolidated the ghetto in a tiny area of the old Jewish neighborhood, along the *Yiddengass*. Word was sent to the factory workers, both at the two glass factories and the Bugai, that we were to take our belongings and go back to the ghetto until barracks could be built for us at the factories. We had been sleeping on our jute mattresses on the floor of the factory for only two nights.

The smaller ghetto was scary. The *Yiddengass* was divided lengthwise with barbed wire tied to posts ten feet apart, as was a parallel street only one block away. This narrow part of the ghetto was called the *kleine blok*. Ukrainian guards patrolled either side of the block, and for the first few nights they would fire their rifles in the air to frighten us.

Afterward, the guards were visible only at the one barbed wire entrance. A Jewish policeman who checked the lists of workers as we came and went manned the gatehouse.

I walked into the ghetto to see people, yet they were not people. It was like a zoo, the human animal caged behind wire walls. It was all kind of unnatural. Some sort of base, primal behavior began emerging. The sacrifices that we would have made for each other before, even among our own families, somehow faded into the shadows of ghetto fence posts.

Some of the people who came to the small ghetto had their own houses to go back to. Even so, they had to open them up to others. I was sleeping with a cousin from my mother's side, another Krieger, Uncle Chemya's son. He and three other men — acquaintances from the first ghetto — were quick enough to "organize" a room when they got to the smaller ghetto.

The first night in the small ghetto, I found out what happened to my family. Walking in and out of the courtyards that lined the *Yiddengass*, I saw my mother's younger sister, Perl. She was waiting for me near the ghetto entrance. I cried when I saw her. She told me where my mother was, where my brother and sister were, and how she managed to avoid the transports.

The day after I went to the factory with the other men, the Germans gathered the Jews of the big ghetto and started calling out names of those who would stay and not have to go with the transport. When Perl heard the name "Raichman" being called, she stepped forward. Her name was not Raichman, of course. The Raichmans had already been transported, and my aunt knew that. She took our cousin Balcha's hand and pulled her along. Balcha was Aharon Dovid's sister. But she did not want to remain behind. She wanted to be with her brother who was already going to Treblinka, and she pulled away from Perl. In this way my aunt saved herself from the transport.

From her I learned that my mother, my grandparents and my brothers and sisters were being held in the synagogue with about 160 other Jews who were flushed from hiding places in the ghetto. Nervous and distressed, in halting half sentences, Perl told me that our family did indeed make it into the hiding place we had so painstakingly built. But soon after the last transport left the ghetto, the Germans came with dogs to sniff out anyone who was in hiding. They took all they found, 162 people, and placed them in the synagogue, under Ukrainian guard. They were held there because the Germans did not want them in the small ghetto. The synagogue, which was outside the ghetto, was the only place large enough to hold such a group.

Perl handed me a scrap of brown paper with pencil writing on it. "Somebody who made it out of the synagogue brought this to me," she said. "It's from your mother."

"*Rateve undz*," the note said in Yiddish. "Rescue us."

Looking at the paper in my hand, I did not know what to do. "How do you get into the synagogue, with all the guards around it?" I asked Perl.

"I don't know," she said, "but people manage somehow."

While we could not stop worrying about my mother and the children in the synagogue, our concern was suddenly and unpredictably unseated by a new urgency, one that was no less dangerous but perhaps more manageable. As I stood talking to Perl, friends of the family slowly came up and surrounded us. Moishe Granatstein, whose wife was a very close friend with my mother, and a handful of others stood around Perl. One by one, we suggested to her that she leave the ghetto immediately. Since so many in the ghetto knew her, she could not successfully maintain another identity. It was only a matter of time, we said, before she would be discovered. The list of women who had not been transported was very short and Perl's name was not on it. In the ghetto, immediately meant it had to be now, and in that moment, we decided we would smuggle her out, tucked among the sixty or seventy men leaving for the midnight shift at the *Hortensia*. Perl would be the only woman among them. With her long blonde hair tucked under a man's cap so large the brim easily slid over her brow, we turned toward the gate.

As our little group fell in with the large march of men, we tightened our circle around her, so that the six of us shielded her from not only the guards, but also from the other men going to the factory. Had others known, it would have certainly increased the risk to Perl, for when it was her time to run, someone else may have wanted to run too. As we approached the Plac Trybunalski checkpoint, we could see the guards counting the heads of the people going by. Our hearts dropped and we began to tremble inside. With no direction other than instinct, we began shuffling around Perl, hoping to confound the Polish guards' counting system. There was a collective sigh when we got one block past the checkpoint. We had managed the most difficult part — getting her out of the ghetto. But there was no time to let down our guard. She still had to make her getaway from the group.

It took us about half an hour to march to the factory. The single file line to enter the *Hortensia's* guardhouse wound around the corner. The routine was to go through this little booth where we were always frisked before entering the factory. To keep Perl from having to go through the checkpoint, we stood together beside the line until it nearly passed us by. The November night was cold and the outside guard, seeing so few people left in line, went inside with the list of names. As I stood near the back of the line, Perl was behind me, hidden around the corner of the building. Silently, we wished each other well and in a moment, she turned and walked away, taking her cap from her head so her long hair hung down.

I knew where she was going. Her older sister, Raizl, had found protection with a Polish farmer and his family only a month earlier. It happened that Mrs. Marcinkowska, the farmer's wife, was a regular customer of my grandparents. Even in these difficult times, with less than perfect merchandise, she somehow managed to come to my grandparents to buy hose. Sometimes she brought from the farm to trade — vegetables, a few eggs, a little piece of butter — and sometimes she paid in cash. Either way, it was illegal for her to have any kind of dealings with us, and she was risking herself to bring us things that were difficult for us to get.

Two days before the first roundup, before the Nazis built the smaller ghetto, Mrs. Marcinkowska and her nephew, Stanislaw Wypych, came to my grandparents' home to get some more merchandise. While waiting for my grandmother to bring her supplies, she noticed my Aunt Raizl and her pretty, four-year-old daughter Halina sitting in the corner. Being four, Halina was of course in a playful mood, although her mother could only smile sadly and no doubt wonder how to save her child from an uncertain future. The farmer's wife then said something that was both compassionate and brave.

"With your permission," she said to my grandmother, "I would like to take the child and her mother to the farm with me, just for a few days, until it is safe for them to come home."

Raizl and Halina quickly gathered a few belongings and while Wypych climbed to the seat of the old, wooden hay wagon, Mrs. Marcinkowska threw what she could on top of my aunt and little cousin as they lay on the wagon floor. With the fading squeak of the rusty steel spokes as the one old horse lazily pulled the wagon down cobblestone streets, they were gone. They were safe.

I do not know what fate brought Mrs. Marcinkowska to our house that day, so close to the beginning of the end. For us it was the beginning of a miracle, for the seed from this one selfless act on the part of a non-Jew allowed just a glimmer of hope to grow.

Perl was gone now, on her way to join Raizl at the farm, but I could not rest knowing my mother, brothers and sisters were still being held in the synagogue. I had to try something. With the help of my two uncles, Michoel Lipschitz and Nachum Naidat, we tried bribing the guards to let them out. My uncles had saved a few gold pieces, and gave some money to a *macher*, a real wheeler-dealer who had connections. This *macher* was supposed to use the money to bribe the Ukrainian guards. I was up all night, the night they were supposed to come out, standing in the shadows of a doorway that faced the canal leading from the synagogue to the small ghetto. With only rags to keep out the November night air, and rats running by me on the street, I waited. I did not mind. I was eager to see my mother.

It was just before daybreak, before I lost the cover of the night, that I left. All the way back to my room, I felt betrayed. We were deceived by this *macher*, or maybe the Ukrainians did take the money and decided not to keep their promise. By the grace of a stranger a life is saved, and by his whim, a life is cast aside. At times a Jew was not worth the money, and at times the money was worth a Jewish life.

Days later, the Germans closed the canal that connected the small ghetto to the outside. I still have feelings of guilt until this day, because some of my friends did succeed in getting people out of the synagogue somehow.

Two weeks before Chanukah, on the tenth of Kislev, forty men were taken out of the synagogue and into the Rakow Forest on the outskirts of town. There, facing the machine guns of the German SS, they dug the large pit that was to be their grave. The next day, all the others still in the synagogue were brought to that place in the forest, where they too were shot and buried in the same mass grave. One person escaped into the forest as the Germans opened fire, a man named Goldstein, a distant relative from Tuszyn. They shot his arm, but he survived and was in hiding until the end of the war. After the war, he told me he saw my mother, my four-year-old brother Yichiel Yaakov and my nine-year-old sister Sara Malka lined up at the edge of the pit moments before the guns began firing.

That morning, the eleventh of Kislev, the Gentile workers who lived in the town ran into the factory. Others stood outside the fences and shouted, "They just killed all the Jews from the synagogue in the Rakow Forest." I dropped my shovel and began to cry. Shovels and tools fell everywhere as others cried as well. Many of us lost members of our families.

Next to me, I heard a Polish foreman say, "Why are you crying? I lost forty pigeons and didn't shed a tear."

Before the shooting, my brother Henoch and sister Hinde managed to crawl from a high window in the synagogue, across a narrow plank and down to the lower roof of the adjacent *beis midrash*. My mother insisted they leave. She wanted to remain with the smaller children. Like others who had escaped, they found their way to the small ghetto.

Four weeks after the shooting in the Rakow Forest I was sitting in the room I shared with Krieger and the others, when we heard someone climb the three flights of stairs and push past the broken door. (There were few intact doors left after the Germans came through the Jewish parts of the city.) Henoch and Hinde walked up to where I was sitting. We hugged and cried. They were looking for a place to hide because we heard that the next day they were going to take away the people who were not registered to work, especially children. We were told at the factory that all shifts had to report at six o'clock in the morning that day. In that way, anyone who was not registered to work would be in the ghetto when the roundup started.

In the room where I stayed there was a big armoire, and we thought about Henoch and Hinde hiding inside it, or even behind it. We came to the conclusion, though, that it was not a safe place. How hard would it have been for the Ukrainians and the Germans with their dogs to find them in such an obvious place? Besides, my roommates were afraid and did not want anyone hiding there, so my brother and sister went back to where they were staying, with my uncles Michoel and Nachum. It was hard for me to turn them away. They were my family. I wanted to be near them.

I had taken this room with Krieger, my cousin, because we were family, even though I had dealt with him only a little before. I was looking for protection, for a big brother. I did not find it in him. He had lied to me since my first day of sharing this room with him and the others. He told me that they were all paying for the room, that I would have to contribute one-fifth if I wanted to stay there. I found out a few days later that there was no rent. Krieger had taken my money and split it among the other roommates. Rather than protect me, because of my youth and naiveté he exploited my sincere trust. But what could I do? I needed a place to stay.

They coaxed me into their card games. The only card game I knew was *k'vitel*, blackjack, and I only played that on Chanukah and *nittle* (Christmas). We played cards on *nittle* because we did not study Torah that day, for it was a day that the Christians studied about the birth of their lord. Card playing, we believed, took one's mind from study.

My cousins played cards all the time, and in time I did too. They used dirty language, and eventually I did that as well. The more I gave in to their ways, the more I left behind. I had to. If I wanted to go on, I had to become one of them. Life was changing quickly. Our definition of what was normal shifted from minute to minute, yet time itself moved so slowly. The constantly changing landscape of life made me question not *what* action would be appropriate, but *when* action was the right choice. The more changes I saw, the harder it was for me to decide whether or not to take action. I was still living with the Talmudic dictum, "*Shev, v'al ta-asse odif.* Be still, and do nothing." Await fate. All this is to say that I accepted my new and changing beliefs as a matter of fate.

After work one afternoon, I was talking with some friends on the *Yidengass* when there was a big commotion as a young man, about my age, with a revolver in his hand, ran past us and into a nearby building. Not far behind him were the Jewish police. When the police ran past, many of us ran behind them to find out what would happen to this man with a gun. As we stood at the bottom of the apartment building stairway, the police came out carrying the gun. They left the man behind. Where was he going to go? While I stood at the doorway watching this show, I smelled something quite unusual. It was the extraordinary aroma of Polish kielbasa. I had never tasted sausage before, and being very hungry, I paid a thirteen-year-old boy a few zloty and bought a sandwich.

With one eye over my shoulder, I took a bite and thought, "This isn't bad after all." Then the doubts came. What if the whole thing is wrong? Who said we have to be religious anyway? Did it help my father, my mother or my grandparents, or the dozens of other saintly men and women with whom my family was blessed? The more I ate the sausage, the less it all seemed to matter.

I still put my *tefillin* on every morning, though the prayers, at times, seemed to have little meaning for me. It was a preoccupation with us to find meaning to our suffering in the words of the Torah and the prayer book. Such an activity gave us solace; it gave us a way to bring the fate befalling our people in line with our wavering faith. *"V'hayu chayecha t'lu-im l'cha mineged.* Your life shall hang in doubt before you," we read in the *tochecha*, the Diatribe in the twenty-eighth chapter of Deuteronomy, *"U'fachadeta laila v'yomam, v'lo taamin bechayecha.* You shall fear the night and the day, and shall not believe in your life." Our life was not in our hands, the verse was explaining. We were afraid for our lives night and day, and the verses were telling us that who will remain alive was not for us to decide. We were being instructed to believe in something greater, even as we watched the lives of the faithful vanishing before us. Yet these verses brought little comfort — only a resignation to our fate. Looking for hope in the tenets of our faith was like grabbing at thin stalks of straw to keep from drowning.

For hope, we turned to Leviticus, twenty-fifth chapter. *"V'hayeta sha-bat ha-aretz lachem le-achla.* And in the seventh year there will be produce for you to eat..." How did this verse bring hope? First, the letters in the word *shabat* (*tav, shin, bet*) are the same as the year 5702 on the Jewish calendar, corresponding to 1942. In the context of the sabbatical year mentioned in the verse, it appeared that 1942 would be a year of plenty, the blessing of abundance. From these letters, we devised the acronym, "*Tavo Sh'nat Bracha. A year of blessing comes.*"

Only a few verses later, we read, "*Bishnat ha-yovel hazot tashuvu ish el achuzato.* In the Jubilee year, every man will return to his property." Here the word *tashuvu* includes the same letters as *shabat,* and includes another letter — a *vov.* We reasoned we could use the *vov* and extend the acronym to *Tavo Sh'nat Bracha U'g'ulah,* that a year of blessing <u>and</u> redemption awaits — if not in the sabbatical year, then in the Jubilee. What awaited us instead in *tav shin bet* was Hitler's "Final Solution."

The morning after my brother and sister had come to find a place to hide, Hinde came to see me, to walk with me to the gate of the ghetto and say good-bye. As we walked down the street, we fell in with the mob of workers, fifteen hundred men, scurrying to the gate so they would not be caught in the roundup.

"Where is Henoch?" I asked my sister.

"He is hiding."

We said very little else as we walked hand in hand. Ten feet from the gate, before I could look up and say good-bye, a Jewish policeman leaped from the guardhouse and grabbed her away from me.

"Give me back my sister," I yelled to him. The tears that Hinde and I had worked so hard to hold back on the short walk to the gate poured out. "Give me back my sister!" I reached for her and he pulled her into the guardhouse.

"*Zai gezundt,*" she muttered from under her tears. "Be well."

With my head low, I rejoined the column of workers heading to the factories. For many years I hoped that she had somehow managed to survive. I never heard what became of her and my brother Henoch. I keep that day of leaving my sister, the twelfth day of Tevet, as their *yahrzeit.*

The two-mile walk to the *Kara* took about three-quarters of an hour. Though it was not far, and though we had nothing to carry, I bore a heavy heart, stooped beneath the burden of sadness that fell on my shoulders like the yoke of old Avramele, *der vasser treger,* the water carrier from Piotrokow. He at least had hope. I had none. He was happy with his load. I was forlorn. His faith was strong; mine was beginning to crumble. I had watched my entire family be taken away and I did nothing.

Physically exhausted, emotionally distraught, what was I to do? Leave everything to fate? So badly I wanted to do something, to feel like I had some control of my destiny. I thought about the many times I had an opportunity to be daring: when the Pole came to the house with a gun and I did not stab him; when I was carrying the crate of guns and did not take one and turn on the German guards; and when I filled bags of gunpowder that were used to clear trees in the Rakow Forest and did not pack away any to use against our enemies. There were many rumors as to what the huge clearing we were making in the woods was for. Some said, "It's so big, it must be an airfield." "No, it's for barracks," still others offered. And later, although we could never confirm it, we could not help but think that this open area was the gravesite of more than 160 of our fathers, mothers, wives and children.

Trying to grab hold of what we had become was like trying to grasp a cloud. Our prayers used to mean something. Our faith used to have purpose. Were we to abandon our faith for the fate that was before us? Many times we tried to find ourselves in the context of our beliefs. We searched the Bible; we recalled the writings of our sages; we analyzed our prayers.

"*Moshul k'cheres hanishbor*. Man is like a fragile shard of broken pottery," we read in the High Holiday liturgy, "*K'chatzir yovesh, u'k'tzitz novel, k'tzel over, v'ch'annan kohloh, u'ch'ruach noshaves, u'ch'ovok poreach, v'chachalom youf.* Like the withered blade of grass, and the flower that fades, as a fleeting shadow, and as a passing cloud, and as the wind that blows, and as the floating dust, and as the vanishing dream."

The world I knew was crumbling away, yet here, in this text, I found the solid rock of courage. I found a way to hold on to that little bit of faith that remained. And in my mind I saw the legless man from Lodz, his tired arms pushing the cart that carried him along the ground as he entered the ghetto shouting, "*Yiden! Zeit zich nisht meyaesh.* Jews, do not despair!"

CHAPTER
13

SPRING 1943

The barracks at the factory were ready in January 1943 and we finally moved in from the small ghetto. By spring, something had happened and we were being sent back to the small ghetto. We began to hear rumors of a Jewish revolt in Warsaw on Passover. On April 19, some of the Jews in the Warsaw ghetto had smuggled in guns and began firing on the Germans. The Nazis quickly subdued them, but because of fears that rumors of the incident might embolden other Jewish prisoners across Poland, we were ordered out of the barracks and back to the small ghetto where we could all be watched. The factories were guarded, of course, but people from outside the ghetto had access to it as well. In the ghetto, there was only one way in and out, and it was surrounded by barbed wire. We waited there under guard and were not allowed to go to the factories to work for three days.

At the end of the three days, the directors of the *Kara* and *Hortensia* were ordered to trim the size of the Jewish work force at the two factories and send some men to other factories around the country. Up to that time, there were about seven hundred Jewish men working. On a warm April day, word was given that all workers were to assemble at the staging area, an empty dirt lot by the small ghetto's entrance. Just beyond the gate, we saw two or three big civilian trucks, open in the back.

We were told to form lines according to who our shift foreman was, so I fell in with the rest of my group beside Wojdela, our Polish supervisor. By that time, with the war already in its fourth year, we did whatever we were told to do: told to sit, we would sit; told to march, we would march; told to stand in line, we stood in line. Vogel, the factory director, was his usual nervous self, pacing from line to line, his bowlegged gait looking slightly ridiculous in the jackboots that were too big for the small man.

Bouncing a leather riding crop furiously against his side as he moved, he pointed at one man, then another, then another. "March!" he shouted as he motioned the people he chose to the gate. Jewish policemen were waiting there to put them on the trucks. In a matter of minutes, the trucks filled up. For each man who was taken, I was afraid for myself. I saw them climbing on the trucks, and was frightened that I would be chosen. The operation moved quickly.

Standing in fear, I suddenly found my eyes peering into Vogel's cold, intimidating stare. It was not until that moment that I realized I was alone. Of the fourteen men that were in my group, only I remained. For two minutes, I stood frozen in Vogel's stare. I did not want to meet his gaze, but I was paralyzed by it and could not turn away. In his eyes I saw everything — I saw death; I saw guns; I saw the empty darkness of an unending nightmare. The spell was not broken until he nodded and walked away. When I heard the truck motors start and watched them leave, I felt myself breathe again.

There was a small commotion as the remaining factory workers prepared to leave for their shift. My Uncle Yidel, my Aunt Raizl's husband, worked at the Bugai, the woodwork factory outside the ghetto. On his way through the gate, he passed me and said, "I'm going to Marcinkowski's, to join my wife."

I looked at him and asked, "Do you think that someday, if I'll have to leave this place, do you think I could also come?"

"No," he said too quickly. "There is a little child there already. How many people do you think he can take in?"

Through our neighbor, Mr. Makowski, I heard that Yidel made it safely. Makowski had gotten the word from Perl, who regularly used this kind man as a courier. In every note that Perl sent me was this line, "Whenever you want to come, there is always a place for you."

For now, I saw no need to go. I felt relatively secure, especially after being spared from the last transport. But even though I felt that Vogel needed to have me around to complete the project I was working on — building the chimney for a new glass furnace at the factory — I would have been foolish to believe, with people dying around me every day, that I was ever completely secure.

I was taken to the *Kara* with my usual shift at ten o'clock at night and we were returned to the small ghetto by seven the next morning. This was our routine. I slept for a few hours after work, then I would get together with others and talk. I met many new people this way. By retelling stories and reminiscing, we supported each other, gave one another hope that the better days we remembered would again be ours.

Yet with all the moral support we were able to give each other, life in the small ghetto was always uncertain. At any moment, a Jewish police-man could harass you for being where he said you did not belong, or a trusted neighbor could turn you in to the Gestapo for having an extra piece of bread.

Food was precious, of course. When I was at the factory, I used to sneak food from the kitchen garbage cans because sometimes that was all that was left after the non-Jewish workers had their share. They always ate first, and sometimes all they left behind was water. If we were lucky, we would find a piece of meat.

In the ghetto, I had to "organize" food for myself, either by trading my belongings, a pair of socks for a couple of eggs or some butter or even a kilo of home-baked bread, or by going to the Judenrat kitchen and pick-ing up my daily or weekly rations. Things like potatoes or carrots may only have been available every other week. Even bread was sometimes only given once a week. The rations never came close to satisfying our hunger. If you could organize it just right with the Judenrat, you could get maybe an extra ration or two. Those with extra rations were big *mach-ers* in the ghetto. They would trade and sell, finding profit even while the rest of us suffered.

The few of us left in the ghetto were all factory workers. It had been that way since the Germans' large transports and the synagogue massacre in 1942. After Vogel's thinning out of the factory workers, those of us who remained were moved to new barracks adjacent to a multi-family apartment building called the *familjakis*. Some of the more influential Jewish workers, like the director of the work camp, Gomberg and his family, and some of the Jewish policemen were housed in the *familjakis*. A fence ran around the outside of the four-story building and included several small buildings. The barracks I was in housed forty people and was one of a pair of smaller buildings near the perimeter of the compound, to the left of the gate as we entered. A small coffeehouse, where ersatz coffee was prepared for the camp, sat between the two barracks. We were only about five hundred yards from the gate of the *Kara*.

There were bunk beds in the barracks, and I slept on a lower bunk. The first time we entered, we were given jutes to fill ourselves with straw from a pile. Because there were no pillows, I stuffed the mattress with a little extra straw on one end so my head could be elevated a little. Along with the new sleeping arrangement we were each given a new work uniform, dark blue coveralls, and a pair of shoes made from canvas with soles of tire rubber. I did not put my new clothing on right away, because I did not need clean clothes for the work I did. Instead, I put the new clothes and shoes under my mattress thinking I would use them only for special occasions — though in reality nothing special lasted for more than a moment, and no moment was special enough to be an occasion.

With my entire shift sent away, I befriended my new bunkmates, two brothers named Weiskopf who, though Jewish, were raised in a faithless home. They confided in me that their family was Bund (Workmen's Circle), the Jewish Socialist organization that was active in the labor movement in Piotrokow before the war. Only a year before, around Purim 1942, the Nazis executed Zalman Tennenberg, the head of Piotrokow's Judenrat and the top man in the local Bund organization. He was arrested with nine other Bund members and, being a Socialist, was accused of conspiracy against the Germans. Hitler had said the Jews would never celebrate another Purim, and to make his point, the Germans took the ten men to the cemetery and there, like the sons of Haman, they were hanged. This was the first group in the ghetto we ever heard about being murdered.

The Weiskopf boys had connections to people in Warsaw, who were in direct contact with the Polish government-in-exile in London. Through secret courier, sometimes Jewish and sometimes not, documents and money were transferred to members of the organization, even those in the ghetto. One day, there was a commotion at the gate, and we heard that a woman from Warsaw was arrested trying to bring in money. The brothers told me that some of that money was meant for them, smuggled from London to disperse to Bund members wherever they could be found.

Being in the Bund also helped the brothers get better food than the rest of us. They shared some with me. The boys also shared some information about the Bund, its philosophy, its structure, how it operates and what they expected to do once the war was over. We did not talk religion because they told me that they never prayed, they never believed. Together we dreamed of what we would do after the war ends, if we survived. I did not tell them about the members of my family who were in hiding, and how one day I hoped to join them.

Meanwhile, my work with the Polish chimney builders continued. I had been with them more than six months, both in the factory and helping in their apartment. I worked more than was required for them, always, according to a traditional, Hasidic way of going beyond the requirements when performing the laws of God. That extra effort helped me because they treated me better. But I was not their friend; I was their Jew. That is what they called me: "Our Jew." I did not like it, but I put up with it because being "their Jew," I was able to eat better and have lighter work. It was good work, and I felt lucky to have it. That is why I worked so hard to please them.

I made sure they knew that I understood that they were superior to me. Certainly I knew that was only the circumstance, but it was a powerful circumstance, driven home every moment of every day. They were goyim, free to come and go where and whenever they wanted. I made them feel important. I thanked them a million times a day for everything they did for me. "Thank you for this....Thank you for that....You are kind....You are good to me....You are helping me....Thank you for protecting me because I am alone....Yes, I will remember your kindness, if I survive." Being deferential to them helped me live.

On a warm, clear, late spring day, I went to my place by the chimney to prepare the mortar for the bricklayers. As I did every morning, I picked up the handles of the dirty, wooden wheelbarrow and rolled it twenty yards, its metal wheel squeaking and wobbling along the rough ground, to a pit filled with cakes of white lime. I loaded the wheelbarrow with shovel after shovel until it was full and heavy. I did not like to make more than two or three trips for the lime. When it was full, I maneuvered it back to the chimney and, after putting a little sand on the shovel to keep the lime from sticking to it, I emptied the wheelbarrow into a wooden mixing container. The large hopper was a little bit longer than it was wide, and about a foot deep. Once the lime was in the container, I slowly added water from a hose, being careful not to splash my skin or eyes because it was very caustic and burned tremendously. The lime, being mixed with water, began to boil. After mixing dry cement with sand two-to-one outside the boiling lime, we slowly added the dry mixture to the wet, stirring with a special tool as we went to keep the mortar smooth. It took two of us to get it to the right consistency. I usually worked with the Polish winch operator, the one responsible for getting the bricks and mortar up to the masons working on the chimney.

Once the mortar was mixed, we worked quickly to get it in buckets and hoisted to the bricklayers. About forty bricks were loaded on each palette and they too were attached to the winch and lifted. Because the masons worked on scaffolding inside the chimney and we were outside, it was necessary for the winch operator to make a white mark on the cable leaving the motor so he would know how far to raise the load. The cable was raised to a pulley attached to the scaffolding with the three bricklayers. They were usually able to build six or seven feet an hour, so the white mark constantly changed.

Although I was primarily assigned to mixing the mortar, from time to time I operated the winch. This day, I was standing near the mixer when the operator turned to me and asked, "Hey! Icek! Do me a favor. Take over for me while I go to the bathroom."

I gladly obliged. After all, it was exciting running this machine, lifting heavy loads two hundred feet. The cable was attached to a palette of bricks, and I waited for the signal from the masons. Soon, they were yelling, "Send them up! Send them up!"

As I wound in the cable, the bricks lifted out of sight. Accordingly, I kept my eyes on the cable, looking for the operator's white mark so I would know when to stop lifting. As the motor wound in, I saw a white mark appear at the top of the door to the chimney. I was prepared to stop the cable when it reached the motor, as usual, but before I got that far, I saw bricks falling around me from the top of the chimney. I stopped the motor immediately and heard yelling. I looked up the chimney and saw the terrible thing I had done. Two of the masons were clinging with their arms to the fresh-laid brick, trying not to fall from the upset scaffolding. A third was racing down the emergency ladder outside the chimney. From all around, people came running. The first on the scene was Kristman, the factory director's son. Among the Jews, this man was known as *der yoyresh* (the dauphin). He ran at me with a piece of two-by-four and began beating me, all over my body, and cursing me, swearing at me. I did not resist. On the one hand, I felt that I deserved it. After all, I nearly killed three men. Also, I knew there was no point in resisting. I knew it was the end for me. "Sabotage!" *der yoyresh* screamed as he beat me. "Sabotage!"

Then, turning to Vogel, he said, "Take him to the office. Send him to the Gestapo!"

Aching from my wounds, blood coming from my nose and my mouth where *der yoyresh* had knocked out some teeth, I walked slowly with Vogel to the office. Tears were soon mixing with the blood as I began to realize that this was it for me. As I walked by a friend of mine, I asked him to get the foreman from the engineers I had been working with on the chimney. Then, I turned and entered the office.

Standing in front of the desk, feeling the pain on my body, I began to say *vidui*, to ask forgiveness, to confess my sins to God before they killed me. "Name," Vogel demanded, and his Polish secretary typed. "Date of birth." I gave them all the details, until the form was filled out. The next thing they would be doing was telephoning the Gestapo.

I said to myself, "This is it. This is the end of me. Nobody can save me. They will say that I am not only a saboteur, but also a murderer, trying to kill non-Jews. Is there any doubt that the Gestapo will put me on my knees and shoot me in cold blood?"

When the foreman from the chimney came in, I fell to my knees, grabbed his legs and his hands and I cried, pleading with him to forgive me. He started to cry too, and went to the director to try to save me. When he was leaving the office, I asked the foreman if I could walk with him. I asked him to find the engineers, the ones who were in the chimney, so I could say good-bye to them. I had worked with them more than six months, and I wanted to see them, to ask their forgiveness for almost killing them. I went back to the office and waited.

Soon, all four of the engineers, including the foreman, came in. I went up to them, still crying. "I never wanted to hurt you," I said, pleading. "It was an accident, a mistake. I'll make it up to you. I'll do whatever you want."

They all walked into the director's office and told him that if I were turned over to the Gestapo, they would stop working. They said they would not complete the chimney if I were taken away. The foreman turned to me as they left the office. "I think you will be released," he told me. These men, people I nearly killed, had saved me from certain death. They intervened for me, those goyim who derided me with anti-Semitic slurs.

The incident gave me a reputation as "the one who pulled down the chimney." The other factory workers pointed at me, but I did not laugh, nor did I brag. I was lucky to be alive after what happened, and I knew that. Had I even shown the slightest smile about the incident, someone would surely have reported me.

The director, Vogel, was furious over the whole thing. First, he was called in to handle it, and then he had to let me go or risk not completing the chimney and losing four master masons. The engineers said they needed me, so I was put back on the chimney detail with them.

When we finished the chimney, I was sent back to the barracks. It took another few months before the whole thing simmered down. There were always new things to worry about. Still, from that moment on, I was scared of every move I took. As for my friends, the ones who I almost killed and who saved me, they considered me a hero. For them, it was an adventure, a way to break up the monotony. Yet an estrangement grew between us, especially between the younger two engineers and me. Any protection I may have had from working with them had dissipated with the tension of the incident.

The work I was given afterward was much harder. Although I tried my best and worked hard all the time, there were still times when I was beaten. I did not like the beatings, but you get used to that sort of thing. As long as they let you live.

CHAPTER
14

ESCAPE

"The Russians are coming closer to Warsaw." This is the news we heard from the non-Jewish workers coming to the *Kara* in the fall of 1943. I began thinking about what to do, where to go. The labor camp was beset with rumors of the Germans moving all the Jews to another camp, but no one was sure what kind.

All the while, I had not lost touch with my mother's two sisters, Perl and Raizl, who were still hiding with the farmer Wypych Marcinkowski about two miles from the *Kara*. Makowski, our former neighbor, was still delivering messages for us so I knew how everyone was getting along. I decided that it was time to join them.

One day the following spring, Kristman, the owner of the factory, brought everyone in the labor camps together to hear a speech. The speaker was very mean looking, tall, dressed all in black with long boots and a swastika on his arm so big it was impossible to hide his allegiance. In his hand he carried a riding crop that he slapped against his boots as he spoke.

He spoke to us in Polish, for he was Volksdeutsch. His speech was a warning. He said they did not know what the future of the factory was, but that they needed us because we do good work. "We know how to smear your behinds with tar," he said, meaning that we would not be able to go anywhere without them telling us where to go.

Standing beside me during the Volksdeutsch's tirade was Yisrolek Rosenwald, who was about my age and whose mother was at

Marcinkowski's farm with my aunts. I turned to him and whispered, "Tonight, we go."

He nodded in agreement. "We will talk after," he said.

When the man in black finished, we walked away, talking in low voices about what it would take to get four people out: the two of us, Yisrolek's brother Pinya and his uncle Avram Jakubowicz. The difficulty was that Yisrolek and his uncle worked the overnight shift at the factory while Pinya and I worked the afternoon shift. That meant that they would have to escape from the factory, and we would have to go from the barracks at the same time. If one of the brothers had failed in his escape and was captured, it would have endangered not only those of us fleeing, but those hiding on the farm as well.

My plans to coordinate with Pinya were a little more complicated than those of Yisrolek and his uncle. The factory had many more options, many more places to jump the fence. The compound was smaller.

I met Pinya a few hours later, before it got dark, in the square where we had heard the Polish Nazi talk earlier in the day. Pinya slept in the four-story family building near the factory gate and I slept two hundred feet away in a thirty-four-bed barracks along the back fence. The least conspicuous spot we found was the area behind the outhouse, where a huge acacia tree outside the fence could hide us. Its branches spread over the concertina wire and the open-roofed latrine.

Pinya and I agreed to meet at the outhouse at five o'clock the next morning. That was about the same time the men for the six o'clock shift at the *Kara* would start moving about the compound. This time of May, the days in Poland were just beginning to get longer, and the darkness had only just settled on us when we separated for what was to be my longest night.

I went up the few steps to my barrack and opened the bare pine door. Inside, I nodded in greeting to the few people gathered around the stove, going through their nightly ritual of story telling and card playing. I turned to the left, walked to the third bunk and climbed into the top bed. I rolled over on my left side and pulled the cover over me. It was relatively easy to reach underneath the jute mattress with my free arm and pull out a brand-new pair of overalls that I was given when I first began working at the *Kara* in 1942. I do not know why I kept these never-worn overalls all that time. I certainly did not do it as part of a long-rang plan. I did not know if I was even going to live long enough to use them.

Every morning when I made the bed, I made sure the blanket held the coveralls closely to the mattress. At the times when we took the jutes out for fresh straw, they lay under my knapsack and other bedding. Unbelievably, I also managed to keep a nearly new pair of sneakers made from old tires and just enough cheap canvas and cord to keep them from falling apart. Under my covers, I put the shoes and overalls on so I would be ready when it was time to go. I was nervous, worried about oversleeping, worried about the risk.

Only one man in the barrack knew what I was up to. His name was Eisenstein, a former neighbor from my grandfather's building, who lived right below the Makowskis. He was around forty years old and extremely intelligent and well educated — a worldly man. Although Makowski had offered to take him in should he decide to escape, he declined because part of his family was in Bugai, and he did not want to save himself and leave them stranded.

Eisenstein was given the responsibility by the Jewish director of the camp, Gomberg, to guard the barrack from any problems among the inmates. Despite this position of pseudo-authority, everyone in the barrack liked and respected him. Because of his connection to my family, I knew he would be a trusted friend and ally.

I had a brief conversation with Eisenstein on my way into the barrack that night, and he agreed to wake me in time (after all, as a guard, he was the only one with a watch) by giving me a signal. Although we had a latrine, it was forbidden for us to leave the barracks during the night to use the facility. Instead, each barrack had a twenty-gallon tin tub on the landing by the front door. When it was filled it took two men to carry it and dump it in the grass. Because the tub was thin metal, it rang loudly whenever one of the men in the barracks used it.

Eisenstein told me that when it was time, he would leave the door ajar and urinate on the tin loud enough to wake me. Most closed the door and usually tried to go quietly. Even with a trusted ally, it was difficult for me to sleep and I made frequent, unnecessary trips to the tub myself. When I saw Eisenstein on the stoop, he motioned me back inside with a brush of his fingers.

But it was not just the fear of missing my rendezvous with Pinya that was making me too anxious to sleep. I wondered about the escape itself, the logistics. Would I be safe? What if I was caught? Where would my protection come from? In reciting the bedtime *shema* that night, I felt the importance of asking, "… let the angel Michael be on my right hand, and Gabriel on my left, and let the Presence of the Almighty be on my head."

The anxious, restless night ended when the first light of the early spring morning came across the compound. Without Eisenstein's help, I knew that it was close enough to five o'clock to start walking towards the outhouse and my rendezvous with Pinya. As it turned out, he left his barrack at the same time and we met in front of a four-story apartment building between our two barracks, exchanging only glances as we headed toward the outhouse and our escape.

In a downstairs window of that apartment building, a Jewish policeman named Herzl Greenbaum was sipping his morning beverage and watching the early activity of the shift change in the yard. He saw us as we met and, curious about our unusually clean work clothes, he stepped out his open window and followed us. We went to the outhouse without a word. He followed us in. Just the three of us were in the latrine, Pinya and I crouching against the wall and pretending to go, Greenbaum just standing there with his back to us, maybe going himself, maybe not. Once or twice he glanced over his shoulder just to make sure we were still there. He finished his business and walked out the door going only a few yards to the center of the compound where he stood, pretending he was not watching us, yet he was watching us from all four sides!

Pinya and I stood and decided to go back into the compound. There was Greenbaum. He knew this was not our shift to work. We walked around like blind mice, not knowing where to go next. I said to Pinya, "I think I'm going to go over to him and tell him that I'm connected with the Polish Underground and if he does not take his eyes off of me, his life is not going to be worth a penny. He'll be killed tonight."

"No," he said tersely. At that second we both looked up. Sweeping outside the door of the kitchen was a junior policeman, one of a handful who were given uniforms and menial work in exchange for a uniform and some police privileges. Pinya and I both knew him as a kind man from a good family. We were ready to trust him on that alone, but under those circumstances, who can be trusted? We quickly dismissed the idea of enlisting him to help us.

"Let's act normal, as if nothing is going on," we decided, "go back to our barracks, get our pot for coffee." We separated, walking to our quarters to retrieve the pots.

The chicory coffee was in a big steel pot that sat in a shack between the barracks. We met there to dip our pots, Pinya with a white enamel one large enough for his brother and uncle, and me with my blue pan with dried bread clots plugging the holes. Greenbaum was still eyeing us from his spot in the compound a short distance away. Somehow I felt that if it were possible for such a miserable man to relax, it put the policeman at ease seeing what appeared to be normal morning behavior.

As we raised our cups to our lips, we both saw the same thing at the same time! An opening, a little space between the wall of this recently built coffee shack and the fence. "Drop your pot!" we exclaimed to each other. Before the pans hit the ground, he was through the gap, and I followed.

Pinya was a little weaker than I, so I locked my hands to boost him up to the roof of the shack, telling him, "When you get up there, don't stand up. Keep low so Greenbaum cannot see you!" Only moments after he got up there, he shrunk back and covered his mouth, gesturing to be quiet. The guard was changing, five Volksdeutschen in jackboots marching by just beyond the fence. We held our breath until they were past. And then he jumped the fence.

Quickly, I planted my new rubber shoes against the wood fence and wires and scrambled up to the roof of the coffee shack, scratching my arm on the wires as I went. And then I jumped too.

We walked about five hundred feet apart, Pinya in the lead because he was from the area and knew the way through the back roads and fields. I kept my cap pulled down over one eye, keeping just enough of the other open to see my way.

While we walked up the small country road that took us away from the *Kara*, others walked by us heading to the factory, local Poles on their way to work. A fifteen-year-old girl who was taking some breakfast to her father saw me and recognized me immediately. She often brought some bread and butter and other food like that to sell to the factory workers for a few slips of worthless Polish currency. I wanted to see her because she always smiled at me, but of course at the time I was very frightened. As our eyes met she smiled at me again and for the last time. "*Idsze z'Bogen.* Go with Godspeed," she said, and winked. I felt relieved.

I left the camp that day in May 1944 with my new overalls, my rubber-soled shoes and a small wallet that I had kept since the beginning of the war. In it were three coins from Purim, a picture from the camp and a few crumbs of matzoh from the *afikomen* of the last seder at my father's house.

My great-grandmother, Chava Krieger, poses with some of her
grandchildren and great-grandchildren in Tuszyn, Poland, in 1937.

The wedding of my Aunt Rikel to cousin Aharon Dovid in the Jewish ghetto, 1941.

The elite work force that served the *Kara* glass factory at the labor camp in Piotrokow. I'm on the far left and the guard Wojdela is on the far right.

The synagogue in Piotrokow where my family was held before they were murdered.

Looking like a typical Polish farmer, I thresh wheat on Marcinkowski's farm in 1945.

Betty and I pose with friends and
fellow survivors on our wedding day
in Berlin, January 22, 1946.

Newlyweds in 1946 at the Feldafing D.P. Camp.

We leave for Canada with son Mark in January 1952 aboard the *Fair Sea*.

I officiate at the wedding of a cousin
in Bogatá, Colombia, in 1956.

Entertaining the audience at a cantors' convention in the Catskills in the 1950s.

Performing with Georgie Jessel at the Cleveland Municipal Auditorium in 1960.

Israel Sun Ltd.

I sing before Golda Meir at a Zionist Organization
of America meeting in Tel Aviv in 1976.

President Jimmy Carter's inauguration day, January 20, 1977.

I visit the Warsaw Ghetto Memorial in 1979 as part of President Carter's mission
to create the U.S. Holocaust Museum.

My grandparents' ghetto apartment in Piotrokow.
Our old bedroom is over my left shoulder.

My reunion with Stanislaw Wypych in Piotrokow, 1979.

Frank Maresca

I am overcome with emotion when visiting the mass grave
for the victims of the Piotrokow synagogue massacre.

While visiting Treblinka in 1979, I examine
charred bones gathered from the pit.

Senator Carl Levin (MI) with Dr. Elie Wiesel and myself at the cornerstone laying of the U.S. Holocaust Memorial Museum.

Shlomo Nimrodi

I perform for Yitzhak Rabin in 1993 at the American Embassy in Tel Aviv.

Betty and I pose before my retirement dinner from
Ahavath Achim Synagogue in Atlanta, 1995.

The Goodfriend family in Atlanta, 1996.

FROM MISERY
TO MISERY

It was less than two miles from the labor camp in Piotrokow to the house where I was to spend the rest of the war. It was a beautiful, sunny day, yet a cloud of fear and anxiety followed me. I could not escape it. I could not liberate myself from it. It was our companion until the end. I was moving from misery to misery along a road of fear.

A dog was barking. Pinya arrived at the Marcinkowski's about five minutes ahead of me, since we wanted to avoid suspicion by walking some distance apart. His uncle, who had left the camp the night before, was anxious to make sure that we had arrived safely. Altogether nine of us were hiding there. Even in this place, away from the abuse of the Germans and my Polish foreman, we greeted each other only in excited whispers, like the flapping wings of nine birds in a small cage. In the back room that was our hiding place, Pinya was with his uncle, mother and brother, and I was with my mother's sister Raizel, her husband Yidel Dzialowski and their baby Halina. My mother's other sister, Perl, whom I had helped escape, was living in the main house, having found favor from Stanislaw, the Marcinkowski's nephew. Being blond-haired and blue-eyed, they passed her off as a cousin from another part of Poland. They called her Marysia.

That day I was given a new name. Stanislaw came in after we arrived and looked at me. Like my aunt, I was fair featured, with blonde hair and blue eyes. I was also young and fairly strong because of my work at the factory. I looked like a real *shaygetz*. Pinya's brother Srulek also had features that could pass for Polish, unlike Pinya, who was smaller and more "Jewish" looking. "From now on, you are Valdek," Srulek was told. "And you," Marcinkowski looked at me, "are named Roman." From then on, that is what all of the Marcinkowskis called me. Even now, when I visit them all these years later, they still call me Roman.

With mixed feelings of relief, gratitude and sadness I greeted what was left of my family. It had been two years since my father died of typhoid, just over a year since the rest of my family was murdered in the forest. We did not discuss any of it. We did not want to open up the wounds. We did not want to multiply the pain. As in the ghetto and in the labor camp, we focused on the present, on making it to the next day. And the fear was still there. What if a German should happen by and search? What if a Polish neighbor became suspicious and denounced us? There would be no next day. We still feared for our lives, and could still see ourselves being hanged or shot or sent away.

In hiding I discovered that misery had taken the love of family and turned it on its head. I saw misery in the labor camp; there I was forced to share sad and desperate circumstances with the strangers around me. Yet a company of strangers in misery will share their food with you, will take their only shirt and tear it in half to give it to you if need be, because the pain of day-to-day living made concerns about material possessions a waste of time. I thought that here, hiding with my family, there would be even more compassion. But when I joined them, I found that in an effort to make the miserable circumstances seem more normal, they were clinging to the same old pettiness, as if none of this had ever happened. In the camp, we were forced to eat and drink out of pans with clots of bread covering the holes. There simply was nothing else. Yet here my aunt had managed to bring a Rosenthal china service for twelve from our home and would not open it up, even for the five of us in our family, not to mention the four others. So we shared a leaky pot between the eight adults. After all, the Rosenthal set was the good china and she was afraid it would break. It did not matter that this is all we had. It aggravated me. It was outrageous to me that even under these conditions she would be so small-minded.

Sometimes I rebelliously thought about going back to the camp because the difficulties were more easily defined there. After we had been in hiding about two months, Marcinkowski started allowing Valdek (Srulek) and me out during the day to help with the farm work. One day he was taking a load of hay to the factory and I had the urge to go with him. I knew it was dangerous, but I did not care.

"Oh, no, Roman. You're not going," he told me.

"I'll disguise myself," I explained. "I'll disguise myself and help you unload."

The whole family yelled at me. I wanted to go back, to see. I would have risked it just for the adventure. But I did not go. If it was adventure I wanted, they reminded me, there was plenty just trying to stay safely in hiding.

One of the first things we did when I got to the farm was dig a small crawl space underneath the floorboards of the room we stayed in. It was something we could pull a rug and table over that would have just enough room for us to squeeze into and have air to breath. Truthfully, it would never have fooled anyone who was determined to search.

One night, the dog began barking from his chain that was connected to a three-hundred-foot run between the house and the road. A man with a gun approached, and my Aunt Perl watched as the old man let him in. We hid ourselves in the place we had dug in our back room. The soldier explained that he was the leader of the local district of the Polish Underground. From time to time partisan fighters from the Polish Underground, the Armia Kraiova — which was the national army of the government in exile — would come by the farm for food. This man said that Marcinkowski had been recommended to him and he asked if he could spend the night.

They fed him, of course, and as he was eating his soup or whatever in the dining room we could hear him from our hiding place in the back. Now the Poles, even those in the AK, are no less anti-Semitic than the Germans. So it was not surprising when we heard him say that for all his hatred of Hitler and the German army, "what a fine job Hitler is doing with the Jews."

We quietly listened to all this from our hiding place. Even when we were out in the room, we never raised our voices, never talked in a normal tone. We learned to whisper. If someone had to sneeze or cough, they used a pillow. It was very dangerous with the baby. The baby could cry. When it was dangerous to come out for days at a time, Perl would sneak food to us.

He saw the closed door to the room in the back and asked, "What's in there?" He stepped toward the door. "May I see?"

"It's just the winter supplies," we heard Mrs. Marcinkowska say, "where we keep crops for the winter."

That seemed to satisfy him because then he got down to business. "I'm here to ask you to do something for your country," he said. "We need a base, a headquarters in the area, and we would like to use your house for men, equipment and supplies."

We could not hear the Marcinkowskis. We heard him add. "To show your patriotism. To honor your country."

Now Mrs. Marcinkowska was an educated woman, self-taught, and an ultra-nationalist. She used to recite poetry by the Polish patriot Adam Mizkiewicz. Four days later, after the partisan had gone and we finally came out of our hiding place, it was obvious she was bothered. "Look," she said to us, "what will I get when I present you after the war? When I say I saved nine Jews will Poland give me a medal? Will they put me in front of the president of the country? No. If I agree to do what the AK asks, then I will know for sure I did something for my country...," she trailed off in her dilemma.

We had to talk her out of it. We told her how dangerous it would be to have arms and ammunition stored here. Her house could be blown off the face of the earth if she did that. We pointed out that she was stuck, that if she denounced us to the Germans, they would kill her too for hiding us. If she gave in to the AK, then it would be dangerous because the Germans may find out and watch the house. It was not long before she came around. Every time the partisans returned, she made up excuses to postpone her decision. In doing so, she was not only protecting us, she was protecting her family as well.

That is why the Marcinkowskis did not discourage the AK from coming around. Despite their anti-Semitism most Poles saw the AK as patriots. Befriending them was good protection. When neighbors started to ask questions about extra workers at the farm, Stanislaw was able to get the partisan leader to go to the neighbors' homes and tell them that the Marcinkowskis were patriots too and to leave them alone.

Meanwhile, when it rained and we were all stuck in our room, days went slowly. On the days we could, Valdek and I were outside working. We spoke quietly to each other while out there, only exchanging a Polish "Good morning" if anyone should happen by.

Stanislaw taught the two of us how to thresh wheat, separating wheat from chaff. With the stalks spread on a clean stone ground, we each took what in Polish is called a *cepy* (two pieces of wood, a short one and a long one, tied together with a leather strap) and beat the wheat hard until the grain separated from the stalk. It went at a steady rhythm with the two of us hitting: tic-tac, tic-tac, tic-tac. If we did not follow the rhythm, it did not work. Sometimes, Stanislaw would join in and the beat would change, tic-tic-tac, tic-tic-tac, still steady like a three-handed piano. Working this way, we were able to finish twenty sheaves a day. The women remained in the house while we worked, sorting peas and peeling and cooking sugar beets to put up sweet syrup for the winter.

Sometimes, when I was working outside, I would sneak into the hen house and steal eggs from underneath the chickens. I would make a pin-hole, suck out the fresh, warm yolk and put the intact shell back under the hen. This confused the old man. I remember him kneeling and praying "Why, God, is my chicken laying empty eggs?" All the fresh food, the warm eggs, the frothy cow milk, I could not help myself. It was so good.

Once Stanislaw came to wake me in the middle of the night to help slaughter a pig. We had to do it at night, because pigs over a certain weight were supposed to be given to the Germans. This animal had been registered, tagged on its ear, and he wanted to kill it before it reached the weight that would make it a meal for a German mess. We walked out to the barn and he handed me a heavy ax.

He made sure the blunt side of the ax blade was down. "Hit it here," he said and pointed to the top of the pig's head. The idea was to knock it out with the back of the blade, not to cut its head off. That would have meant too much blood loss, and bloodwurst is a delicacy in that part of Europe. It was not pleasant. I hated the site of blood anyway. I closed my eyes and hit the pig hard.

Stanislaw worked quickly, getting up every drop of blood before it turned cold. He did not waste one piece of meat, bone or skin. He showed me how to turn the hide to leather for horse reins. He took the rump and smoked it to have ham for Christmas. He showed me where the best back of the pig was, the bacon, measuring to show that it is three fingers thick. I was surprised how clean the animal was inside. Slaughtering the pig did not bother me as much as you might think it would, being a Jew, because it was something my benefactor asked me to do.

Even as I helped him make the bloodwurst, preparing the casings, making the sausages with the different colored gelatins, I was not bothered. I was out in the barn when he brought me a steaming hot piece of the cooked wurst and the big knife he used to cut it. "Roman, here." So I tasted a piece and for all the guilt, it was so heavenly I asked for another piece. I thought the sky was going to fall on me, or like the punishment of Korach when he mutinied against Moses, the earth would open up and I would sink right into the ground.

By September, nearly all the grain was harvested and all the peas stored for the winter. Staring out the window of our room at the cleared fields on the horizon, I listened to the sound of the autumn breeze trying to penetrate the panes. Did the wind come to carry us on its wings to freedom, to a new life? Or was it the haunting sound of bad tidings, of the unexpected, still to come?

Or was the wind blowing by our window carrying the sounds of a far away shofar, heralding the days leading up to Rosh Hashana? We did not have a calendar in Nazi-occupied Poland in 1944, but an old formula we were taught in cheder said that if you know the date of Passover, you can easily figure out the rest of the holidays.

Likewise, cheder taught us how to prepare for the *yomim nora-im*, the Days of Awe that begin with Rosh Hashana and end with the last shofar blast on Yom Kippur. We observe the holidays with awe and dignity, according to our tradition. But here in our small room, afraid to talk, afraid to sneeze, how does one prepare for the Days of Awe?

We began in our memories of the not-distant past, of families being together, rejoicing. We celebrated in the illusion of the festive times, with the aroma of mother's fresh-baked challa, the delicious fish, the apple and honey. And every bit of soup the nine of us sipped out of the one bread-patched tin plate was like manna to that illusion of home.

As for the spiritual preparation for the High Holidays, when one has to give an account for all his deeds, his omissions, his transgressions, and ask God for forgiveness for all sins committed, that was entirely different. There our illusion was eclipsed by emotion, and inner struggle overpowered our nostalgia.

How can we, with clear conscience, approach the Almighty on this Day of Judgment and ask forgiveness for all our sins? What sins? Have we not paid enough for our sins, for all those we have committed, for all those we might commit? Is not the sacrifice of 28,000 Jews in Piotrokow enough? Or the 162 martyrs murdered in the forest, my mother, my brother, and my sister...my God, is this not enough for atonement?

Why bother with observing Rosh Hashana, the Days of Repentance, Yom Kippur? Yet we were Jews and, we reasoned, no matter what fate may bring in the ensuing days, if the Nazis were to discover our hiding place, at least we were Jews until the very last moment of our lives. With that thought in mind, the five men crowded in the corner of the room, our backs to the crucifix on the wall, and we began our prayers. We prayed a bit louder than a whisper, without prayer books, so that when one would forget the liturgy, the others would prompt him so as not to miss any of the prayers.

With trembling hearts we concentrated on the meaning of every phrase and every word. "*Avinu malkenu,*" we recited, "Our Father, Our King, repeal the evil sentence that may be decreed against us. Our Father, Our King, avenge before our eyes the blood of Thy servants. Our Father, Our King, bring glory to Israel Thy people."

We were uplifted spiritually to the highest degree that a human can aspire to achieve. Suddenly we were like the Maccabees who raised arms against their oppressors. We too defied our oppressors, not with an army but with the only weapon we possessed — our prayer. The little invisible spark inside us suddenly ignited, and that was something not even the Nazis could take from us. That is the last Rosh Hashana we commemorated in the time of our despair under the Nazis.

This is how I passed my time at the Marcinkowskis' — working when

I could, praying when I should have. I shared a pair of *tefillin* with the other men. When I saw that they had managed to bring theirs when they fled here, I was devastated that I had chosen to leave mine behind at the labor camp barrack. I did not want to take the risk of having them on me in case I was searched. So I left the *tefillin* my father had given me at my Bar Mitzvah, the ones he had created by one of the most pious and out-standing scribes in Poland. I was reminded of that every morning when I put them on and faced east to pray. Of course in every prayer we asked for our safety and the safety of those we loved. Even Mrs. Marcinkowska, when she knelt in front of one of the crucifixes hanging on the wall in every room of her house, prayed to Jesus that we be guarded as well as she and her family.

CHAPTER
16

LIBERATION

Fall turned to winter in 1944 and we heard only bits of news. Aunt Perl had brought back a few slivers about the war when she went into town, to the market. The snow fell, the calendar changed and our uncertain life in hiding went on.

Then, one January night, I was awakened by the drone of bombers. I looked out the window of the room where we hid and saw the sky lit with flares. The Russians were bombing the city. It was an eerie feeling that three of us, Srulek, Avrom and myself, shared as we sat at the window watching the display. Yidel cowered in the corner with Raizl and the baby. We were not familiar with the game of war. Were they Germans? Were they Russians? Why were they dropping flares before they bombed? We had never experienced the war this closely. Piotrokow was in the middle of nowhere. The Germans just rolled in when the war began. We never saw planes dropping bombs. We really had no idea what that meant, that this nightmare was so close to being over. We were only two days away from liberation and still not sure we were going to survive.

At this point we sat down to write an account of what happened here, at this farmhouse during the war. Three men of different ages sat down in the room where we had been hiding and began to write our accounts in Yiddish. On whatever paper we could find to write, we listed the names of the people who spent the war at the farmhouse. It was no more than a ledger, an accounting of how nine Jews counted their days. We planned to put the words in a jar and bury it beneath the floorboards, in the space we dug when I first arrived. We put in our names, the names of our families, our family history and then certain personal feelings about why we were there. We collaborated on it, so that if nothing were left at least something should be left. Even then we could not believe there would be a brighter day, that we would actually be free.

As the day wore on, the roads filled with fleeing Germans. The Russians were very close and we could feel the excitement. We sat in the back room still working on our lists and journals while bombs were falling and cannons were firing. Once again the dog started barking and running to the end of his leash, as if someone were approaching. The old man went out to see and came back in running. "Germans," he shouted. "The Germans are coming! German soldiers!"

We went right into the hiding place beneath the floorboards, all of us except Perl who continued in her role as Marysia. The Germans banged on the door, Gestapo style. We thought this was it. "They are coming for us," someone whispered. "We've been discovered and they are coming to get us." We prayed they would not find us under the floorboards covered with a carpet. If they were serious about looking, and the Germans were always serious, they would find us. No doubt the hollow sound of the floor would have given us away. We held very still as Stanislaw opened the door to see what they wanted.

"Come with us," one of them said. They were not there for us — they were there for him. They needed him. More specifically, they needed something he had. "We want your horse and your wagon. Load it up." They needed transportation. They were pulling back and needed anything that could move. They took him and a horse and a wagon and headed towards the German lines.

The next morning, Stanislaw came back. He said he had only gone a few kilometers. "So crowded," he told us. "The road stops more than it moves." He left the horse and wagon behind and being a very smart young man, he ran away. The Germans did not bother trying to find him. They had their own problems. It was chaos. Besides, he did not want to go with the Germans. He wanted to stay with Marysia (Aunt Perl). Even after liberation, after it had all ended, he sought her out.

The next day there were more Russian planes. In the barn, we were digging a big ditch to hide the winter stores from the Russians. Marcinkowski was afraid the Russians would raid his house, and we dug the ditch to hide everything that was in the attic and the cellar, huge earthen jars filled with beans and sugar beets, wheat and corn, bread and meat. We also hid blankets and other items that become extra precious during a war. The Marcinkowskis were not rich people. They did not know if they would have to flee the Russians, and wanted to have something there when they returned.

With the night settling in and the planes gone, it was quiet except for the sound of our rakes in the straw. While we were working, two people from the city, some acquaintances of Stanislaw, came by with their wives. It was safer to be outside the city in case the Russians came in at night to bomb. Srulek and I quickly hid ourselves behind the doors of the barn.

Stanislaw came out and said, "Don't worry. You'll sleep here until they fall asleep. I'll come get you and you can sleep on top of the oven in the kitchen." There was a nook on top of the oven where people used to put their dough, a warm place, to let it rise.

So with rats for company and only steaming piles of cow manure to keep us warm on this cold January night, we curled up in the straw to sleep and waited for the call to go inside. The rats crawled all over us while we tried to sleep. We even killed some of them with a pitchfork. Finally Stanislaw came to take us quietly into the kitchen. The strangers were in the other room when we came into the kitchen and crawled up on top of the oven. The door was closed, but we could hear them. Immediately I recognized the voice of one of them. I grabbed Srulek's hand and said, "Oh, my God! It can't be." Then we heard it again, and I was sure. It was Mrorzinski, the assistant director from the *Kara* who always wore a beaver collar coat and high boots. He beat everyone, even me, with the riding crop he always carried. They were toasting and drinking to the gratitude they felt to Hitler for "doing away with the Jews."

"One thing he is doing right," he chided my protector as they drank together. And we heard it all, Srulek and I, from our little nook.

We were very apprehensive already, with this bastard Mrorzinski in the next room. But then, without warning, the kitchen door opened and in he walked. Now because of the Russian bombers there was a blackout, so every room was pitch black, especially the kitchen, and we did not see him, but we recognized his voice immediately. Suddenly Srulek and I were really crouching into each other. It was as if we shrunk in half. We did not dare move. We did not dare breathe. The stove was just to the right of the door where he was standing. Then we heard a scratch and saw a spark from a match head. Mrorzinski was trying to light a match. I suppose there was some food on the stove he wanted to warm up. Srulek and I grabbed each other's hands. It felt as if my heart was going to leap from my chest. We knew if he were to see us that he would kill us. He would kill us!

But the match never ignited. He tried again. Then again, this time with a few choice Polish swear words. He never got the match lit. Swearing a few more times, he turned and left the kitchen, closing the door behind him. As soon as we were sure he was not returning, we slipped back to the outside and went to sleep with the rats in the barn.

The next morning, Mrorzinski and his companion left to join the throngs of refugees walking along the roads away from town. He just wanted a place to spend the night, in case the Russians bombed the factory.

Later that morning, Srulek and I were finishing hiding the stores in the barn when more Russian aircraft began to fill the sky. Then they began to dive and strafe the retreating Germans. There was the *ack-ack* of anti-aircraft guns, but that did not stop their buzzing. Srulek and I dropped our rake and shovel and started to dance.

We could not believe it! The end of the war. We did not understand, or even care about the ramifications, about what will be tomorrow. I could not have cared less what was going to happen in the next hour! As long as the Germans are defeated. Finally defeated. The Russians are here and are going to liberate the city.

We were euphoric! We danced. Yes, we danced! Our dance turned into a song "*Loz es fallen! Loz es fallen!* Let them fall! Let them fall!" The old man fell to his knees and prayed, "Please not on me, not on my family."

It was January 18, 1945, and within a few hours the first Russian tanks were in the city square. People came and told us. We were curious, but we were also afraid. We were not up to being the first ones to greet the Russians. We decided to wait one more night before leaving.

When the next day came, Srulek and I were ready to go into the city.

It was a good thing to be able to say, "I'm going to leave the house."

"Roman, Valdek. Come here. I want to tell you something before you go." It was the old man Marcinkowski. He had some things he wanted to say to all nine of us. He was anachronistically somber in this time of celebration.

"You are all free. Free to go," he began, then took a deep breath before continuing. "But where will you go? Home? There is no more home. There is nothing out there. There is no place for you to go. This is your home now. It will always be here."

Again he paused, looking at each of us. He looked at me and at Srulek. "Roman, Valdek, you are strong young men and perhaps, by chance, you could have survived working at the glass factory." He looked at Rachel, the baby, who was now almost six years old. "But the little one here, the baby, how would she have survived?" The tears welled up in his eyes, in all our eyes. She would not have, of course. The Germans would have taken her immediately. We all sat in the quiet noise of our tears for a long while.

RUSSIANS AND
REVENGE AND THE REST

Srulek and I left the somber discussion about our future with
Marcinkowski and went to see the Russians who had liberated us. When
we got to the square in Piotrokow there was a lot of looting going on.
Whatever the Germans had left in their warehouses, like huge sacks of
sugar, everyone was grabbing. In the middle of this melee, Russian soldiers were walking around, checking out the town and enjoying the adulation of the crowd of mostly Poles. They spoke with whomever would
stop them. They were extremely friendly.

I knew only one word in Russian: *Yevrei*. It means "Jewish." We
scanned the crowd for Russian soldiers who looked Jewish and any one
we saw we ran up to and asked, "*Yevrei?*" Sure enough, we found one
almost immediately. He was from Baku, on the Caspian Sea. He would
not let us go. "Show me where they are! Any German who did you wrong.
Show me. I'll take care of them." He took the gun from his holster and
handed it to me. "Here," he said. "Here's the gun. Kill the Germans!"

I had never held a gun in my hand. I was afraid. I looked at the gun.
"All right," I said, then tried to act nonchalant as I looked around. "I don't
know where they are. They must have run away."

Actually I really did not know. The Germans who were running the
camp were taken prisoner immediately by the Polish Underground, the
Polish civilians and the people who worked in the camps. There was one
Polish collaborator, though, a policeman, who I was looking for. We
called him the "*grobber politsiant,*" because he was round like a barrel. His

face was like a wild pig. He was the "phantom" of the ghetto, always walk-ing around with the Gestapo man Williams and his dog, pointing out the Jews. Maybe he managed to change his clothes and blend in with the crowd, but I knew I was not the only one looking for him. I do not know if he was ever found.

The Jewish soldier from Baku told me that as the Russian army was driving toward Piotrokow, liberating one town after another, they came across a group of refugees coming out of the camps in their striped con-centration camp uniforms. One of his army buddies was leading a column of German prisoners and threw a gun toward the surviving remnants of the concentration camp. "Here! Why don't you get rid of them? Do it now!"

"Not one of them did it," our new friend from Baku said. "Not one would take the gun and kill the German prisoners."

Those who were looking for revenge, though, found there were other ways to get it. While we were in the square a group of militia came by. I recognized one of them as a Jewish man who had been in the camp with us. He had run away and was liberated only a few days before in a town four hundred kilometers away! He was already wearing a gun and had grenades hanging from his belt.

"What are you doing?" I asked him.

He looked at me like a general about to take over the city. "I'm going to take revenge," he said.

If it were only to get the *grobber politsiant* I was ready to sign up. After all, the Nazis killed my family. So we got in line, Srulek and I, at police headquarters to register and to get arms. Maybe it was the way we looked, or maybe the way the other Poles waiting with us looked at us like they knew we were Jewish, but as the line moved forward, we began to get this very peculiar feeling that we were not in friendly territory. It slowly dawned on each of us that maybe this was not the kind of crowd with whom we would enjoy being comrades in arms. Their faces looking at us brought back memories from before the war, when all we had to worry about were Polish anti-Semites running after us yelling "Dirty Jew! Go back to Palestine." They were the same faces that once took my father's hat from him on a streetcar and threw it out the window, just to make fun. It may have even been the same people.

We were almost at the door, ready to register and get our weapons, when like magic we both turned to each other, Srulek and I, and said, "What are we doing here? Look at these people. Do we want to do that? Let's get out of here."

It was not long after getting out of the line to join the militia that out of the forest staggered the remains of a group of partisans. I could count what was left of the battered fighters on my fingers.

It was then that I thought of going home — not to the farmer's house, where I slept on the floor — but to my family's house in the old ghetto area of Piotrokow, where we used to live before the war. Walking up the road to the square apartment building, I entered the courtyard. I was afraid to walk up the steps. I went alone. Perl and the others were still on the farm.

I turned my eyes to the second story, to the windows of the living room and the kitchen that overlooked the courtyard. The white curtains we had were gone. These new curtains were as colorless as the lifeless windows. No smiling faces of children. Not Henoch. Not Hinde. Not my smiling mother. They were empty.

I went up the stairs and knocked on the door. There were people living in my home already — non-Jews who had moved in as soon as the big ghetto was closed in October 1942. I told them who I was, that I used to live there.

"I am not here to take back the apartment," I assured them. "I just want to look around, to reminisce." I walked from the entry hall to the main room and quietly glanced around at what had been the center of my grandparents' home. The new tenants had changed it so that it was barely recognizable. My heart lamented to see that this apartment where the sound of my cousins' laughter used to mix with the tone of my grandfather's *gemorrah nigun* as he studied, this room where we sang *zmiros* at the Sabbath table, now echoed with a sad silence. I turned to go, but asked if I could check the shed. Like everything else, the gold coins we had hidden behind a few bricks in the wall less than two-and-a-half years before were gone.

The only thing I could take from there were the memories I brought in, echoes of a vibrant family turned in such a short time to an empty shell. There was nothing for me here, and I set about looking for a place to stay. I knew that my rich great uncle Hershel Pacanowski, the one with the roofing factory, had a house on the fine thoroughfare named Third of May Avenue. I also knew it was next to the local headquarters of the now-abandoned German High Command. I thought maybe I could set up a place to live there, and stay.

I walked to the center of town and up to the little hut where the superintendent lived on the premises and told him who I was, that I wanted to stay there. "Ach," he said with a wave of his hand after he let me in, "Stay here? There is nothing here. Nothing."

That meant I had to organize furniture, including a bed. I wanted to sleep in a bed. Between the camp and the farm, it had been three years since I had slept in a regular bed, with a regular mattress. I went next door and started taking things from the old German High Command building. I found a mattress and I carried it back to the house. I went back and grabbed a sofa, a chair, back and forth I went. Dressed in my old blue overalls and sneakers, with nothing but a beat-up old jacket to keep me warm, I kept carrying whatever I could find over to the house from the German headquarters.

I had no identification, no money. We did not use money anyway. Who knew what was good money then? We organized furniture. We organized food. If one group was coming out of a warehouse, we were right behind them, hauling sacks of potatoes, carrots, whatever we could find. The Russians were free with their bread and their lard.

So there I was coming and going with items from the German High Command, and as I was carrying out maybe the last mattress, a Russian major saw me in the gateway. "Stand and face the wall!" he yelled in a Russian that was close enough to Polish for me to understand. He pulled out his gun and put the cold steel barrel against my temple. "So you're a German. You are the one hiding here," he said with a frightening certainty.

"I-I-I'm not German. *Yevrei!* I'm a Jew! A Jew!" I stammered out a reply. "I am Jew from Piotrokow!" I tried in my broken Russian to explain, but the only word I could think of was *konz-lager*, meaning one from the *konzentrazion*, from the concentration camp or labor camp. I had already learned that the Russians knew what the term *konz-lager* meant.

"You are not a Jew. All the Jews are dead. They killed all the Jews. You are no *konz-lager*. You are a spy."

Just then, in front of the courtyard of this house, I saw something I had not seen in years. An old woman, maybe around sixty, dressed in a fine suit, impeccable with hat and gloves. She was out of place for a war, but not for the kind of street I remembered Third of May Avenue to be. "Madame," I shouted to her in Polish. "Madame, please! Do you speak Russian?"

She saw the situation immediately. "Yes, I do," she said.

"Please explain to this officer that I am Jewish and that my uncle was Hershel Pacanowski," and I pointed to the house next door. I told her my aunt's name, and the children's names. "Please, tell him I am not a spy."

When she heard my uncle's name, her face lit up. She was a friend of the family. Quickly she explained to the officer that indeed I was a Jew, and indeed she knew Pacanowski who lived next door. With a grunt and a sneer, he holstered the gun.

What fate that brought this woman by just at this time!

After dropping the last mattress, I ran back to Marcinkowski and told Perl and Raizl that we had a place to stay. Perl came back with me and we moved in before the sun was even down. Raizl was a little more stubborn, and definitely afraid. "Who knows?" she said. "The Germans might come back!"

All this in one day that was so long and so short at the same time.

The next day, Perl had gone back to the farm to get a few more belongings and some food. When she returned she told me that Stanislaw was going to be coming by in the evening. She was certain he would propose. The two of us walked across the street and sat on a bench in the park. The conversation was very simple.

"What do we do?" she asked. "What do we say?"

"*Emmes*. The truth," I said. "The truth is best."

"Who speaks? Do we both speak?"

"If you like. We should tell him the truth about who we are, who he is."

Perl listened as I spoke.

"We tell him that out of respect for our family, who died so tragically, that they be able to rest in peace, this cannot be. We tell him that we respect what he has done for us and will love him all our lives for that, that we are thankful." Perl nodded. Both of us were sobbing, lamenting over this.

"He is a religious man, and we are religious." These were terms we felt he could understand.

This was when I knew I was grown up, when my youngest aunt came to me for advice. She did not even ask her sister.

It was almost eleven o'clock when Stanislaw came to the door. We were all sitting on the few pieces of furniture I had scavenged. He came in and sat with us, looking at Perl, whom he called Marysia. We sat in silence for a moment, and then he began, talking to me. "I care for her so much. I will treat her right. I will take care of her, find a trade, open a butcher shop."

He was such a kind and simple man, a farmer who believed deeply in God and the almanac. He cried as he spoke. "I will be a good and kind man to you, Marysia."

I entered the conversation. "You are one of the kindest men on earth. We owe our lives to you. But this cannot be," I said, not in a lecturing way, but with all the love I felt, for this was our truth for him. "It is against our beliefs, our religion that our parents were raised in. And now we do not even have a grave to stand over, to pray for them. We cannot disrespect them or our God in this way. It is a sin for us. We hope as a religious man you will understand.

"We will always be grateful. Anything you need, anything we can we will do for you, but not this. Not this. Please understand."

In a sad silence Stanislaw rose and shook hands with me and walked out the door.

And that is how I grew up. After being liberated from the Germans I was liberated again. In the space of five agonizing years I had gone from being sixteen to being twenty-one, with no time in between to test what it means to be independent. I was never a teenager. I never lived that life. I was depended on to take care of my family when my father died, when I was only eighteen, but I was not independent. A twenty-one-year-old man in Europe is a man, mature in all respects. Now I was free to be that man. I was no longer surrounded by barbed wire, no longer forced to labor or die, no longer forced to hide and survive. I was free to do what I wanted, whenever I wanted. I was a liberated Jew and free to be a man. I was no longer afraid.

MAKING LIFE
LIVABLE AGAIN

"I shall not die, but I will live to declare the works of the Lord."

— Psalm 118:17

CHAPTER 18

BACK TO LODZ

A few people started coming back from the liberated European camps, pouring into the cities and the towns from Auschwitz and other horrors. Looking into their faces was like seeing someone come back from the dead. Everyone had his own baggage, his sack full of *tsoris* that he carried around. Every face was a jumble of emotions, like a mess of puzzle pieces or a knotty ball of twine. They were all set on looking for someone, now searching, now waiting, waiting and asking, "Is it really over?"

I was living in Pacanowski's apartment in Piotrokow with my aunts Perl and Raizl, and my Uncle Yidel, Raizl's husband. The Russian soldier from Baku, the Jew we had met on the first day of the liberation, needed a place to sleep and was staying there as well. He spoke a fluent Yiddish and we sort of became friends. He was stationed for quite a while in the city. He intervened on behalf of a Jewish couple from Moscow, a doctor and his wife, who needed a temporary place to stay before returning to Russia. The huge apartment on Third of May Avenue was packed with people. After about ten days, I was ready to get out. While I loved my family, they needed my help with so many things that I felt my new freedoms getting more and more congested.

I had the idea of returning to Lodz to see what had happened to my father's side of the family. They had all been in the ghetto there and I wanted to see if I could find somebody, a cousin, an uncle, even a second cousin. Maybe by a miracle someone was alive.

It was a snowy day at the end of January 1945, and the drifts were up to my knees. The trains did not run. They still were not up, as the war had ended in this part of Poland less than two weeks before. I heard that other people were walking wherever they needed to go. I also heard that for a little vodka the Russians would take you anywhere. So I pulled on my big cloth boots I had scavenged and started down the highway, planning to walk the forty-four kilometers to Lodz. On the way out of town I stopped at Marcinkowski's and took a little moonshine from his still.

I walked alone for a long time, passing the looted bodies of dead German soldiers in the snow banks beside the road. Finally I saw three others walking the same direction. They were quite a bit older than I was and non-Jews. They were Polish-German refugees who, I soon discovered, were also going to Lodz. "I have a bottle of vodka," I told them. "We can use it to flag down a Russian army truck. I'll wave the bottle and maybe they'll stop."

After five kilometers, though several military trucks passed us, they did not stop for me, my companions or my bottle of vodka. After ten kilometers, they still did not stop. The snow was deep, and hour after hour we walked. A Russian on a motorcycle passed by and looked at us with a shrug. He could not even take one of us if he wanted to.

After about twelve hours we arrived in the town of Tuszyn. I knew the place because my mother's grandmother Chava had lived there before the war. I had visited her many times. On the way into town, a Polish militiaman stopped us. He was young, in his twenties, and had hand grenades in his belt and a Russian machine gun on his shoulder.

"Papers," he said, and held out his hand to receive our documents. The three men I was with dutifully handed over their papers. They were Poles released from Russian prisons. They may have been Polish Germans, since those were the first freed by the Russians in Poland. They had their papers. I had nothing. The militiaman looked at me.

"I don't have any papers," I said to him.

"Who are you?" he asked.

"I'm Jewish. I'm going home. I'm going to Lodz." He looked at me and I kept talking. "I have family here, in Tuszyn. If you are from here, if you were born here, you must have known the Kriegers. That's my great-grandmother's family. And the Sterns. Do you know the Sterns?"

The young militiaman smiled, just a little. He was listening, not talking, and then he said quietly, "Go, with Godspeed."

The four of us continued into town. We had agreed before we even reached Tuszyn that once in town, we would stop and ask a farmer to put us up for the night. But once the three men I was traveling with found out I was Jewish, things changed completely. It was nightfall when we reached the outskirts of the city, and whatever bond my companions and I had formed during the day faded with the sun. They turned to me as they headed down to knock on a farmhouse door. "Find your own place," they said, and that was that. It was like I did not exist. I went from thinking that these older men were helping me to being alone. I realized I was continuing on my own.

I had no difficulty finding a small farm with a kind old woman. She fed me and gave me a place to sleep. The next morning, I hitched rides on hay wagons from town to town over the last twelve kilometers or so. I was excited and anxious to see the city again, but what stuck in my mind as I entered Lodz was the sight of Russian pilots in their leather bomber jackets, wearing their insignia.

Heading through the center of town towards my own neighborhood, I looked from face to face, scanning the crowd for something or someone familiar. "*Amcho?* Are you of my people?" I asked someone I thought I recognized. "Ya," he said back.

"Tell me," I asked him, "where is the Jewish community?"

"Ah!" he declared in Yiddish. "You have to go to the committee, to register. Come! I'll take you."

He took me to the place where every Jew returning to Lodz came to register. It was a place to find family and friends, to get a meal and a place to stay. The food was already there from American relief organizations such as the Joint Distribution Committee (which we called the Joint). It came from Americans and was delivered by Russians.

Mirsky was the man in charge of the registration group. The Russians had started in Lublin organizing committees like this one, and continued as they went through Poland. In this way they could control the refugees. The other purpose of the committee was to see what other Jews were still alive in the city. When the Russians liberated the Lodz ghetto in January

1945, there were 830 souls who by some miracle managed to survive. Just before the Russians came in, the Germans had taken a detail of Jews out to the nearby cemetery to dig a mass grave. The liberators came in before the last 830 Jews of Lodz could be executed and buried there.

I arrived in Lodz at the very end of January, and was one of the first to actually return to the city. I was given registration number 840. I was also given some clothes and a little food. From the courtyard near the registration office and inside where it was a little warmer, I watched all day as the Jews came back. Every day a few more returned.

My first day back in Lodz I met a redheaded man, a Jew, who lived in the city not far from me before the war. He took me to stay with him, in the apartment of a German-Polish family.

Two days later I had recovered my strength after all that walking and went back to the committee. I wanted a place of my own, without staying with another family. They told me about an apartment across the street from the police station. "It's a big apartment," they told me. "You will have to put some other people in there with you."

One of the next people in line was a partisan, another Lodz native. He needed a place too, so they put us together in this apartment. From first sight I could tell I did not like him too much. He was not my kind of person. Our upbringing was different and I found it difficult to communicate with him. But what could I do? They gave me an apartment. I could not say no.

And what an apartment! When the superintendent let us in we saw that it was filled with everything from food to linens. The Germans had lived there and left all this stuff behind. There was even ammunition. The kitchen was filled with plates and utensils. The cupboard was filled with food, but I was afraid to touch it. I thought, maybe it's poisoned or something. I would not eat it.

After one night in that beautifully stocked apartment, I left to organize some other food and get some decent clothes. The first thing I did was find a man in a Russian uniform. I knew where most of the German Poles lived, and I knew that if they saw a Russian uniform, they would get scared and do anything we asked. The man was not a soldier in the army; he was a partisan in the underground who fought alongside the Russians, so he had the uniform. His name was Moishe Cohen, and he was a distant cousin of my uncle, Yidel Dzialowski.

Together we marched a few blocks and up a few steps to a door. I remembered a German family used to live there. We knocked. "What do you want?" they asked, once they opened the door and saw us both standing there.

I looked just inside the door and saw a bike. "I want a bicycle," I said. I did not even know how to ride it. I just wanted to take from them.

"Oh. You can't have that," they said. "It's my son's."

I said, "You say I can't have it, but I'm taking it." And that is what I did. Even though I was not an experienced rider, I could push myself along, so now I had some transportation. I took the bicycle back to the apartment, along with other things I had organized. But every time I went to bring more things, the man I shared the apartment with took them. So when he went out, I took the things that he had brought in. We had a big argument.

"Look," I said, "I don't need you. I'll do my own thing."

I went to Cegielniania 17, the address of my Uncle Yidel Dzialowski, Raizl's husband, to see what had become of his apartment. Peeking inside the windows, I saw that it was empty. I had become quite bold by this point. I walked straight to the superintendent and announced, "I am the nephew of Dzialowski. I want to use his apartment."

"Well," he said, not very pleased with my tone, "the apartment is empty now."

"Don't give me the business. Open the door." Then I threatened him. "I'll call the army. They'll search your apartment and see how much you have taken from here and they'll arrest you."

Just like that, he opened the door and let me in. It was a beautiful two-bedroom apartment that I had all to myself, but it really was empty. Not even a bed. I had to start organizing again, so back to the streets and knocking on the doors of Germans.

Around that time, while I was organizing and looking for people, I went back to the house where I grew up, but it was gone. The same thing with my father's parents' house. I walked into the field where the ghetto had been. It was in ruins. Scattered on the ground were documents and money and piles of books. Secular books and religious books.

I went to where the synagogue had been, where it had burned down. In a building next door, in an undisturbed room, were stacks and stacks of books. I had not gone looking for books. I was looking for people. I was looking for food and clothes. But I had a knapsack and began taking books. For the next few days, a few times a day, I would come by and take books back to the apartment. Somehow, in my mind, I thought that perhaps my family had hidden some of these books. I finally had to stop because the bookcase in Dzialowski's apartment was filled to overflowing. There were Hebrew books and Yiddish books, secular books of poetry and holy texts. There were books from the father of Zionism Theodore Herzl, the poet Dovid Frishman and Jewish historians Dubnow and Gretz, including all the volumes of the latter's *De Yiddeshe Gashichte, The History of the Jews*. Though I would leave all those texts behind, some from the nineteenth century, I was able to find the same printing of Frishman's books years later when I came to Atlanta. There were some valuable books there. God knows what happened to them. Even with all the books and the gratification I had from reading them, or even having them, I needed a different sort of commodity, one that I could get something out of immediately.

I went back to the people my father used to do business with, the Schlegels, the Biedermans. They remembered my father, and though they were German, they were very nice to me. They fed me. They gave me raw yarn for making textiles. I was able to sell this yarn right away to get things I needed.

There were others I wanted to see, with whom my father had done business, but I did not want to go to see them alone. I intended to hurt them, to take revenge on them. These were the people who abandoned my father, and worse. One in particular was the man named Schmidt who, on Rosh Hashana in 1939, had led the Gestapo to our house. It was Schmidt who had them drag my father to our store and make him open it. It was Schmidt who took everything in the store. This one I wanted to see alive.

I remembered the address because my father used to take me there when I was eleven or twelve years old. I took someone along with me because I was afraid to go by myself. My blood was pumping so loudly in my head that I did not hear my fist pounding the door. The door opened and there he was, still sitting at his old loom and weaving. My heart pounded when I saw him.

"Schmidt!"

The old man turned, startled. He had been old when I first met him as a child; he must have been in his eighties by now.

"Do you know who I am? I'm Gutfraind," I announced with a sadistic triumph.

He dropped everything. His face turned white and red and blue at the same time. I walked over to him, picked him up by the lapels and slammed his head against the frame of the loom.

"Please," he started begging. "Please don't kill me."

"I'm not going to kill you. Look at me! I look like a ghost, right? A ghost come back from the dead. Do you remember what you did?" My fists clenched even tighter around his lapel.

The old man was trembling. "Please," he begged between whimpers, "please."

There was a hand on my shoulder. It was the friend I brought with me. "Don't do anything. You've given enough punishment already. He didn't kill your father."

"No, he didn't," I said, "but he had the chutzpah to bring the Gestapo into our house and take my father out and steal his merchandise."

"I'll give you anything you want," old Schmidt cried. "If I did anything wrong," he stammered, "it was not of my doing. They asked the Germans to lead them to the Jewish people who were no good. It was not my fault." So he blamed it on the authorities, as many others would come to do.

"I don't want anything from you," I told him. "I just wanted to come and see you. I wanted to see how you suffer." And I dropped him and walked out.

A few days later I was back at the street near the committee. It had become a meeting place, where people had come to find each other.

Suddenly, I heard my name. "Itchele," a girl was calling. I turned, and there was my cousin Kalcza (Carmela) Wajnrib. She was a few years older than I. I remember her father had a beautiful tenor voice. He was a brilliant man, an astronomer. He died in Treblinka, along with her mother and two sisters. One of Kalcza's sisters was married to a cantor before the war. They were all beautiful girls. It was such a miracle to see her.

"Do you have a place?" I asked.

"No."

"Now you do," and I took her back to Dzialowski's apartment. She brought a friend along as well.

Within a few days the time had come to let my remaining family in Piotrokow know what the situation was here in Lodz. There was no way of writing letters to notify them. But they would be worried, so I had to find a way to go back there.

By this time the trains were running. I went to the train station with some food and a few zloty that were just starting to be exchanged as currency for some restaurants and groceries in the city. The only train heading in the direction of Piotrokow was a coal-fired locomotive. Just the locomotive, no train cars. The engineer said, "If you want to freeze on the nose, you are welcome." I had to get there, so I bundled up and sat on the nose of the locomotive, holding tightly to the front of the engine. At the switching station in Koluszki I boarded a freight train that took me to Piotrokow.

I found my family still at Pacanowski's. "Uncle," I said to Dzialowski, "I found a place in Lodz. It's your apartment where you lived!" He could not believe it.

I only stayed a few days because it was not long before I started hearing, "Itchele, do this for me. Itchele, do that for me." After all I went through in Lodz, all the real leadership and resourcefulness I had demonstrated to myself, they were treating me like a child. I decided I was not going to fall into that again. I was twenty-one and I missed the independence I had in Lodz.

"I'm going back to Lodz," I told them. "I have friends there, a place. My cousin is there." And I left.

By the time I got back to Lodz the second time, many more haunted survivors had returned from the camps. Everyone needed to look to the future, to make life livable again. Nobody wanted to talk about the last five years. The door was closed as if it had all happened a thousand years ago. We were people waking from a nightmare, a distant hellish dream that no one at the time wanted to recall. All anyone wanted to do was take advantage where they could without reaching too far into what was left of their self-respect to get it, rebuild what was left of their lives, and trade what they could with farmers and others to feed what was left of their families. In this way they returned to Lodz.

With this latest influx of survivors, the Lodz Jewish community was starting to take shape again. That meant there were places of prayer, a place to find a minyan. I went to every place I remembered. I looked for the *shtiebel* where I used to pray with my family before the war. It was known as *dos groyse shtiebel* at Zachodnia 56. It had been outside the ghetto, not far from where we lived. It was, of course, gone.

I was desperate to find a remnant to which I belonged.

CHAPTER
19

COMMUNITY BUILDING

One day, as I continued to look for what was left of my family, I thought about my uncle, Rabbi Elazar Lipschitz [ל״ז] and his wife Shevele. Elazar was one of the six recognized rabbinical authorities in the Lodz rabbinate before the war. Many cities had a chief rabbi, usually one man who was the authority for the entire community. But Lodz had not had one since 1918, when the last great rabbi, Eliyahu Chaim Meisels, died. Since then, the community had been unable to find a suitable replacement, so there was an ongoing consortium of six rabbis chosen from among the different Lodz congregations. Rabbi Elazar was one of them. They helped in matters of law, in the *beis din*, the community tribunal that applied Jewish law.

Elazar's wife, Shevele, was the daughter of the first Alexander rebbe, Reb Yechiel Danziger. She was known in the community for her regal bearing, her personal involvement in the community and her knowledge. She was the sister of Yismach Yisroel [ל״ז] and Tiferes Shmuel [ל״ז] (whom I am partly named for), two great and wise leaders of the Alexander movement.

So I went to look for my uncle Elazar, whom I had not seen since the cold January night in 1940 when he and his family stayed with us before everyone moved into the ghetto. I went to their address at Dzielna/Narutowicza 7 to see if they were still there, by some miracle. I did not expect them to be. Every place I had gone since my return to Lodz was not how I remembered it. Some of the Jewish houses were empty, but most were now occupied by non-Jews.

I walked up to the second floor, turned to the right. There were people inside. I could hear their voices. I held my breath as I opened the door. Inside was a room full of teenagers singing songs of the Zionist pioneers and listening to speeches in Polish, Yiddish and Hebrew — a lot of Hebrew. There were boys and girls from all segments of Jewish society. The speakers were all from different organizations too, and talked about Palestine and repatriation. The group called itself *Ichud*, which is Hebrew for Unity.

After this first chance encounter, I found myself coming back to these gatherings again and again. My new friends would come up to me on the street. "What are you doing Saturday afternoon?" they would ask, and we would hop on the streetcar and go to these meetings. Word-of-mouth was the way it had to be done. Lodz was under Russian occupation, and it was dangerous to announce or pass out invitations to Zionist meetings. It was dangerous for those attending and especially for the people who hosted the meetings in their homes. I liked going because I heard revealing things about Zionism and the movement's leaders. We talked about sociology, about life on a kibbutz in Palestine; we talked about the politics of Zionism, the ideology of the movement's founders, their aims and goals. We spoke of spreading the love of *erets yisroel*, the land of Israel, and I found that I was sitting with my mouth open through most of it. That we should be talking about returning after two thousand years of Diaspora was amazing to me.

"I'm going to kibbutz next week," one of the kids would say.

"I'm going next week as well."

"I'm going next year."

"I'm going to be smuggled into Palestine."

To talk in such terms! For someone with my background, it was a discussion of messianic proportions. "Now?" I found myself saying. "Already? How wonderful! What an opportunity this is. Someone must be doing something right." I often went twice a week to those meetings, to listen, to hear, to get some modern inspiration. I say modern because my father would never have allowed me to join an organization like this.

There were speeches about how if there had been a homeland for the Jews, if our parents had had the foresight, none of the past few years would have happened. We would have all been in Palestine. It played on all our sympathies, and at the same time it gave hope for a new beginning. I was raw. My mind was looking for something on which to build my life. I had only been liberated a few weeks, and when we walked the streets the war was still around us, our world still filled with soldiers and weapons and fear. I did not believe that everything was normal yet, that it ever would be. I did not believe that war would not start up again any day.

The Zionist meetings injected me with hope. They goaded me by creating the possibility for community. I was young and hungry for knowledge, for a return to a little bit of Jewish culture. All of us in the group were in the same boat; we had all stopped our formal education at an early age, many earlier than I.

The meetings were not a place for Jewish education, though. It was more of an education for Jews, because regardless of whether you were practicing or not, we all went through the same thing, and the idea was we all had to stick together. We had to work together to create a home to go to, for none of us had a home. It became our goal. I became involved with the community at these meetings, involved with Zionism, and it was there that I began to make friends.

→— —→

One night the Joint brought an old Yiddish film to the community. Everyone who had come back to Lodz was there. I spoke with as many as I could; it was not a question of knowing them before or not. We needed one another. Soon I had found a group of three people my age and we began to talk.

After many little get-togethers, the conversations came around to organizing, to acquiring the goods we all needed to survive and maybe try to do some business. "What are you doing this Saturday and Sunday?" one of them asked me. I shrugged.

"We heard there is an opportunity to organize, to go into Breslau and bribe the Russian soldiers guarding German stores. We get the merchandise, bring it back and sell it."

We had nothing to lose. At the time the trains were moving pretty frequently, and with a little bribery we were able to get a seat on the top of the train, on its roof! Every time a bridge came up we had to stretch out low so our heads would not be chopped off. The real insanity was that we did this more than once, every time we went in to Germany. It was an hour and a half each way and at night we were freezing.

In Breslau, there was a four-story department store that had been bombed by the Allies. All the floors were in the basement. By bribing the Russian guards, I was able to get into the rubble and find some bolts of fabric. Then I went to someone who had a truck and in exchange for transporting the booty into Poland for me, I offered him a piece of the sale. Sometimes I would barter merchandise, like cloth for jars of honey.

It was after my first trip to Breslau that I found my family had come back up to Lodz from Piotrokow. I stayed in Lodz a while. With my new friends, I went to see films and concerts. Growing up I had only been exposed to Hasidic music — *nigunim* and *zmiros*. I had never gone to hear a musical concert and I had not enjoyed singing since before the war. Up until this time I was like a Jew in mourning, fasting from the pleasures of hearing and singing music. Even when I sang in the ghetto it was not as a free man. Now that I had survived, my heart was so filled with pain and sorrow, I thought there was no room for the joys of music. Walking the streets of the city where I grew up, and realizing what I had lost, how could I open myself to the enjoyment of it? It was only through the insistence of my friends that I had even gone to a show where the Russian Red Army Choir performed. It was only a few steps away from Uncle Yidel's house. They gave a concert conducted by the great Alexandrov. Watching the singers up there on stage, I began to envy them. I wished I could do the same thing. I had never heard a big choir like that before. When the show was over, I told my friends that I used to sing.

"You used to sing?" one of them asked.

I nodded.

"Do you know opera?" another asked. These were educated young men.

"Sure," I declared, and at their insistence I began to sing. "Yai, bu bai bai bai bai bai bai bai..." It was a *nigun* composed by Getzel Zeide for the Rosh Hashana service only a few years before.

The boys started laughing. "That's opera?" they asked between chuckles.

"Well," I said, embarrassed now, "that is what the man who composed it told me."

My friends went on to tell me of a conservatory in Lodz, and I thought about going, but the necessities of rebuilding my life and the enthusiasm in recapturing my lost youth distracted me. I traveled with my new, worldly friends from city to city, sometimes for business, sometimes for fun, and lived from day to day.

Every time we returned to the streets of Breslau I saw a sea of young people. Everybody was looking for adventure. We stayed with a German family, five young Polish Jews out for business and excitement only days after the war ended. One of my friends knew someone who knew someone, and for the price of a slab of bacon in a war-ravaged town, we had a place to stay. And they were happy to have us, to show they had nothing to do with anything bad the Germans had done to the Jews.

Looting bombed-out stores was not the only way to get merchandise to sell. Our biggest business deal started with two bottles of vodka. I traded the vodka to the Russians and they gave me horses. We got a covered wagon filled with other merchandise and paraded the horses in front and behind all the way back to Lodz to sell. We had no problem crossing the border because we had bought false papers through connections in Breslau and Lodz. The Russian papers, signed and sealed, said that we were comrades on our way back to Russia. We also had two people with us who spoke Russian.

In order to complete a big deal like this we had to form a kind of syndicate with two others. They knew where we could get a lot more horses. Because of their help, we divided the portions seven ways instead of five. Even with the extra partners we each got a great dividend. Horses were very expensive at the time. We took in as much as fifty thousand zloty for each horse. That allowed our organizing and our adventuring to continue.

Every day one of our little group came up with ideas of how to keep things going, sometimes for business, but more often for fun. Little by little our lives were coming together. One day a friend from the labor camp, whom I had not seen since he had been taken away to a concentration camp, returned to Lodz. His name was Adasz Jolinger and he had been my grandparents' neighbor in Piotrokow before the war. His father was an artisan who would turn wood for Torah scrolls and other decorative purposes. Seeing him brought back some painful memories, but like others from the labor camp I had met in Lodz since the liberation, I tried to think only about our future and how we could be successful. Still, I knew his family and asked him about them.

"My father is alive," he said to me.

"Really?" I asked. "Where is he?"

"In Berlin. I heard he was seen in Berlin." He paused for a moment. "Come to Berlin with me, Itche. I can find my father and you can do business there."

I spoke with my five "partners" and we all agreed to go to Berlin. After all, it was another new adventure.

CHAPTER
20

BERLIN

The next day, we went to the rail station and, just as we had before, found our usual places on the roof of a train headed to Berlin. We had to do this to get into Germany undetected. In order to stay in Berlin, though, you needed a special visa because of the four powers occupying her immediately after the war. This was no problem. We only had to say we were German Jews instead of Poles, and since hardly anyone at that time had documents, it was easy enough to declare that I had been born in Frankfurt-Am-Main. Sure enough, a day after we arrived in Berlin, my friend Adasz found his father living with a German woman.

Because of all our dealings in Breslau, my German had improved to near fluency. We could all speak it now. It was not long before we were going back and forth between Berlin and Lodz, buying, trading and bartering as we had in Breslau. The five of us had rented rooms in someone's apartment. At that time, you could not get your own place unless you evicted a German, and since we were transient, we decided not to get a place yet. We continued in our trading, earning enough to pay the rent, but clothes and food were not a problem, either. We might have eaten a little better than others because we got to know the Jewish chaplain of the American army.

Being in the parts of Berlin under American control was a lot different than being in the Russian-occupied areas of Germany and Poland. With the Russians, there was plenty of food, but beyond that there was a certain air of distrust between us. The Americans, though, were a lot more open. Whatever they had they gave to you with a full heart, no strings attached. Anything we wanted, we could have.

I thrived in this air of freedom. As a result, I did not return immediately to my traditions and my background, though on Friday nights I would walk to a little *shtiebel* to pray. There the unbridled freedom I was experiencing collided with my past. It hit back and I fought it inside me. "I can go back to that way of life anytime," I said to myself. After all, I was not strange to it, and it was not strange to me. I lived in the declaration, "Let me enjoy life now, with no obligations." I was not obligated to man or to God.

At this time, I had a choice between the *yetzer hara*, the evil inclination, and the *yetzer hatov*, the good inclination. In the past, I would have considered the other side of the story — that is, what if I do this and not that? What can happen if I choose to do the wrong thing? I was now in a time of not thinking about such things. There was no ritual in my life. I did not keep kosher; I ate what I could find. I had a thoughtless day-to-day existence and there was no thinking about the consequences.

My lack of concern went back to when I first ate what I knew was strictly *treif,* when the farmer gave me that warm piece of bloodwurst from the freshly slaughtered pig. I had thought that something was going to strike me when I ate it. When it did not, I said, "What the heck!" Whenever I thought that maybe my actions in this new freedom might be an aspect of *yetzer hara,* I just fought it off and told myself that I would do things as they came, and so I did.

Then, in late summer 1945, I was walking through Berlin and met someone on the street who changed my life. He was with someone else I knew, and we were doing introductions.

"This is Aharon Saurymper," my acquaintance said.

I said, "Wait a minute. Didn't you live in Lodz? My God! My uncle and aunt rented an apartment in your house when they got married."

"Oy!" he said, stumbling in surprise. "Sure."

This man knew my family, my background. He kept up the religion as strongly as before. "What's happening to you?" he asked me. "Where are you going? Have you completely disassociated yourself from your past? You completely forgot where you came from? Don't you know what kind of family you come from?"

He went on to describe me as *farblunjen*, lost. He asked me how I had become so ruined, *kalle gevorin*, spoiled, like a bad piece of meat. But he did not insist. At first I discounted what he said, but we got to like each other and he sort of brought me back to my roots. He took my hand and led me. He was sincere and wanted to help me in anything — in business and in life. He was fifteen years older than I was, and I respected him. He became my mentor.

Aharon had been in Berlin long enough to establish good connections in the German Jewish community. He was able to easily obtain the ID cards we needed to get certain things like food. Specifically, he was able to get the red ID card for my friends and me. These cards were given by the *Judesche Gemeinde Zu Berlin*, the Jewish Community of Berlin, and were marked "*Opfer Des Faschismuss*, Victims of Fascism." Having a red card entitled you to more food than others, including the Germans.

Aharon began taking me to services on Friday nights at the house of a Jewish chaplain, Rabbi Joseph Shubow, from Boston. The chaplain and our five partners became very close. He wanted to do so much for us. He provided us with gefilte fish in cans and canned meat — the stuff sent by the Jewish Welfare Board for the Jews in the American army. Because of our involvement with Aharon and the chaplain, we became active in helping establish the first Joint Distribution Committee office in Berlin. Around the same time, the United Nations Relief and Rehabilitation Administrations Agency (UNRRA) was opening Schlachtensee, which eventually became the displaced persons camp on the outskirts of Berlin. Most of the three hundred refugees in the DP camp were Jews who survived the war by escaping to the Soviet Union.

Organizing was something I had become very good at, and Aharon knew it. I had even done a fair business with Germans in Berlin, when they were more afraid of us than we were of them. One day, Aharon asked me to schlep some challah over to the DP camp.

"I'll tell you what," I said. "I know a baker who lives on a street where everything is blocked off. He's a German baker. The doors and windows are boarded, but I know he is in business, that he's working."

How did I know? I used to rent his three-wheeled cart because I did not know how to drive and I needed to transport merchandise. I had seen this three-wheeler one day, driving down the street, filled with sacks of flour. I stopped him and asked, "How would you like to make some money?" and I told him to take something from one address and deliver it to another. It was as simple as that. In this way I got to know him and do business with him. I told Aharon that I would go see this baker and find out what we can do.

"We need three hundred loaves of bread," I told the baker when I found him.

"Ach," he complained, "I don't have the flour for three hundred loaves of bread!"

I said, "I want you to do it for me and we will pay you for it. If you are going to continue complaining and not do it voluntarily, then I'm going to force you."

He just stared at me. "Now," I continued, "would you rather see me coming over here with half the army and lock up your place and take everything you have, or are you going to do it?" I remember how excited we were when we transported the challahs to the DP camp.

Then, the DP camp needed a Torah. The Berlin Jewish community had buried three or four hundred Torahs in the Jewish cemetery of Weissensee in the beginning of the war, and they unearthed them after the liberation. The Torahs were stored in the Jewish Community building. We retrieved one and brought it to Rabbi Shubow.

I was successful at organizing because I worked with everyone, and everyone I worked with gave me a new connection. I went home at night to the apartment room I rented with the others and there were girls to cook for us and we enjoyed radio, conversation and records. We had one Jewish record. It was the first time I had ever heard the world-famous cantor Hazzan Yossele Rosenblatt. The record was of two of the most famous prayers of the High Holidays — *Hineni* and *Kol Nidre*. We had an old wind-up Victrola and must have played that record twenty-five times a day.

Sometimes, despite the curfew, we would walk over to nearby friends' places and talk or play cards. While we were too busy to think about long-term relationships with women, sometimes we met some girls we liked and wanted to be with. The girls who helped us in the apartment were friends with my partners (and they eventually married them).

I had met girls since the war ended, before coming to Berlin, but it was a day-to-day, hour-to-hour kind of deal. You saw a girl in the morning and forgot about her by the afternoon. There was too much going on. I did not have time to dwell on relationships or even give them a chance to gel. But now that I was spending most of my time in Berlin, I was beginning to feel differently. It was the next step toward normalization in my life. That is how I met the woman whom I describe as my "first love." It was August when I met this girl in Berlin. She was less than two years older than I was, and she was beautiful. She had blue eyes and blonde hair; I fell madly in love with her.

We were introduced through a friend from my hometown. Her name was D'vorah Lipschitz, the same as my mother's family. We spoke about family background, of course, and found we came from very different upbringings. We talked about everything. She was intelligent, well read, and though her Yiddish was not the best, we spoke a little of it together — but mostly we spoke in Polish. She also spoke German quite well. She was not Hasidic, but traditional. She was in a concentration camp, though I do not recall which one. What she did in the camp, I did not know.

I wanted to buy her something, and kept picturing her in a blue dress my aunt Perl used to wear. I felt she would look exquisite in it, with her deep blue eyes and long blonde hair. I also was remembering how good my young aunt looked when she wore it.

In the early autumn, I was planning to return to Lodz on a business trip. I had some money, and I trusted D'vorah to keep it until I returned. "Why don't you hold on to this for me?" I asked her. "I'll be back in two weeks." I wanted to bring her with me, to meet my aunts. This is how much I was interested in her. She refused to leave Berlin, though, and cried when I left. If love were not so blind, perhaps I would not have done it, but I gave her the money to hold for me and went on to Lodz.

When I got to Poland, my aunts insisted I stay for Rosh Hashanah. Considering the last time we celebrated that holiday, I was not too enthused, especially since I wanted to get back to Berlin and D'vorah. Then I remembered what she had said as I left: "Pray for me." Because of that and my aunts' insistence, I stayed. It turned out that, although there is a proscription against unmarried males leading High Holiday services, the Lodz community asked me to conduct services for Rosh Hashanah. People had started coming back, but there were still only a few thousand in the community at the time. They wanted me, they said, because many still remembered my voice, and they all knew my background.

While in Lodz, I told my aunts about D'vorah, about how much I loved her and wanted to buy things for her. "I don't have the money for gold or silver," I told my aunt Perl, "and I don't want to start with that kind of stuff."

"What would you like to give her, Itchele?"

"Well," I said, "she needs clothes." Perl just nodded and I continued. "You know that blue dress of yours, the one I like so much?"

"I know the one. I like that one too."

"Isn't it too small for you? I mean, it doesn't fit you, and she would look so good in it; I mean, she needs clothes anyway." And Perl gave me the blue dress.

"Come back after *yontif*," she said, "and I'll come with you to Berlin to meet this girl."

After Rosh Hashanah, I returned to Berlin with the dress. There was no D'vorah, but there was a note. "I cannot explain why, but I am sorry," the note said. It went on to explain that she had found a Polish army soldier and had to leave. "Please let me know where you are and I will send you your money. I'm sorry. I never wanted to hurt you."

"What the heck!" I said to myself. "I'm not even going to answer her. If she can do something like this, then she is not worth it." And she really wasn't. It turned out that she liked to flirt. She was an attractive girl, very popular. This bothered me very much. I was jealous, of course, and disappointed. I was looking for someone to lean on, to combat the loneliness of my new life. I was a very successful organizer, but I could not adjust to many of my friends' idea of a relationship. For them it was one girl today, another tomorrow. I wanted to find somebody.

A few days later, I met another friend of Aharon Saurymper with whom I became immediately close. His name was Yisroel Gepner [ז"ל]. One day, we saw each other on the street and he told me there were three Jewish girls staying in the apartment where I usually rented a room.

Aharon and Yisroel had an apartment above me in the same building.

"Three Jewish girls?" I asked them. "Where did they come from?"

"It's a long story," Yisroel said. "You'll find out."

"Where are they?" I asked anxiously.

Yisroel pointed to a nearby restaurant. "They're over there having lunch."

It was October 10, 1945, when we walked into the restaurant to meet the three Jewish girls. We walked over to the table and introduced ourselves. The girls were nurses working in the Russian army hospital outside Berlin. Their names were Esther, Ida and Betty.

CHAPTER
21

BETTY

I did not see the three girls again until almost a month later, when they came back from their duty at the Russian hospital. That night, we threw a big party. Twenty-five people were in the little apartment we rented in the Russian sector. We had a lot of vodka, schnapps and plenty of food. We did not realize how much noise we were making, but we were having a great time.

It was after midnight when we heard a knock on the door. When the door opened we were faced with four Russian soldiers standing there with machine guns.

"What's all this noise?" the officer asked.

"We're having a party," we said, then added a small lie, "a birthday party."

The officer looked at all of us in the room. "Who lives here?"

"I do," I answered. The soldiers then took what was left of the food and the vodka, and they took the girls to the command post because they were wearing their Russian army nurses' uniforms.

We sat in the apartment and wondered what to do. It was maybe one o'clock in the morning. As the night dragged on, we came up with a plan, but even with all my organizing ability, there was nothing I could do in the middle of the night. There was no one we could go to. Then, at about 3:30, the door opened and the girls came back, escorted by soldiers who dropped them there and left.

The girls told us what had happened, which of course sounded like a typical Russian government story. They were told to sit down as soon as they got to the command post. People came and went, and they continued to sit. Nobody knew why they were there. Nobody paid attention to them. Finally, the post commander came in and asked, "What are these girls doing here?" When no one could answer him, he sent them on their way, but not before they asked for an escort. After all, they would be on the streets of Berlin in the middle of the night during a curfew.

But there was another problem. While walking back, the soldiers made a date with them for the next day. The girls had to promise to meet them.

"So you promised," I said. "When are they coming to pick you up?"

"Ten o'clock in the morning."

I said, "Don't worry. We'll be out of here before then."

When the sun was just coming up, I went down to the street to find some transportation. I saw the three-wheeled, wood-burning coal truck making his morning deliveries. I went up to the driver. "I need you and I'll pay you well," I said to him. "Take furniture and belongings from here and take it to this address in the American sector." At that time, of course, Berlin, although divided, was still an open city. It was no problem going from sector to sector. By seven o'clock in the morning we were on our way across town, getting a little dirty in the back of the coal truck, but we got everyone out. We went to the apartment I had on that side with Aharon and Yisroel.

Now that we were together, we started spending more and more time with Esther, Ida and Betty. We spoke of many things — politics, news, Palestine — things that held our interest because they concerned our common future. We all became so compatible. But when it came to the war, none of us spoke of how greatly we had all suffered over the past five or six years; we spoke of the mundane things, and laughed at the memory of a stupid capo or foreman who guarded us. The detail, the real meat of the suffering, was within. We felt it. We felt it every day and every night. We just did not talk about it. It was too fresh.

After a while, Yisroel and Esther had begun to form a bond, and I found that I was beginning to click with Betty. There was a chemistry with her that I did not share with the other girls. She was intelligent, straightforward and very attractive. She represented the different kind of relationship I had been looking for. It was like day and night between being with her and even imagining the kind of relationships that were occupying others I knew. I was very, very much in love with her.

Under these conditions, with both of us being alone, things were bound to happen quickly. We were young — she was eighteen and I was twenty-one — but before November had ended, we wrote a letter of engagement. I did not remember how to write the *t'naim*, the letter of conditions before you get married that is a contract of what each family will provide. Since we had no family to provide these things, certain traditional language had to be changed or omitted.

The third girl, Ida, was a rabbi's daughter, Rabbi Tsvi Tabori from Shaulai (Shavel) in Lithuania. She knew the law, spoke Hebrew fluently and even studied Talmud. She knew the text of the engagement letter by heart and wrote it out on a piece of paper for us. I still have that letter. We set the date for the wedding: Tuesday, January 22, 1946.

It was a huge task at that time, in that place. It was going to be one of the first Jewish weddings in Berlin since the war ended. Our friends were very excited. "Don't worry," they said. "We will help you. We will organize it."

Betty realized that we had access to enough linens and household items so she did not have to go out looking to create her trousseau. She found out from the German Jews where the local dressmaker was and she went there with her friends to have her gown made. There were no stores open yet where she could just walk in and get a wedding dress. It did not matter that Betty had no money. I was doing very well and had enough money for two weddings.

One important thing I had to do was find an apartment so Betty and I would have a place to live after the wedding. As I said before, the only way I could get my own place as a Jewish refugee was to evict a German. Aharon knew the commander of the district in Berlin where we wanted to live. The American command had a list of Nazis, those who were actively involved with the party under Hitler. The list included addresses. A week before the wedding, the commander gave us two of his soldiers and we walked two doors away from the headquarters to evict a Nazi

family. I walked in to the apartment and announced, "You have five minutes to take any belongings you can carry in your hands and leave."

"We're innocent!" they cried. They were not innocent. We had the
list. It felt good, this little bit of revenge I took.

The wedding plans continued. Our friends had rented a beautiful hall
in Berlin that was owned by a Jew named Wolff. It was a nightclub called
Kreuzberger Hoff. I helped by getting the liquor through the PX, through
Jewish GIs from Brooklyn, and through the chaplain, Rabbi Shubow. We
did not send written invitations. We invited everyone we knew, which at
the time was barely more than thirty friends and family. Betty found out
that her sister was alive and living in Munich, and she came. I invited my
aunts from Poland, but they did not come. I never found out why. Maybe
they did not like the *shiddach*, the match. Maybe they had someone else
in mind for me, someone they felt it was their responsibility to choose
since my parents were gone. Their not coming disturbed me, but I did
not call off the wedding because of it.

Meanwhile, Saurymper and Rabbi Shubow said to me, "You have to
invite more people. You have to invite everyone who wants to come." So
I went out and invited anyone I could find. There were almost three hundred guests at our wedding. They all came because it was a real *simcha*, a
celebration that was important to affirm after what we'd all just been
through. There were representatives of the four powers, including Jewish
American officers and soldiers, British Generals and Jewish Russian officers and enlisted men, the Jewish Brigade who served the British army in
Palestine, even a delegation of Swedes that had come that week to deliver
CARE packages to the Joint Distribution Committee. There were even
some German civilians there, people we did business with. I still have one
of their gifts, a copy of Gottlieb's painting, "The Jews in the Synagogue."

Everyone had a good time. There was plenty of food and music. The
wedding was done in the old, traditional way. You might call it Hasidic
because of how strictly the laws and customs were followed. Aharon even
made sure that Betty and I did not see each other the week before the
wedding; he had a *shomer*, a guard, watching us.

The former rabbi of Lydda, who was in the nearby DP camp, performed the ceremony. I wore a white *kittel*, a ceremonial robe, according

to tradition, and Betty had a white gown. We both fasted on the day of the wedding until after the ceremony. I had a simple gold band for Betty, as is the tradition. There was even a ritual bath, a *mikvah*, available for us before the ceremony. The ceremony was Jewish to the utmost and the party went on until four in the morning.

It was a little over a year later that Yisroel Gepner married Esther.

CHAPTER
22

TRACES OF A
FAITHFUL PAST

As Betty and I began our lives together in Berlin, I continued in my business dealings while she was busy in the apartment or spending time with friends. Sometimes we would go to the movies, or listen to the radio. We also did a lot of socializing, partying and dancing. I had not known how to dance with women because of my upbringing — it was something I had to learn. Betty and I were both *shtetl* people, raised among our own kind, restricted either geographically or culturally or both. We had never been exposed to the cosmopolitan way of life.

Berlin was certainly that, even though at the time the city was not normal. It was a city where even though the war was over, it continued. There were streets you could not go through, and times when you could not be on the streets at all. The apartment that Betty and I had in Berlin was filled with items left behind by the Germans we evicted — nice things — but I was using other people's beds, other people's towels.

One night, around two o'clock in the morning, I heard stones plinking off one of our windows. "Who would be doing such a thing in the middle of the night?" Betty whispered to me. I got out of bed and walked toward the window. "Be careful," she said. Not knowing what was going on, we both thought it could be some hooligans. After all, this was Berlin and there may have been some disgruntled Nazis prowling the streets looking to take their frustrations out on Jews.

I opened the window just a crack at first, to peak at the stone thrower. It was our neighbor from across the street, Mr. Geffen. "I'm so sorry to bother you, Herr Gutfraind," he said, trying not to shout. "My baby is sick. There is something wrong and he won't stop crying."

I had seen his son before. He was a fat baby with wispy red hair. "*Nu,*" I said, "so what do you want me to do about it?"

"I know who you are, where you come from," Geffen explained. "I need you to *shprach an ein horeh*, say a blessing to remove the evil eye from him." When I was growing up, it occasionally happened that my father would chant certain mystical incantations that directly asked the angels for their help in things such as curing an illness. He had taught me how to invoke the names of the angels in prayer for such a purpose, but it was something that was rarely done.

"What is your son's name?" I asked Geffen. He told me the Hebrew name. "I will say it. When your son yawns, that will be a sign that the prayer helped," and I closed the window, prepared myself and began the prayers.

Within a couple of hours Geffen came running back, shouting his thanks. "*Hot ge-helfen,*" he said. "It helped."

With everything else that was going on in my life, I put the incident out of my mind. I had no reason to expect that more than twenty-five years later I would see Geffen again, but that is exactly what happened. In 1972 I was in New York for a convention, and I stopped in to a kosher restaurant to eat. I was ordering my food when I saw a familiar face. He looked at me from behind the crumbs in his beard and smiled broadly as if he knew me too. Suddenly he became very excited and ran up to me "hepping" as he tried to speak. "Gutfraind, is that you?" he asked. I nodded. As soon as he came up to me I knew who he was. "It's me, Geffen. Geffen from Berlin. You remember?"

"How are you?" I asked him.

"Fine. Fine. Yes. Yes," he said impatiently. He pointed to his dinner companion. "Do you know who this is?" he asked me.

I looked over and saw a robust man in his twenties with a bushy red beard. He was quite a large young man. It was then that it hit me. "That's not —"

"Yes! That's my son! He is the one you prayed for twenty-six years ago. See how healthy he is? He has not been sick since." I looked at the young man and smiled. He was still fat.

⭤ ⭤

In Berlin in the early days of our marriage, Betty and I began to think about our future. I thought about going to school to study music. I talked with friends about taking piano lessons. I had to make money, though, because Betty and I were thinking of the immediate future. Life was still very unsettled — Jewish refugees were still showing up after the war, and we never knew who we might find from our families.

Most of the refugees in Germany were from Poland and Hungary. We knew there were many potential Polish and Hungarian émigrés who wanted to come out of Russian-controlled Germany into the West, where they would have the opportunity to emigrate to Palestine. The leaders of the Zionist groups in Berlin seized on our enthusiasm and asked Betty and me to take a group of 175 Eastern European refugees from Berlin's Russian zone west to Allied-controlled Germany. We both had a facility with language, with Betty having worked in the Russian army hospital and me doing business with Germans since the war.

Risking the chance of ending up in Russia or the Russian zone permanently, I organized a moving van and driver, and Betty and I were able to take the refugees across the river into the Zailsheim Displaced Persons Camp, near Frankfurt.

We did not return to Berlin but instead stayed in the camp, surrounded by so many other Jews from all over Europe. I found many who knew my family, my background, and by extension, me. In that way, I was drawn into the religious life there. Still, Betty and I only went to regular Sabbath services occasionally. We held on to the feelings that we had a complaint, a complaint against God for everything that happened during the war. Even though we said things like "thank God," "with God's help," we still questioned our faith. Deep down we were asking, "Why? What help?" It was, by now, a sadly old, unanswered question: why? We could not go to other survivors for help. Everyone went through the same *tsoris*. It did no good for me to go to a neighbor in the DP camp and ask, "Look, how do *you* feel about God right now?" What am I going to do with his answer? All we could do is talk, reminisce about a time when we had faith in our community and in a God that would deliver us from our enemies.

There were people at Zailsheim that I went to Yeshiva, even to *cheder*, with. "Do you remember that rebbe?" we would ask each other, casually reminiscing over our lost past. We spoke about Lodz, walking down certain streets before the war, going to the *mikvah*, young boys holding hands on our way to *cheder*. Yet details of faith we did not go into. "What is your feeling about God? What do you think?" No. They had their feelings; I had mine. It was a problem to even think about adjusting to a religious life. Still, God finds a way, and circumstances came up that addressed this particular problem for me, in a way that gave me the answer for myself. The answer lay in who I was, how I was raised.

It was Rosh Hashanah in 1946, the only High Holidays we were in Zailsheim to celebrate. There were about 250 people at the service. The rabbi was Rabbi Volgelernter, a chaplain in the American army who was also from *va'ad hatzalah*, an American Jewish relief organization created by Orthodox rabbis. When I walked into the large military-type building where services were to be held, I saw there was a big tumult. People were punching and wrestling with each other. "What is going on here?" I asked the person next to me.

I was told that before the morning prayers had even begun, there was a dispute between two men who both wanted to be the *hazzan* for the service. Who knows how it disintegrated, but people's nerves were on edge here in this small DP camp. For many, life as a displaced person was just a continuation of life as an inmate. For many, they would be inmates the rest of their lives. So these two men were fighting and others took sides and joined in the melee.

Finally, Rabbi Volgelernter jumped up on a long table and shouted, "Control yourselves! Have you no shame? Just think! What if the Germans were to come in now and see how we fight among ourselves after what has happened to us, after what has happened to our people by the hands of the Nazis? What would they think? What would they say?" That quieted the congregants a bit, but the situation was still unresolved.

Romek Zale, the *gabbai*, or rector, of the congregation, knew my family and me before the war. He was a director at Esla, one of the largest stocking manufacturers in Lodz, and had done a lot of business with my grandparents in Piotrokow and with my father. He was also a close friend of Aharon Saurymper. Zale knew I liked to sing. He approached me with another *landsman* from Piotrokow, Henoch Laznik. Zale was obviously agitated by the situation and had gone out of the building to gather the calmer minds to form a minyan somewhere else. He and Laznik came back into the room and said to me, "We want you to *daven musaf* at a minyan for Polish Jews." I was grateful to be away from the inappropriate behavior that was taking place in this room, especially on such a holy day. I was also honored by being asked to lead prayers, particularly this portion of the Rosh Hashanah liturgy. Still, I hesitated.

"We know the circumstances," the *gabbai* continued, "that you are not observant like you used to be, but we forgive you. You should be our *shaliach tsibur*, our messenger. And you know," he added, "you can always repent. You can always do *teshuvah*."

Starting to do *teshuvah*, the repentance process, is what Rosh Hashanah is about. This man said the congregation forgave me for my lack of observance, so in this way I was already absolved from my fellow men. He was giving me the opportunity to ask forgiveness from God. Then he said something that struck a note. "I bought an *aliyah* for you. I bought you *maftir*."

Bidding for the honor to participate in some portion of the holiday services is a way to raise money for the congregation and other charities. It is a tradition that is still practiced in many synagogues. That Zale would buy me the honor of coming up to the Torah for *maftir* hit me hard. Honors at a High Holiday service are the most coveted, and *maftir* is one of those honors that brings in some of the highest bids. "Me?" I said to myself. "An honor for me? Nobody ever bought an honor for me, even before the war. Who am I? I'm just a kid!"

I went up for my *aliyah* and I cried. I cried more than I prayed. I poured my heart into the *musaf* service that followed. "*Hineni he-awni mimaas*, Here I am, a humble man poor in my collection of good deeds," the service begins — intoning the cantor's humility before God as he prays on behalf of himself and the repenting congregation — and I repented through my tears. After that, there was no reason for me to run away from my religion, for to do that would be to deny who I am, and would accomplish nothing. Little by little, I was drawn into community activities.

There were several organizations already established at Zailsheim, mostly Zionist. There was the Mizrachi organization, the Labor Zionists, the general Zionists and the Agudah. The Agudah had already formed a small kibbutz in the DP camp. People came to the camp all the time to talk about Zionist idealism. Almost everyone in the camp was waiting to go to Palestine.

As my involvement in the camp's Zionist community grew, Betty and I wanted to help as many refugees as possible. We were committed to all who wanted to be able to go to Palestine, and that included ourselves. We did not even think about America as a first choice. Betty had family in America — uncles and aunts in New York and Boston whom she did not know — but I had no one, so we did not think about it. We were part of the growing Jewish community in the DP camp, and we were active in it.

I went to the Hasidic wedding of our friend Aharon Saurymper, who married a girl from the Agudah kibbutz. It was a traditional Hasidic wedding, like I had seen years back: the groom gave a small discussion on the week's Torah portion in a separate room from the bride, but was stopped with a "*yesher koach*," a "well done," before he had a chance to finish, so as not to engender the evil eye; women danced with the bride up to the *chupa*, approaching the groom who was already there; and, of course, men and women sat separately, with a divider between them.

Between the old-fashioned wedding that brought back so many memories and my experience at Rosh Hashanah services, something began to hit home. I was not ready to declare that I was giving up all the things I did from the day I was liberated until now. I was not ready to go back to being a "good boy," and doing things the way I did back home, but something I felt, something good, brought me back in a little bit. I started to go to the daily minyan and I officiated at services. That made us not only active in the organizational life of the DP camp, but we also took a decisive turn toward religious life.

After Rosh Hashanah, Betty and I thought about being with family. Betty and her sister Pola were very close. Betty was the seventh of nine children, and Pola was her next oldest sister. They went through much of the war together. She lived in Munich and we spoke about being there with her. As far as Betty knew, Pola was the only surviving member of her family. They had an older sister, Judy, who had married and moved to Paris before Betty was born, but they did not know if she survived. Betty never met her, and all we could do is send letters to her last known address hoping to hear from her. It was then that we spoke of starting a family, having children. We agreed to, but not before we settled down in some sort of stable place. Being with Pola was a start to that. It was more important now for us to be with family and to make a fresh start than to return to the money we might have been able to make in Berlin. We thought we would be with Pola, then go to Palestine or America, so we all moved on to the Displaced Persons camp called Feldafing.

Feldafing was a former German camp that was used for Russian POWs toward the end of the war. It was not far from Munich, in a scenic forest where we could see the snow-peaked Bavarian Alps rising. The camp itself was on flat terrain.

We saw these beautiful views from the windows of our barracks, which were wooden shacks with wooden floors. Makeshift walls separated the building into rooms. There was a sink that we worked hard to keep clean and a toilet outside. For activities we would go to the movies the camp showed or take the train into Munich to see the opera.

The UNNRA ran the camp, though it was under American supervision. Pola's husband Zundel, whom she had married in the Kovno ghetto and miraculously met again after the war, spoke English well and helped us with getting things such as food and cigarettes. They also gave us clothing to help us in this transitory place.

My questions about my faith continued. I thought that I would build a Sukkah, a booth for the Festival of Booths. Why I suddenly had the urge to do this I was not sure. I was so back-and-forth with religion, fighting with myself over whether I should continue what I remembered from my upbringing or rebel and let go of what I knew was part of me. As I gathered the spare boards and whatever else I could use as materials from around the DP camp, I remembered building the Sukkah every year with my father. This one was not the best-looking Sukkah I had seen, but I had made an effort to express a part of me that I knew I would never lose.

I wanted to change my life, my personal way of life. Betty and I were part of a large group of Eastern European Jews who were used to the *shtetl* life — small, and mostly poor, Jewish communities outside the city centers of Europe. So I was in a transition, moving from one life to another I did not yet know. I was certainly displaced, transitory — and a Displaced Persons camp was where I had to be to restage my life.

It was during this search of how to rebuild my life that I walked into a Mizrachi meeting. Up to that time, I was trying to reconcile my new found interest in Zionism — a movement that emphasizes the importance of a modern Jewish state where all Jews could lead a modern life — with my traditional Hasidic background that said that our return to the Holy Land would be part of the Messianic era. The Mizrachi was an organization of religious Zionists that said you could be a Zionist and still not compromise a traditional, religious life.

I said to the Mizrachi man, "Why do we have to change? I think Palestine is making a big mistake with modernization. We are an ancient people. God doesn't change. I think we are getting ourselves in trouble, trying to be like the rest of the world. We are unique, and the way we live has always been unique.

"We have lived in ghettos and in *shtetlach* all through the *gallut*, the Diaspora. Why should we have mechanics and modern machinery now, after all this time?" I asked him. "Should we not be following the teachings that say the Messiah will come and take care of everything?"

He smiled at me. "It's Torah and *avodah*, learning and work," he said to me, emphasizing the rabbinical notion that the world is supported by work and learning. "There can be no world for us without the machines and technology of the world we live in now."

The more I began to think, the more it began to make sense to me. "Maybe this is what I want to do. This is who I want to be," I said to myself. "At home, maybe it was a sin to be a mechanic and a Hasid, but here it is no sin to be a mechanic. After all, we are going to Palestine, to the land where my father should have gone. They need mechanics in Palestine, to support our people. There is no sin in that."

I went to learn a trade at the local ORT school. It was a way I could serve my family and my people. There, I learned how to make tools. I worked with my hands all day, filing on the hammers and other tools, with the promise that eventually they would let me on the machines. I assumed that was what I would do — I would go to Palestine and be a tradesman. Betty and I both were developing a passion for Zionism, but we did not have a plan. We had an opportunity that seemed to be a way we could make a life together.

Then it happened. After all the months of trying to reach her sister Judy in Paris, we finally got a letter back. It was early October 1946, and suddenly we were on our way to France — and what we were sure was our next step on the journey to Palestine.

CHAPTER
23

PARIS

It was not widely known, but in 1946 the French government had given tacit approval to the Zionist organizations in Germany to smuggle Jews in and forward them to Palestine. Even though the French were not for the establishment of a Jewish state, there was a feeling in France that they, more than any other group of people, understood the suffering of Europe's Jews. The British, who ruled Palestine, and the United States did not support an independent Jewish state either, but unofficially and secretly, the U.S. allowed its army trucks to be used to smuggle the people from Germany to France. The groups ended up somewhere near Marseilles where, with the help of the second immigration to Palestine known as Aliyah Bet, they were prepared for the move to the Holy Land. They were loaded into boats and Aliyah Bet smuggled them in under the nose of the British.

I found the opportunity to leave for France in early November. Betty waited behind so we could be sure I made contact with her sister Judy before I came back to get her. The operators of the transport took the identification I had picked up in Berlin — the red ID cards belonging to the "Victims of Fascism" — and the papers of everyone who was beginning this journey to Palestine. It was night when we boarded the trucks and headed for the border. As the truck pulled up to the crossing near Strasbourg, the driver told us not to make any noise, nothing to tip off the border guards that there were people in the truck. The drivers were Americans, dressed in American army uniforms and probably had papers saying they were carrying goods for the American army. The trucks were U.S. Army trucks, complete with insignia.

We crossed with no difficulty and camped in Nancy, just inside France. There, they had hot meals waiting for us and new identification papers. There were also trucks warming up to take us on to the port at Marseilles, where we were to stay at another camp before being loaded on the boats to Palestine. After the meal, though, I did not stick around. With only a piece of paper with a scribbled Paris address, no French money and not being able to speak the language, I took off for the train station and went to Paris.

I got off the train in Paris and looked at the address. Judy had said in her letter that it was not far from the station, but I did not know Paris, so I thought the best thing to do would be take a taxi. I showed the taxi driver the address and he nodded and started to drive. He drove for about a half-hour, and suddenly started looking at the street signs and asking to see the piece of paper again; he did not know where he was. He just saw a green-horn and thought he would take me for a ride. I saw a police station and signaled the driver to stop. "Police," I called to the gendarme standing nearby. "Police!" I showed him the address and he directed the driver. Of course I had only German and American money, so the taxi driver waited for Judy's husband, Yisrael Kochavi, to come down to pay him.

Judy greeted me at the door, and even though she had never seen me before, or Betty for that matter, in five minutes we were family. She lived in an ORT school where she was the supervisor and the cook. This was one of the first ORT schools in France. It was in the mansion that used to belong to Baron Ginsberg, the organizer of the first ORT school in the world. The ORT turned the building into a school for mechanics. "Mechanics?" I said with surprise. "I took mechanics at the ORT school in the DP camp." I thought I could continue here, but I did not arrive on Judy's doorstep with the intention of staying. I had to get back to Betty.

"You are not going back into Germany," Judy's husband insisted.

"Well, I can't leave Betty there."

"She'll just have to find her way by herself," he told me, "and when the time is right you can send for her."

Judy's husband was a British subject, since he had a passport from

Palestine, and during most of the war he was treated like a British POW. Eventually, though, the Nazis deported the Jews from his camp, Drancy, to Auschwitz and Birkenau.

"I'll stay, but in a country like this, a civilized country, I'll have to find something to do." I walked the streets of Paris, trying to adjust to this modern city. I had heard about it, of course, even when I was a child: a big city, a fantastic city full of stories.

Yisrael, my brother-in-law, insisted I learn the language, and he tried to teach me, but his accent was heavy and it was hard to understand him. I learned more walking down the Grande Boulevard, listening to the French as they strolled and did business. Eventually I enrolled in the Alliance Francaise, a French language school for adults. I was not the only Jew there. It was not long before I was able to pick up a newspaper and read and understand it. Between the streets and the other students at the ORT school and the paper, I was adjusting to the language well, albeit with a lot of mistakes.

Soon the joys of life in Paris began to transform me. I started to conduct myself as a Frenchman — with my dress, my walk, my actions, the atmosphere, everything. "What a beautiful world this is," I said to myself one day. "The past is gone. There is nothing to lean back on or push back against. There is only forward, so why not adopt new customs, the Parisian way of life?" I had been in Paris less than six weeks, and already I was a Frenchman! I could not wait for Betty to arrive so I could share this wonderful new life with her.

One day, while walking the streets like a Parisian, I met others from Poland who had made their way to this magnificent city. Some of them were in the labor camp, the *Kara*, with me in Piotrokow. "What are you doing with yourself here?" they asked me.

"For the time being, nothing; but I'm going to the ORT school and thinking of going into mechanics."

"Mechanics? Ach," they said. "Don't go into mechanics. This is not work for a Jew. What will you do? Fix cars or machinery?"

"It's honorable work," I said, but I knew that in the ORT mechanics class there were more non-Jews than Jews.

"The best job for you," they insisted, "for any of us in this city, is a tailor, or a pocketbook maker, or a furrier."

Now I had experience with tailoring before the war because I was starting to use machines to make stockings for my father's store. I thought I could go into tailoring. Yisrael supported me because he had a friend who was very successful at tailoring. The ORT school, it turned out, offered courses in tailoring so I signed up to learn how to tailor with a machine. I walked into class and there were piles of pre-cut coats and jackets. There was an old man in the room who started to teach us how to stitch with a machine, how to make even seams. In two weeks, after ruining about half-a-dozen pairs of pants, I finally learned how to sew on a machine.

I wanted to waste no time in putting my new education to the test. "If I know how to sew on a machine, now I think I can make a living," I said to Yisrael. He offered to help me. He did not know how to use a sewing machine, but I taught him what I had learned after my ORT class. We found a Paris contractor whose only work was making short and long pants for the North Africa market.

"We'd like to take some work out," we said to the contractor. There was a shortage of skilled tailors those days, especially those willing to take work home.

"You? You know how to sew?" he asked. We nodded. "Alright," he said, "Here's a package of pants. Let me see what you can do. If you bring them back and do a good job, then I'll give you more. We'll give you so much, you won't have time to breathe!"

We took the package of about thirty pairs of pants to the house where we set up two machines and went to work. Well, you do not become a tailor after a two-week course; we ruined quite a bit of the merchandise the contractor gave us. We finally called in a friend who was a tailor to show us how to make a pocket. I never understood how you have to make a pocket just the opposite way to make it look good. Anyway, we ruined quite a bit, and when it was time to deliver, my brother-in-law looked at me.

"You go. He doesn't know you. You deliver it," he told me.

I shrugged. I did not want to deliver bad merchandise. I was afraid of what the contractor would say. But I put the bundle over my shoulder and walked over to the office. I carried the pants up the stairs to the third floor. "Here are your pants," I said, and I dropped them on the table and ran out. I was afraid he would take a look at a pair of pants and throw me out, maybe even hit me for ruining his merchandise!

We still needed to work, so Yisrael thought we should try again. He went to the contractor and asked for more work. The guy laughed. "You didn't have to throw it on the table and run out! You could have waited. I would have told you, 'You did this wrong, A-B-C; this is how you fix it; this is how you do it better.'"

Yisrael smiled. He explained that I was ashamed of the bad job we did, that I was young and shy. The contractor still needed people and relented, giving us more work. Only the material in this batch was not as good as the first one. I am sure he was saying to himself, "If these guys are going to ruin my merchandise, at least let them ruin the material that isn't worth much."

Little by little, our sewing skills improved. Eventually I became a real wizard at it, turning out twenty pairs a day. That was a lot because we made them from scratch. I worked fourteen or fifteen hours a day on the machine and became very fast once I got used to it. I was young and healthy and enthusiastic. I looked for anyone who might have bought my pants, anyone on the street who might be wearing them, but they all went to places like Siberia or South Africa. From pants, we moved up to coats and coat linings.

By the time Betty took her transport across the border in January 1947, Yisrael and I had quite a business going. The days leading up to her arrival were like years. We had been communicating by letter so I knew she was on her way, and I lay awake nights worrying about her being transported safely. When she arrived, Betty stayed with me at Judy's until we found a place of our own to move into and make a nest. Betty helped with the sewing by learning how to sew on buttons. From the two machines we started with, we grew to four, then six and finally eight. I became a contractor myself with a sub-contractor. I hired people to help with the work, and then we took the coats to a friend of mine who made buttonholes and in this way we delivered a finished product. Betty went to language school and together we made a living.

Changes happened every day. Socially, culturally, Betty and I embraced Paris life. There were Jews there who were able to survive the war in the underground, whose homes were still intact, with the same furniture and the same fine things as before the war. There were non-Jews who welcomed us into their apartments, after just meeting us on the street. You meet someone on the street and you start talking. He invites for a drink, and you go. You invite him to your apartment, and he goes. There was no such thing as a stranger.

On Sundays we got together with groups of young Jewish people and sang songs; we used to go on hikes. We had a good time. We went dancing four times a week, even after a sixteen-hour day at the machines.

It was a beautiful city, with museums and unbelievable public art and architecture, and it was a friendly city, with everyone using each other to help heal the scars of the German occupation. We did everything the French did — eating fish and shellfish, eating non-kosher meat, fine pastries and drinking wine — and doing everything included waiting in ration lines for the wonderful staples of French food.

Like most Jews in Paris at the time, I attended synagogue only during the High Holidays. I even made some extra money as a soloist in the choir. I auditioned with the cantor and he hired me. But my connection with the Jewish community was more social and intellectual than it was religious. The freedom of thought and freedom of living, the openness of the French non-Jews to us, drew me into a society I had never been exposed to before. The French felt that the war left us with much in common. I allowed myself to be a free man in an open city, where faith was not as important as fraternity.

Most educated Jews in Paris then were very far left, politically. There were many who were socialist and even communist. Though my politics were more centrist, I went to lectures with my friends to hear famous French Socialist leaders such as Maurice Torez and Jacques Duclos. Like reading the newspaper, these events were interesting and informative, and full of intellectual discussion.

The open minds and liberal society in Paris changed something in us. Betty and I decided that we no longer wanted to go to Israel. The feeling had actually begun in the DP camp at Feldafing. The leadership of the various Zionist organizations was constantly battling for power over the others. A bureaucracy began developing before we knew it, and then it was like in the ghetto, with this committee or that committee in charge, telling us all what to do to survive in Palestine. We had already survived; we were not ready to exchange one struggle for another.

In November 1947 we received word of the United Nations Partition Plan for Palestine. Within days, posters went up all over Paris's Jewish neighborhoods announcing rallies in support of a Jewish state. We followed crowd after crowd, through the streets and the Metro, and went wherever the Jews went. We attended rallies with the leading Zionists including Moshe "Klein-Greenbaum" Sneh, Moshe Sharet and Abba Eban, whom I had heard speak in Paris the year before.

When Ben Gurion declared the independent Jewish state of Israel in May 1948, Jews from all over the world volunteered to help fight in the War of Independence. Many embarked from the staging area near Marseilles where the Haganah, an Israeli paramilitary group, trained them. My cousin Enrique Kerpel and his friend Chayim Glogover came all the way from Bogotá to train. Enrique came with suitcases full of suits and ties, tuxedos, all kinds of clothes that were inappropriate for someone joining a fighting group. I asked him why he brought it all and he said his mother wanted to make sure he had enough clothes! A week later I received a telegram from him that he had been robbed of all his clothes and money, right there in the camp.

I went down to bring him a few francs and some clothes. He was filthy. I got him showered and took him to a barber. Before I left him I asked, "Why are you doing this? Why did you come all this way? To maybe get yourself killed?"

"Itche," he told me, "this is the least I can do after what happened to your family, to my family. This is the least I can do." He wasn't worried about not returning alive. I gave him and Chayim each one of the *machatzis ha-shekels,* the two remaining half-mark coins I had carried with me through the war for luck. Enrique went on to become commander of the South American battalion and returned safely to France a few months later.

In February 1949, Betty gave birth to our first son, Serge Marcel (whom we now call Mark). The tailoring business was going great, but there was another mouth to feed and a lot more time needed to pay attention to the baby. A few months later, our old friend Aharon Saurymper came by for a visit. He was in Paris for a World Jewish Congress conference. He saw me sitting at the sewing machine hours and hours a day.

"What are you doing?" he asked. "This is not for you! Come back to Berlin; you won't have to do this kind of work. I guarantee you'll make more money and work not even half as hard. You'll be much better off."

I explained that we were waiting to save some money to go to the United States, Canada or even Australia. He interrupted me. "If you are thinking about emigration to the United States or any other place from here, forget it. The people who are getting visas are in the DP camps in Berlin. From here you won't get anywhere."

It was a hard decision, but by the beginning of 1950 I decided to follow Aharon's advice and I left Betty and my son in Paris and returned to Berlin. I stayed with Yisroel Gepner, who had married Betty's friend Esther shortly after our marriage. When I got there I saw that Aharon was right. People were making money in Berlin doing almost no work. I did not have to work sixteen hours a day. It was simple — you bought from one person and sold to another, and made a profit. Everybody had something that someone needed, whether it was scrap metal, nylon stockings, whatever. I traded anything I could get my hands on. Before the year was over, I went to Paris to collect Betty and Mark and we returned to Berlin.

CHAPTER
24

BERLIN AND DESTINY

In Berlin, people were still living in the past, in the way of the *shtetl*, compared to the cosmopolitan lifestyle we had in the big city of Paris. When I first returned, I looked down on them. Their manners irritated me. Their way of dealing bothered me. Maybe it was because I was already living a normal life in Paris, with a job and a wife and a son. My life was moving forward, and here I was surrounded by the old DP mentality — the mentality of displaced persons waiting to get somewhere, waiting to get out. Some of them never got out. They were stuck in Berlin, and stuck in their own thoughts of always being in transition.

Betty and I tried to keep living the Parisian lifestyle in Berlin, but it did not work. The city was too different; our old friends had different priorities. Slowly we began to slide into the religious life that we had begun before we went to Paris. Shabbes became Shabbes — Friday night meant traditional Friday night meals, and Saturday mornings we went to the synagogue to pray and participate. We went to the synagogue on Rickestrasse in the Russian sector. It was the only Jewish house of worship not burned down during Kristalnacht in 1938 because it shared its walls with the two adjacent apartment buildings.

One Pesach morning during prayers, the service suddenly came to a stop after we had only completed the first part. I was sitting with my friend, Yisroel Gepner, so I turned to him and asked, "What's going on? Why haven't we started the Torah service?"

"The cantor took ill," Gepner said. "They don't have anyone to read the Torah. Maybe you should go up to read."

I knew from my upbringing, of course, that we would not be able to finish the service without the Torah reading, but I did not want to do it. "I should go?" I asked him incredulously. "No. I did not come here to do the Torah reading. I came to pray."

But Gepner kept insisting, to the point that I felt guilty, as if it were my fault that we could not continue the service. Before I knew it, he had gone up to the *gabbai* who was standing on the *bima* with the other members of the synagogue's committee, the *Vorstand*, and told him I could do it. The *gabbai* approached me, looking concerned. "Herr Gutfraind, we need a Torah reader this morning. Could you do it for us?" he asked. I saw from the sadness in his face that I was the last chance for the congregation to continue the service. I reluctantly agreed.

After the Torah reading the members of the *Vorstand* said, "As long as you are up here, will you lead *musaf* for us and finish the service?" When the service was finally over, the leaders of the congregation approached me. "You have such a wonderful voice," they said. I thanked them and was ready to wish them a "*gut yontif*" and go home. Then they asked me the question that was the turning point of my life. "Please," one of the leaders said, "we need a cantor. You'll only have to work once a week, and the rest of the week you can do whatever you want."

I had never thought seriously about being a *hazzan*. When I was a child I used to play "cantor and choir." It never occurred to me to make my living by anything other than business, as my father had, but it had always felt good to sing. I enjoyed opening my heart to the meaning of the prayers and expressing them with my voice. The adulation was nice too. I accepted the position. As a result, the congregation sent me to the conservatory in Berlin to study. They sent teachers to our apartment, piano and music teachers, so I could learn the right way to sing. That is how I became an official cantor in Berlin. The way the "cantoring" business worked in Berlin was that the *Judische Geimeinde Zu Berlin*, the Jewish Community, would assign where I was to work. Each week I would go to them and they would hand me a schedule. I would lead prayers one week in East Berlin and one week in West Berlin. Between my love of the proper chanting of the liturgy and the musical knowledge I gained at the conservatory, I became very good at it and I enjoyed it.

My life was beginning to make a plan for itself. All that time when I did not know what was going to happen, what the next step in my life would be, my future was being created in front of me. And I was unaware of it while it was happening. To me, making plans was still something to fear. I was afraid to make goals or think about dreams. When I was in the ghetto and my family was still intact, my thoughts were, "Will I ever see my sister's wedding or my brother's Bar Mitzvah, or his wedding? Will my father be comfortable so that one day he will not have to work so hard? Will I have a normal family ever again?" How could I make plans even after the war when my life was interrupted and so many of my dreams fell away? I had no teenage years and no continuity of what we call a normal life. I did not see any of it — no weddings, no Bar Mitzvahs, no *nachas* from my parents for the grandchildren I was to bear them. I could not make any long-range plans.

I only knew what my plans were as they occurred, as they fit into the puzzle of the pattern of my life; they flowed with which city I lived in, or which environment. Every outcome could have been the plan, and we often thought "Maybe this is it," and at the next step, "Maybe this is it." When I was a tailor in Paris, I thought I would be a tailor for the rest of my life. I learned the machine, I knew how to get work, and I knew that on Friday I dropped off the finished work and got new work. I expanded my business and thought, "This is it. This is what I am going to do." But that was not it. Even in the Paris we enjoyed so much, Betty and I were still looking for a place to raise our family, a place that would really be "it."

We were able to function in Berlin, but we were not happy. We thought about leaving the way people were leaving every day. Post-war Berlin was not a place for a Jew to make his future, and since we had a family already, we were anxious to move on to a place where we could honestly say we had begun our lives again.

We applied for visas to the United States, but the Polish quota was a terrible number. They told us we would have to wait three years for our number to come up. It was not easy unless you had someone to send you an affidavit of sponsorship, saying that they really needed you and your skills. We had no one in the U.S. at the time to send us one. We applied to Canada also, since the quota was easier, and decided that whichever came up first we would take.

When the Canadian immigration officials came to Berlin to interview people toward the end of 1951, we were called to the consulate. As the hours drifted by we watched people come and go. Every Jewish family who came out of the office was refused a visa, and it seemed that every non-Jewish person who applied was granted one. It turns out they were looking for lumberjacks, and there were no Jews in Berlin at the time who even were close to capable of that kind of labor. Ten hours later we were still waiting to go in. It was already eight o'clock when Betty turned to me.

"Why do we keep sitting here? Let's go home," she said. We were both frustrated and tired of waiting.

"We've waited this long," I said, "How much longer could it be? Let's just sit another few minutes." It was only a couple of minutes later that we were finally called into the office.

We sat down and, after a few pleasantries, the woman there asked me to show her my hands. "You're not a laborer, are you?" she asked, after seeing my smooth palms.

She asked me what I did, and I told her, "I'm a cantor and a businessman."

The woman looked at our paperwork. "It says you are a tailor too. What do you make?"

"I make pants, whatever I can."

She turned to speak to the others in the office. "He is a tailor who makes pants," she said to them, speaking in French, so I interjected in French as well, "Yes, when we were in Paris."

"Oh, so you speak French also?" And with that we had our visa to Canada. We were the first Jewish couple to get a visa from them that day. It was time for another life, another change.

"At least we speak one of the languages," Betty and I said to each other as we left the consulate that night and made our way home. It was January 1952 when my wife and son and I boarded the boat in Bremen bound for Halifax. She was called the *Fair Sea*, and there were three thousand other souls on board going to Canada.

PART IV

FINDING MY CALLING

"Songs have been to me as your laws in the house
where I have sojourned."

— Psalm 119:54

CHAPTER
25

MONTREAL

The voyage to Canada was the first time in my life I was on a ship at sea, and the journey was pretty rough. I did not know anything about sea-sickness. They told us to eat bread to keep from getting sick. Most of the three thousand on board were ill, including Betty and Mark. Somehow I managed not to throw up.

There were only about three hundred Jews on the *Fair Sea*. The rest of the passengers were Ukrainians, Poles, Lithuanians, Hungarians, Romanians, all nationalities looking for a better life after the war that devastated Europe. It made for an interesting journey. They separated those who kept kosher from those who did not. There was a Hasidic rebbe from Hungary traveling with his court, and he immediately asked anyone who kept kosher to make themselves known. I fit in well with the Hasidim on board both because of my upbringing and because by this time Betty and I were back to our roots, after my involvement in the Jewish community in Berlin as a cantor. We kept the laws of *kashrut*. At the Hasidic rebbe's request, there were separate tables set for those of us who kept kosher. There was no kosher meat on board, of course, but they fed us herring and all kinds of fish. There was enough food and even some fruit for Mark, who was three years old. After ten days on the *Fair Sea*, we landed at Halifax.

Before we left the boat, the Canadian immigration authorities came on board and let us know where we were going. "Gutfraind," the man called out in German. "You are going to Winnipeg."

"Winnipeg?" I asked. I had never heard of Winnipeg. "Where is Winnipeg?"

"It's about four days by train," he said.

"That's too far. Where else?"

"Toronto. It's only a two-day train ride."

"Toronto? Toronto sounds Italian. I'm not going to Italy," I told him. I knew that Romek Zale, the *gabbai* from Zailsheim, was in Montreal with his family. "We would rather go to Montreal. We know people there, we have friends." So they sent us to Montreal.

In Montreal we were welcomed by the JIAS, the Jewish Immigrant Aid Service, and given a room. It was in the old part of the city. The JIAS had my dossier and sat down to interview me as soon as we were settled. "What are you," he asked me, "a tailor or a *hazzan*? I see on your papers that you are a cantor. Well, I can get you a job as a tailor right away."

I saw this moment as an opportunity to finally express what it would take for me to feel fulfilled. Since Berlin, I had felt that my fulfillment came from being a cantor. For me, it was destiny that I was in that synagogue in Berlin on a particular Jewish holiday morning when there was no one to read Torah. I believe to this day that being a cantor was why I had survived. It was why God watched over and protected me. "I'd rather not," I told the interviewer. "I'd like to try 'cantoring.' I'd like to be a professional cantor."

"This is very difficult," he said. "There are so many cantors here. Other jobs I can find for you."

"You know," I said, "I'll take whatever comes first." After all, I had a wife and child to take care of. I spent the next few weeks interviewing with various companies for tailoring jobs.

While I waited to find permanent employment, Betty and I went to Esplanade Avenue every day, where other immigrant families came to find lost relatives and friends. Even now, seven years after the war had ended, people had hopes of finding somebody. On Sunday, the square was black with people, wall-to-wall, who simply had come to look. Sure enough, we found friends that we knew, and they found friends. Once again Betty and I began to form a community; once again, we asked ourselves, "Is this it? Is it real or just another fantasy? Are we going to settle here or is this just another place we stay for a while until we go somewhere else?" We were ready to settle down and move forward with our lives.

Eventually I found a job as a tailor. It paid thirty dollars a week. That may seem pretty small now, but grapes were only ten cents a pound then, tangerines were thirty, and everything else was very, very inexpensive. We were sick the first day from all the grapes and tangerines we ate! The tailoring job was not for me, though. I disliked it the minute I walked into the factory. It was like a sweatshop, with the foreman standing behind me yelling all the time, giving me orders. "Do this! Do that! You're too fast! You're too slow!" I knew I did not want to stay there long. I worked a week, just to get the feel of it, to see if I thought I could make it there or not. I could not take it. I quit after the first week.

I looked for other jobs. I looked in the field of merchandising and business. I went door-to-door asking, "Do you need anything done?" I was willing to do manual labor, anything. From time to time I auditioned to be the cantor at any number of little synagogues in the old section of the city.

One day during this search, my dear friend from Piotrokow, Shalom Malc, who had come to Canada two weeks after we did, asked me if I wanted to go to the fresh produce market with him. We hopped the streetcar down to the market. I am not sure why I went. The weather was awful. It was bitter cold with snowdrifts up to ten feet high! But I always like being around the smell of fresh oranges and grapefruit hanging in the air there, so I went.

As we browsed the outdoor market, chatting between ourselves in Yiddish, we walked up to a vendor to buy some fruit. He was bundled up in a raccoon coat with a hood so tight I could barely see his mouth. I spoke French to him and from beneath his fur I saw a smile. "What's the matter with you?" he asked in Yiddish. "Can't you speak Yiddish, or are you afraid to speak Yiddish?" Just like that our faces lit up. "Why are we standing out here in the cold? Come on into my office."

We went into the man's office and he took off his coat and gave us a drink. "My name is Malin," he said. "Sit, sit. Tell me something about yourselves. What did you do in Europe? What did your family do?" He turned to my friend first. He was very interested in survivors, in how many survived and how much of our family was killed.

While they were talking, I looked at his bookshelf. I said to myself, "This can't be! Look at all these Jewish books in the office of a produce market!" There were books by Engels and Marx, in Yiddish. That someone who is an owner of a market should have such things I did not understand. How can one be a capitalist and a communist at the same time? I decided to leave it alone for the time being.

Malin turned to me. I told him what I did, what skills I had. I did leave out the cantorial thing though. I did not think that being a cantor would get me a job with produce. I did not realize, though, that my friend had already told him I was a *hazzan*. When the two of us were done talking he turned to my friend and said, "You, I can give a job tomorrow. Do you want to start work tomorrow?" My friend nodded. Then the man turned to me. "You," he said, "I have to see."

"Why do you have to see?" I asked.

"Well, it's a long story," the fruit man began, "but I write music on the side." Before I knew it, he had reached into his desk and pulled out a piece of music. He wrote a *kiddush* for Friday night. He loved cantorial music. "I will have to see you at my house. I'll get you something. You won't be sorry." I had nothing to lose, so I agreed to go to his house. After all, he might really have something for me.

The discussion was winding down, so I thought I would ask him about his books on communism. To me, a man of means probably did not get that way by sharing his profits with his employees; it was like an atheist whose shelves are lined with Bibles. It was great there was free speech here. He could read whatever he wanted. Certainly he would not have been able to do that if he were in Russia. "About your books," I said, "it's very interesting to see Yiddish books in a Canadian fruit market, but I don't agree with their content."

"What do you mean you don't agree?" He was pretty incredulous. "Do you know what a power Russia is? Do you know what the Russian government does?"

"Do I know? I lived under it in Poland and in Berlin. True, they liberated me, but I don't agree with their philosophy, and if you were in Russia you would not like them either." Here I was asking this man for a job and arguing political philosophy with him. I saw he was getting very upset and I decided to drop it. "That's an interesting opinion you have. Let's leave it at that." I said, "When do you want to see me?"

The next day I was at Malin's house. He sat at his piano, and with one finger plunked the melody of one original piece after another, making marks on music paper that looked more like bird droppings than notes. I sat and listened admiringly. "If I get a job as a *hazzan*, this is the first composition I am going to sing — yours." Maybe it was a little self-serving, but it seemed like the right thing to say, and it made him smile.

"Well," Malin said, "let me see. I have a son-in-law living in Sherbrooke who is the president of a synagogue there. If you like, you can be their full-time *hazzan*, but they do not have a big congregation. You would daven maybe once a month. Otherwise, you can sell for my son-in-law. He has a big department store. His name is Shechter."

"I'll give it a try," I said.

"Good. Good. In two weeks you can go and daven in his synagogue, and on Monday, if you want to sell, then you can." He told me they would pay me fifty dollars to lead prayers, which was a lot of money.

I came to Sherbrooke by bus on a Friday morning. Shechter was waiting for me. He said, "Why don't you take it easy? I arranged a room for you at the inn. Go clean up and rest. Tonight you will have dinner with us and tomorrow we'll go to *shul* and meet the congregation. Everybody is coming. On Monday, we'll see, maybe you'll want to go out and sell." His plan was that I would be a clopper, sort of an assistant peddler. The peddler had already purchased the goods and it was my job to go door-to-door to sell it. I was anxious to get started.

I said, "It's early now, only nine in the morning. *Shabbes* doesn't start until 4:30. I don't mind trying to sell today."

"No, no," Shechter said. "Everybody is in the market today because it's Friday. The housewives go out to buy for the weekend. You won't find anybody at home."

"I'll tell you what," I countered. "My philosophy is that if I do bad today, I have an excuse — it's Friday. If I do well, then I'll feel better on Monday. I'll be happy."

He reluctantly agreed. He had someone hand me a sample case packed for an assistant peddler, and then he gave me an order book. He took me to a place about twelve blocks away and said, "Here, try this street. You're on your own. I'll come back in three hours to pick you up."

It was very cold and, despite my fur coat and boots, the wind and snow were blowing. I girded myself against the chill and started knocking on doors. I said to myself, "It's so cold. Who in their right mind would answer?"

I knocked on the first door. "What do you want?" the woman asked. "I wonder if I could interest you...."

"I don't need anything. Go away. Not today." And she slammed the door. Again and again and again this happened, two, three, four, five times in a row. I put the sample case down and said to myself, "I must be doing something wrong. Let me try a different approach."

I knocked on the next door and the woman said the same thing, "I don't need anything."

I said, "I'm not going to sell you anything today. Just do me a favor and let me come in for a few minutes. It's very cold." And she did. She offered me a cup of tea and as I sat there with her, I started a conversation. I looked at her drapes. "Very nice drapes you have," I said, and she nodded at the compliment. "You have very good taste," I continued, "and I can see that you are a good housewife and a good housekeeper." She thanked me, and I went on. "I have in my suitcase a tablecloth that will go with these drapes like nothing else. It's magic."

I opened the suitcase, and as I removed the tablecloth I reiterated, "You don't have to buy. It's simply that you were so kind to let me come in and warm up, I have to show it to you. There's no obligation." And I spread the cloth on her dining room table.

"You're right," she said. "It goes together," and she went to my sample case and began to look through it. "What else do you have?"

I felt better already. Even if she does not buy, I thought, at least I see how things work. I made a sale, not a big sale, but a sale. I sold her nylons, some pillowcases and the tablecloth, of course. I said, "You don't have to pay for it right away. You can pay it out over time."

"Oh, that's nice," she said, and signed the order. I thanked her a million times for letting me come in to her home, and as I walked out the door, she shouted behind me, "Please, button up. Don't catch a cold."

I felt great! The next door I knocked on I made a sale, and the next one, and the next one, and the one after that. There was not one call I made after that where, as long as they were home, somebody did not buy something, even if it was only for a few dollars. I felt great! It was an accomplishment. I did it!

I did my job, and by 2:30 I was at the place Shechter said to meet him and get picked up. As I got into the car he said to me, "Well, was I right?"

I said, "You were 100 percent right. One hundred percent."

"I told you to wait until Monday," and he went on to tell me again why Fridays were bad for this kind of selling, all the way back to his office.

When we were inside I said, "Well, that is your opinion, and you may be right. I did not do much, but here." I threw the receipt book on his desk.

"I don't believe it!" He said it again, "I don't believe it! For most people going around knocking on doors, to sell $350 it takes them a week. You sold it in a few hours." I made 10 percent commission. "Are you going home after *Shabbes*?" he asked.

"Yes, I'd like to go home Saturday night," I said, and he wrote me the commission check right there. The next day I conducted services at his *shul* and went home. I told the hotelkeeper to hold the room, that I was coming back Monday to stay for a week.

When I came back to Sherbrooke on Monday morning, I brought some kosher food with me because it was not available at the hotel. I went into the office at the store and picked up my merchandise. After a few hours, I called the hotel to see if Betty had left any messages, if everything was okay at home. There was a message to call her in Montreal. It was urgent, the message said, very important. When I called the house, Betty told me, "The president of the Shaare Zion synagogue called to say he wants to see you tonight." Their assistant cantor of thirty years had become ill and was retiring. One of our friends from the boat, Solomon Gisser, had gotten a job as the main cantor at Shaare Zion as soon as he stepped off the boat. He had a lot of experience, and was cantor in Europe before coming to Canada. Gisser went to this *shul* and told them about me. So here I was, again starting what I thought might be a lifelong career in selling, or at least a job for the foreseeable future, and again being interrupted.

We spoke on the phone for a while about it. "What do you think I should do?" I asked Betty.

"This seems like a steady job," she said. "What can you lose?"

I went to Mr. Shechter and said, "I have to go home. I cannot tell you why, but something came up and my wife wants me home." I took the train back to Montreal.

I went that evening to meet the president and vice president of Shaare Zion — just the two of them — at the synagogue. They asked me what I knew from law and liturgy, and then they opened up a *Chumash*, a Bible, and asked me to read. It was not long before they offered me the job. I thought about my recent success at sales and the money I made at the *shul* in Sherbrooke the last weekend. "It depends," I told them. "How much does it pay?"

"Well, the basic salary is fifty-five dollars a week, but with special functions, you can expect to make as much as a hundred."

Fifty-five dollars was more than the thirty-five I made at the sewing factory, and more than the one-day commission I had made so far selling. A hundred dollars a week was very livable in 1952. "Let me talk it over with my wife," I told them.

"I don't know what to tell you," Betty said later when I told her. "It looks good and it's a steady job. You won't have to worry about anything, like going out in the cold and knocking on doors." So I accepted the job. We settled down and both thought that finally this was the "it" we'd been looking for.

In the beginning I looked at the job at Shaare Zion as simply a vehicle for making a living. I no longer had to worry about having a regular income; that was one aspect of it. The other aspect was personal satisfaction — that I could live as a Jew after all the ups and downs, after all the crises of faith I had had since the liberation.

"This is where we are going to build our future," Betty and I said. "This is where we are going to live until the end of our days. This is where we are going to raise a family. This is where we start a normal life." It was March 1952, only two-and-a-half months after stepping off the boat. I was twenty-seven years old, still young for a man establishing a normal life, but my life experience was that of someone who was a hundred. Because that is where I finally began to define who I am, I still consider Montreal to be home.

It is amazing that after all the traveling we did, all the different cities, Montreal was so stable. The fact is that the other people who came off the boat with us in Montreal all still live there. They did not move, as I eventually did, because of their business. Had I been a peddler in Sherbrooke, as I had started out to be, then I probably would still be there. Compared to the Paris we loved and the Berlin we tired of, Montreal was a more permanent place, not a place for souls wandering in transition.

We loved the involvement of the Jewish community, the *yiddishkeit*, even in the small but growing Montreal of those days. The community gave us something to anchor ourselves to. It helped both of us grow as people, and I began to gain a name for myself. I bettered myself by going to school.

I went to night school to learn English, to keep my now-normal life going forward, but I only kept it up for a few weeks because I could not stand the teacher. I kept comparing her to the language teacher I had in Paris, at the Alliance Francaise, and finding fault in every way she taught. I ended up teaching myself English at home, by reading and listening. But I wanted to accomplish more than learning English. I wanted to achieve something.

I enrolled at the Conservatory of Music at McGill University in Montreal, and subsequently at the French-speaking Conservatoire Provinciale. They both gave me scholarships — McGill's was called the "Barbershop Quartet Scholarship" — so I went to school for free. At McGill I learned music theory, harmony and everything that had to do with my craft. At Provinciale I became involved with opera, learning repertoire and drama, including diction, acting and fencing (complete with sword and mask). I did it to better myself, to be a more complete singer. I went during the day, because even though I was a full-time assistant cantor, I only had to be available mornings, evenings, weekends and holidays. I did not neglect my job at all, and took my studies seriously.

Except for language classes, I had not been in school since my education was interrupted in 1939, when I was only fifteen years old. Here I was in a classroom, not fearing the teacher the way I used to because he did not treat us like children or pupils. The teachers were professors, and this was serious business. I knew why I was in class, and my entire approach was different because it was something I wanted to do. I was more mature and I knew that in order to accomplish something I had to work hard.

Part of that hard work included taking voice lessons. My voice teacher was named Rhea Lensens Hennings, a tall, distinguished Belgian woman — much older than I — who was married to the personal physician of the royal family of Belgium. She had reddish blonde hair and brown eyes, and always wore proper dresses. All our lessons were in French. When she spoke, it was always with authority, and she required, even commanded, respect. I always addressed her as Madame Lensens.

She was an important influence on me, sort of a mother type. She also liked Betty very much, and she came to our house often, or we went to hers, for four o'clock tea and pastries. She followed my career for a long time, and when it came time for me to audition for different singing engagements, such as operas, I always asked her, "What shall I do? How shall I do it?" She came to every audition.

Madame Lensens advocated that I sing and interpret classical French and German lieder, oratorios, rather than opera. I studied that repertoire with her for years — pieces from composers like Schubert, Schumann, Brahms, Bach, Beethoven and Mozart for the German, and Fauré, Hahn and Duparc for the French. She arranged for me to tape an audition at the CBF, the French-Canadian Broadcasting Company, so they would have my voice on file in case they needed a baritone. A Belgian conductor who came to Montreal and needed a soloist to sing Bach's Cantata No. 82 — the only Bach cantata written for a baritone soloist — heard the tape and called me. This, of course, was the kind of music Madame Lensens approved of for me. It was to be a live radio performance with a large chamber orchestra. I kept my appointment with him, and he liked the way I pronounced the German, and the way I sang it.

"You're going to do it," he said.

This was my first radio performance on the CBC, and to say that I was nervous would be an understatement. They reminded me over and over again during rehearsals that it was live — there would be no repeats, no starting over — and that the first run is the only run. I worked very hard preparing for it. When the show was over and I read the reviews, I was overwhelmed.

The years I spent in Montreal were four of the most productive and beautiful of my life. It was a place of culture and achievement for me, for my friends and especially for my family. Our second son, Enoch, named for my brother Henoch, was born there in 1953. There were excellent schools where he and Mark would be able to receive a good Jewish education. The congregation at the synagogue was large — fourteen hundred families — and getting to know them gave us a community, and allowed me to make a good name for myself.

Culturally, my love of singing and performing gave me access to not only the Jewish community, but also Montreal's non-Jewish French community. I gave recitals under the auspices of the French bishop. I gave operatic performances and was exposed to such great personalities as Wilfred Pelettier — a former guest conductor at the New York Metropolitan Opera — who was the director of the Conservatoire de la Republique de Quebec. I was invited to join a special society of French Quebec, La Societé De Bon Parler Francais, The Society of Good French Speaking People. This was high society in the French community, and was one of the more obvious marks of what I was able to accomplish there.

My love of singing made life in Montreal so wonderful that even when I had opportunities presented to me, business opportunities where I was told I could make three times more money, I brushed them aside. I was very happy and fulfilled.

The rabbi at Shaare Zion, Rabbi Maurice Cohen, and his wife Rochelle were important influences on our life in Montreal. He was the most refreshing human being we had met in our New World. He was tall and very distinguished, with dark eyes and a kind, smiling face. His dignified dress and walk caused people to stop on the street and watch him go by, a Homberg sitting smartly on his head and a folded umbrella keeping steps with his stride. And despite the fact that he was born in Massachusetts, Rabbi Cohen's Lithuanian parents taught him to speak a beautiful Yiddish. It was as though he were from the old country.

Maurice Cohen's influence was manifold. Being ten years older, he was somewhat of a mentor to me. He taught us a new way of practicing

Judaism — the Canadian/American way of Jewish life. Shaare Zion was a Conservative congregation. To me, hearing some of the prayers in English was strange, but he was able to keep it meaningful even though it was not in the traditional Hebrew or Aramaic. He showed me that it did not diminish the prayer's power.

He had a way of dealing with the congregation that I had to learn to follow, but not imitate. I love people anyway, so being comfortable with them was not a problem for me, but Rabbi Cohen had a more secular education than I did, and so had a broader knowledge of how the congregation understood Judaism. I had to adjust and adapt, and he taught me how to do that through his own observance.

His observance with his family, for example, was new to us. Specifically, the way he dealt with his children around the table, everyone having a voice and an opinion and not having to restrain it for the sake of his opinion. Still, he spoke to his elderly father with the same respect he expected from his children, and I liked that. Betty and I tried to be as modern as he was, but certain things you cannot take away. We remembered the way our mothers and fathers used to deal with us, and we could not help but do the same with our boys.

The rabbi also helped me with my English. Just listening to him speak was an incredible lesson in learning to speak the language the proper way. I asked him to help me. "Please correct me if I say something wrong," I requested from him. "I won't be offended."

I counted on Maurice Cohen's opinion as a mentor and a friend. When I decided to go back to school, to go to the Conservatory, I asked him, "What do you think?"

"By all means," he said, "if a person has a chance to study, he must improve himself. It's your field. You have got to go. I'm sure you'll do a great job."

Later, when I was exposed to the public through radio recitals, I asked him, "Rabbi, what do you think? Should I sing a Bach piece on the radio where I have to mention Jesus' name?" Whether it was radio or doing the opera, he backed me up and gave me moral support. He did not find it to be sacrilege.

"You do it for interpretation only," he said. "You are interpreting the music. You don't have to believe what you are saying when you are singing. As long as you do the text musically correct, the way it is written and composed, then you are bringing out music. You are bringing out culture."

This was certainly a more generous response than some of the congregation members were giving me. They used to call Betty while I was singing on the radio and criticize, "How could he? How could he do a thing like this?"

Betty already knew what to say. We would never put the rabbi in the middle of it, of course. We never said, "Rabbi Cohen says it's okay," but Betty used the rabbi's reasoning. "It's culture; it's music. He doesn't have to believe what he says. It's just a matter of musical expression."

One day I came to my voice teacher, Madame Lensens, with some news. Many of the others who were studying opera with me at Provinciale and performing with the Conservatory's company were going to Covent Garden in England to join permanent companies. Around that time an agent contacted me and said he wanted to manage me and my opera career. I did not know what to do, so I went to Madame Lensens to get her advice. I sat with her for hours as she put it in perspective for me.

"You have a job and you make a steady living," she began. "You have two small children. Can you afford to do this? You are going out into the world now on an 'if' basis. The way up is very difficult unless you have tremendous financial support to go to the Met or City Center. Even then I would not advise you to throw away the livelihood you already have. You can keep singing, but the difference is if you go to work at an opera you will wait for an engagement. You'll work, say, twelve weeks out of the year. What will you do with the rest? Wait for a concert? You cannot get concerts every week — you are not there yet. Can you afford to become a vagabond and let your family sit and wait until you get an engagement?"

I sat and listened to what she had to say. She concluded by saying, "You can do it on the side. Sing as much as you want, and it can be supplemental to what you are doing now, but do not throw away something that you have, that you like and are comfortable with. Stick with what you are doing and continue with your studies." I listened, and I took her advice.

There were other ramifications Betty and I were concerned about, though, when it came to the lifestyle of those who performed opera. After one of the opera performances for the Provinciale, we were invited to a party. These were artists and performers in the early 1950s and they were quite bohemian. Jazz music was playing and the dress was very casual — women wore loose sweaters, men in shirts with ascots. Everybody was affectionate, with a lot of hugging and kissing. I knew it was just part of being in theater, having to dress up in costumes and make-up, and need-ing to dress down. It was part of that life, part of the scene. Betty's reaction was more direct. "Is this the way we are going to live?" she asked. "Like gypsies and bohemians? Is this the way we are going to change?" It was the complete opposite of the way we wanted our lives to be, and despite our attempts to defend what I was doing as culture, the voices of my critics in the congregation were asking us to turn away from it completely.

It all came to a head when I was invited to appear on live television in the opera *Rigoletto*. It was my first television performance, and I was in the title role. The director was Otto Werner Mueller, who went on to lead con-ducting at Yale University. I asked for advice from as many people as I could about the role, about the opera and about performing on live televi-sion. Coaches and other singers gave me a lot of help. While I felt prepared for the role, I was not ready for the backlash from my congregation. A young woman named Sylvia Stahlman, who was a beautiful girl, played the Gilda to my Rigoletto. We had some scenes that were meant to be roman-tic, and even though it was just a play, the reaction was unbelievable.

They called Betty all night. "Did you see the way your husband was sitting with that girl?" they asked incredulously, "Did you see the way he held her?"

Rabbi Cohen backed me the whole time. "I don't understand you people," he told the synagogue board when they complained to him. "This is art. Performing art."

The next thing I knew, I was meeting with the president of the con-gregation. "This has to stop," he told me. "Make a decision. Either you remain a cantor or you want to be an opera singer. If you want to be an opera singer, then you cannot be our cantor. We will not permit it." He even tried to sweeten the deal by offering to send me to school in New York to accomplish myself as a cantor, "but you have to forget about the rest of it. No radio programs, no recitals and no opera."

Well, even though I had already decided not to go into opera full time, I was not going to stop doing recitals or radio or even the occasional opera on the side. That was Madame Lensens's advice, so that I could sing all kinds of music. It was around that time that I received an offer from a synagogue in Boston. I said to myself, "Why should I go around being miserable and unsatisfied?" Within days I handed in my resignation. They could not believe it. The board thought I would fall for the threat that the president made and drop the other music and stay with Shaare Zion.

We had another reason for going to Boston in 1956. Betty's sister Pola had moved there with her husband Zundel. Even though we had many friends in Montreal, we had no family other than ourselves.

Rabbi Cohen's support was unwavering. "By all means," he said. "Go. You are capable of doing something better than what you are doing now. I hate to lose you. I hate to see you go, but how far is Boston from Montreal? Not far. We will still be friends." He wrote a letter of recommendation for me to the congregation I had applied to; he was the only one out of the entire congregation to do so. He was interested in me bettering myself, the same expectation that he had of his children and himself.

Bettering myself in Boston meant continuing my music education as well, so Pelettier, from the Quebec Conservatory, wrote a letter of recommendation for me to the head voice coach at the New England Conservatory. We were excited to move to Boston, on to the next adventure. Still, we never knew how much we would miss Montreal.

CHAPTER
26

BOSTON

We considered Montreal our first home. It was the first time we had a chance to live like normal human beings since Germany and the problems we had getting our lives started after the war. Now in Boston, for the first time I felt like we did not make the right choice. We had trouble with the landlord, trouble with finances and trouble with the congregation.

The landlord's name was Mr. Cyker, a survivor who was able to get on his feet quickly after the war. He bought a lot of property around Boston. He was also a member of Beth Zion, the congregation I worked for in Brookline, but I certainly received no deferential treatment because of it. He had the old, bitter mentality of someone constantly fighting with life; it may have been his experiences in the camps, but I think he was just a miserable character. He never fixed anything. There was no heat, and, as most people know, the winters in Boston are quite severe. We walked around the apartment all day in sweaters and blankets, and even called the health department on him to show how we were forced to live with two small children. He gave us trouble for one thing after another.

The only good thing about coming to Boston was meeting Helmut Wulfuss, the voice coach of the New England Conservatory of Music. He was a German Jew in his sixties who had come to America before the war. I have never met another coach or music teacher quite like him. He was my coach in lieder and knew everything by heart. Wulfuss often fell asleep at the piano while I was singing, and if I made a mistake he would correct me as he slept! He was a most unusual man.

What really saddened me, though, was being largely forced to neglect my music career while in Boston because my main preoccupation was providing for my family. Mark was seven years old and we sent him to the Maimonides School, a private school, so he would get a Jewish education. It was expensive. I was only getting paid sixty-five hundred dollars a year, and could not manage. I had to supplement my income, so I arranged to sell plumbing supplies. In my free time, I called on hardware stores all over that part of New England and sold them wrenches and fittings. It was miserable, but I had two children to take care of.

The financial situation forced me to go to the synagogue and ask for a raise. Neither the rabbi nor the president of the congregation was sympathetic. I showed them how impossible it was to pay my rent, to feed my family and to send my children to school on what they were paying me. I told them I was looking for another job. The president, Joseph Sargon, said to me, "If you cannot live up to your contract because you are doing other work, then I will terminate your contract as of tomorrow." I had a three-year contract. They gave me a day and docked me the last two months of the first year.

"That's fine," I told him. I already lost more in my life than two months' salary. It was no problem for me to cut relations immediately. "Just put it in writing," I said.

About a week after that happened, the annual Cantor's Convention was held in the Catskills. I told the placement committee that I was available and looking for work. A committee from the Community Temple in Cleveland, Ohio, was at the convention looking for someone, so the placement committee introduced us. They invited me to come back to Cleveland with them for an audition. I did not go one *Shabbes* without a job. One day I was in Boston, and the next day I was in Cleveland. We were in Boston nine months.

CHAPTER 27

CLEVELAND

Once in Cleveland, I took immediately to the rabbi, Jack Herman [ז״ל]. We grew very close and the relationship between the rabbi and the congregation and me was ideal. They accepted Betty and me with an outpouring of appreciation. Once again, we decided that this was it. "Cleveland is where we begin anew," we said. "This is where we are going to make our roots, and this is where we are going to stay. We will do what every other family does: build a normal life together with the rest of the community. Enough running; enough looking. Enough! Enough!"

Cleveland was very good to us. What made the city so appealing was that the most involved people were the same ones who put down the welcome mat for us when we arrived. In 1957 Cleveland was a city with a thriving, vibrant Jewish community. I was thrown into the tide of activities from the first day there. And I was immediately accepted by the other cantors as a peer on equal footing. Part of the reason I had the freedom I did to perform in Montreal was that, for all the success I had there, I was only the assistant cantor. While I was a friend to the other cantors, I always felt that they were "big shots." In Cleveland, everything fell together like pieces in a puzzle. It was a good feeling for the children, for their education, and we embraced the community, especially the members of Community Temple.

With the help of so many new friends, I reached a point where I felt part and parcel of the Jewish community. I was satisfied personally; my family grew to three sons with Perry's birth in 1959, and there were places to send my children to get a Jewish education. And I was satisfied professionally as well. Unlike in Montreal, I was able to continue doing concerts and programs, and also continue my education in music and theory. I went to the Cleveland Music School Settlement, and I drove out to Baldwin-Wallace College in Berea twice a week for voice lessons. I was able to do all this at my own expense. Most of the concerts I did were for worthwhile causes in the community and not for compensation. I performed for different organizations, such as Israel Bonds. At one Bond Dinner Golda Meier was the honored guest and I performed with Georgie Jessel. During that performance, I sang a song to a little boy who sat on my knee. It was a nostalgic Yiddish melody about an elder teaching a child the *aleph-beis*, the Hebrew alphabet. It was called "In *Cheder*":

"Come closer to me, my little boy
And give heed to the sound of *komets aleph aw, komets beis baw....*"

When I finished the plaintive song and the audience applauded, Jessel stepped to the stage and with a histrionic flourish, bowed on his knees and kissed my feet. I thought he was just doing shtick, until he looked up at me and there were tears streaming from his eyes. At the end of the program I signed my copy of the sheet music of "In *Cheder*" and handed it to him. The little boy I sang to, by the way, was named Howard Bender, and he grew up to be an opera singer.

There were also times I got to perform with comedian Lou Holtz, Cantor Moshe Koussevitsky and many other prominent names. At the community celebration for Israel's tenth anniversary, I performed with other local cantors, and Rabbi Abba Hillel Silver spoke. I became friendly with my colleagues and integrated into the community.

One of my best friends in Cleveland was another survivor, Sender Wajsman (ז"ל), who was the director of the Peretz Shule, the Workmen's Circle School, also called the Yiddish School. Among other things, the organization championed the continuation of Yiddish culture. Sender admired my ability to interpret music and called on me many times to interpret Yiddish songs. I participated in the annual Workmen's Circle Third seder, a special mock Passover seder done all in Yiddish. Sender was not only a great influence on me professionally, but from the time I came to Cleveland, we hit it right off.

Sender was especially instrumental in helping me select the Yiddish songs for my first record album. The record came about when a young member of my congregation — a newlywed — came up to me. He looked like Tony Curtis. His name was Mike Lipton and he worked in the Cleveland office of Jubilee Records.

"Cantor," he said, "I have an idea." I nodded and he continued, "You know that the top-selling records these days are Mitch Miller recordings." At that time, the bandleader Mitch Miller had achieved great success with a television program called "Sing Along with Mitch." The similarly titled records had reached the top of the charts. "How about doing a record for Jubilee called 'Sing Along with Isaac?'"

I became very excited and I agreed. "Let's do it," I said, "but let's call it 'Sing Along in Yiddish.'"

In a matter of days I was in the studio recording a selection of familiar and nostalgic Yiddish melodies. Like Mitch Miller's recordings, the album included the transliterated lyrics on the back cover. The first day that the record hit the shelves in Cleveland it sold two thousand copies. I think that was it. I never made money on the record; in fact, when I went to New York to collect my royalties for the ones that sold, they opened their ledger to show me that I owed them money for the studio time! Well, it was my first album and I learned that I was not a record executive. I was a performer.

Performing at events was one way I could contribute to the success of the community, but in order to help people, in order to get involved, I needed to do more. I wanted to reach out to people in the community, not for their glory or mine, but for things that were worthwhile. It is part of the way I was raised. At home *tzedakah*, charity, was always a part of our lives. We were not wealthy, not even what I would call comfortable, but we still had eleven *pushkees* at home for collecting coins for various charities, including the charity that collected dowries for poor brides, a couple of Yeshivas and the Jewish National Fund. They were always there, and we always had a coin or two to drop in them. When I was young, my grandparents encouraged me to go from door to door in Piotrokow

collecting money for a poor relative. In Lodz we went to large manufacturers to ask for contributions to one charity or another. We only
walked away with nothing when we came across people who were simply
against everything, or if someone was against giving charity because it
would hurt his pocket. What I always try to convey to the people I talk
to is how worthwhile it is to give, not for yourself, but to improve someone else's life, or to support a worthy cause. That is how I approached
involving myself in the community.

The first group I found was an organization of survivors, not from my
own town, but from other parts of Poland, from Hungary and many,
many people from Lithuania. The name of the organization was the Kol
Yisroel Foundation. At the time, in 1957 and 1958, when we got together
it was mostly for social functions. As an organization, though, we had
talked about doing something to remember those who did not survive.

In those days the Holocaust was far, far removed from the minds of
most people. When it came down to things like the observance of Yom
Hashoah or educating people about the fate of Europe's Jews, nobody
thought of it and nobody wanted to touch it. The interest was not as
prevalent then as it is now. On the one hand the subject was a matter of
sensitivity to the survivors, and on the other hand, there was apathy in the
community — it did not concern them.

For some, keeping the memory alive meant doing things like visiting
concentration camps such as Majdanek and Auschwitz, and bringing
back pictures and stories. There was a member of our congregation,
Maurice Salzman, who did just that. During his lecture at the synagogue,
I had to carry Betty out of the room when he went into detail about gas
and teeth and the ashes of the crematoria. It was shocking, but it was a
story ready to be told and I had to convince people of that. If we wanted
the world to remember, if we wanted our children to remember, we needed
to build a monument. If we left it to posterity, I was sure that fifty years later
it would be as if the Holocaust never happened.

We were treading new ground. Cleveland was one of the first communities in the country to get involved with a Holocaust memorial project. We had an architect come up with an idea for a black marble monument. The cost was estimated at fifty thousand dollars. That was a lot of

money when we started the project in 1959. The community had been so welcoming to me when I first arrived, and it was time to repay the favor and put my connections to use. The Bramsons, who owned a cemetery on Northfield Road, donated the grounds for free. Now we had to raise the money. I specifically chose to ask Jews who were not survivors to participate, so that it had the support of the entire community. There was a man named Israel Taslit, a writer and lawyer who was very active in the Jewish community. I met with him and got to know him. He was a man who had a heart and a feeling for Jewish causes. He introduced me to Albert Levine, another lawyer. "The only thing you have to do is ask," Mr. Taslit told me. "Talk to the man and he will not refuse you. That's all you have to do. Just talk to him."

I met with Mr. Levine and told him a little bit about my background and what I went through. Then I told him why I was there now. He was a strong supporter of Israel, so I talked to him about the parallels. "Now that we have a State of Israel," I told him, "we have a place to go if this should ever happen again. But how will we know what is happening? How will we remember? You must have had cousins there, or a grandfather. How will your children remember what happened to them?"

It was not difficult to convince him to contribute to something I believed was worthwhile. Another man Mr. Taslit told me to "just talk to" was Harry Robbins. I convinced Mr. Robbins after the first moment I spoke with him. We became such close friends that he would do anything I asked of him, and he was not even a member of my congregation. We finally raised the money and set the date of the dedication for Yom Hashoah in 1961.

Some months before, we wrote the Polish government requesting something from the camps, some remnants from Auschwitz or Treblinka or Majdanek. With their cooperation, we received six quart-sized mason jars filled with bones and ashes. The night before the dedication we asked for ten volunteers from the survivor community to come to the Berkowitz-Kumin Funeral Home. We wanted only survivors for what we were doing. At the funeral home, Sam Berkowitz had prepared six bronze urns for us. We transferred the ashes from the glass jars into the urns. As we quietly sifted and poured, watching chips of ivory bone tumble through the black ash and into the urns, we were all lost in the same thought: "Maybe this is my mother, my brother, my sister." There was no ceremony — only the sound of sifting ash and the occasional plunk of bone hitting the narrow mouth of the bronze urn.

The next day, there were a thousand people at the dedication. We organized a very moving citywide mixture of Jews and non-Jews. The mayor of Cleveland, Mayor Celebrezze, was there, and there were representatives from the local military, from the civic society and from the Jewish Federation. A processional of flags moved from the cemetery gate to the memorial. Six survivors carried the bronze urns and placed them in the monument where they remain. This is the shrine they use now in Cleveland to mark every Yom Hashoah.

As a cantor, part of my satisfaction came from my work at the synagogue, especially working with the children. It was in Cleveland that I discovered that I derive a satisfaction from children because I believe that if I can impart just a minute bit of education to them — that they know a little more than they did before — then I have accomplished a lot. I worked with them in an individual, though informal, way in the classroom. I felt more of a parent to them than a teacher. I felt part of them and their lives, and I thought it was reciprocal, that they felt the same way towards me. I taught history and Bar and Bas Mitzvahs, and always felt that the children enjoyed being with me. Many trusted me and came to me for counseling for one thing or another, especially when it came to marriage. I had as many as a dozen girls come to me over the time I was in Cleveland and ask me about marrying someone from another faith.

Typically the girl came to me and said she was "madly in love" with a particular boy. I knew the parents, of course, and they were traditional people. I tried to talk her out of it. I did not go to a psychology school and did not have a degree in counseling, but I used common sense and approached it based on our traditions. I told the girl about our history, our background, and what might happen if she were to marry a non-Jew. There were a lot of arguments and rebuttals: "Love is stronger than anything else.... Love can conquer anything and everything...."

But I did not play on the love aspect alone. "The human being is a creature of faith, and there has to be some sort of compatibility," I said.

"They have to be compatible with one another and even then, during the smallest argument, an anti-Semitic remark might come out, no matter how much you love each other. You never know. He gets mad and says something like, 'This is what happens when you start with Jews.' He might even call you a name. 'Dirty Jew,' he might say, 'Kike.' This could happen." I told her, "You have got to weigh all these possibilities, the pros and the cons, and make your mind up, to see if you really want to do this thing." Then there was one more point I would make. "If you are in love with this boy, would you convert to Christianity?"

"No," was the answer she would usually give.

"Then," I pointed out, "there is already a loophole. If your love is so strong, why not convert to Christianity?"

"Well," she said, "I am a Jew."

"Well, if you are a Jew, then you have to live like a Jew. Would he convert to Judaism?"

The answer to that question often varied. If she answered no, or "If I asked him he would," then I said, "But he would not come forward on his own and say 'I'll do anything,' even if it were just for love and he did not really believe." Sometimes I succeeded and sometimes I did not.

I also received satisfaction from helping two people in their decisions to become rabbis. One became a Reform rabbi, and one a Conservative rabbi. They came to me and acknowledged my influence in them becoming people who wanted to minister to their congregants, whether as the result of a direct relationship or the relationship I shared with their family. These men watched me as I worked with the congregation. I took my profession very seriously. If I noticed a grievance on the part of a member of the *shul*, I made it a point to approach them on my own, based on my own instinct, to initiate a dialogue. "Why aren't you happy? Is there anything we can do to improve the relationship?" Nine times out of ten I was successful in assuaging their concerns. This way I have of handling people, of helping them with their problems and their relationships, was not something I went somewhere to learn. It is within me, and I am compelled to help people, impart what I can to them. I do it because I love people. Maybe sometimes that is not so good. Maybe I am covering up for my own ego, but I strongly believe in helping people for their own sakes, and not for any personal gain. I always cared more for others than for myself.

———

In Cleveland I really excelled. With all our involvement in social, cultural, and humanitarian activities in both the Jewish and non-Jewish communities, I could have stayed there indefinitely, without any new aspirations or new ventures, and the status quo would have been fine. In Cleveland I could have said, "This is it." But the status quo meant that professionally I was going nowhere. I let it be known to the proper people in cantorial circles that if something good was available, I was interested. Because the status quo was comfortable, I was looking for something very good — a uniquely involved congregation and community.

Without knowing it, the answer to my quest was in my hands many times. It is common among synagogues and temples in North America with similar affiliations to send copies of their bulletins to each other. I often looked through these newsletters for musical ideas and presentations, ones I could appropriate for my own use in Cleveland. Among the bulletins we received at Community Temple was one from Ahavath Achim Synagogue in Atlanta. I was very impressed with the level of activity and involvement the bulletin demonstrated. I even mentioned to Betty once that a congregation like that is worth looking into. A short time after I submitted my name to the Cantors' Assembly to be considered for other positions, I received a telephone call that there was a vacancy at Ahavath Achim, if I was interested. I let them know and within two weeks I received a call from the rabbi. He was very sweet on the phone.

"Cantor Goodfriend, this is Rabbi Epstein from Atlanta. Your name was submitted to us that you are a *hazzan* and you are interested in changing congregations. We would very much like to hear what you have to say and, if you are still interested, we would like to interview you."

I said to him, "Rabbi, before we go any further, I have to know from you a few things. What type of community is Atlanta, and the foremost question, is there a day school? This is what I believe in for my family and this is where my children go and this is what I want to be able to give my children. If there is no day school, then we have nothing to discuss."

He smiled on the phone. "Yes," he said, "there is a day school."

"Then we can continue our conversation," I said.

He said, "How about sending a tape of your voice, whatever you select, and the committee will listen to it?"

I said, "Rabbi, personally I do not believe in a mechanical introduction because one of us will be cheated. If I send you a tape, I'll probably select the best tape that I have and it will sound very good. But you would not know whether I am that good or I just sound good on that tape. A tape is just that — a good reproduction. One of us will get the short end of it."

"Alright," he said, "you'll hear from us."

After two more weeks went by and I did not hear from them, I decided that maybe that is the way they operate, and I made a tape for them. At the time cassette tapes were not yet popular, of course, so I made a reel-to-reel tape. I picked a few impressive songs, some liturgical and some secular, some with choir and some alone, some with orchestra or piano accompaniment and some a capella. That was in February 1965. Well, February passed, and March and April and May. I watched the bulletins every week, and saw that each week they had candidate after candidate auditioning for the job in Atlanta, and I had yet to be called. Around the end of May I received a package with my tape and all the papers and clippings, with all the biographical material, even the letter I wrote them. Looking at the package, it seemed they had not read the letter. The tape was certainly not opened and listened to. "Well," I thought, "that's it. I guess I'll stay where I am," and I began to negotiate a new contract with Community Temple.

One Sunday evening at the end of June I got another telephone call from Rabbi Epstein. He apologized a thousand times for the delay in getting in touch with me. "Cantor, I am so sorry. I heard from Cantor Sam Rosenbaum [the executive vice president of the Cantors' Assembly] that we would be making a big mistake by not inviting you here to audition," and he asked me if I could come down on Tuesday. That was only two days away.

I checked the calendar. "I'm sorry. I cannot come this Tuesday," I told him, "but I can make it the following Tuesday." We made arrangements, and the following Tuesday I told my congregation I was going to visit family in Boston and went to Atlanta by myself to audition.

Auditioning to be a cantor is unlike any other audition, even for other kinds of performing jobs. You have to be prepared for all kinds of opinions from a variety of people. In fact the reason my tape was never listened to was because one of the board members saw my resume and said, "This is not possible. There is no way that one man can possess all these skills. To read the Torah and sound the shofar and be able to perform the entire liturgy and be active in the congregation? It's too good to be true. He must be lying."

But a cantor is not interviewed by only one person. There is an entire congregation to impress, and every one of them has a different outlook as to what a cantor should be, what he should sound like. Maybe there are particular prayers that one individual likes to hear from a cantor or he is used to hearing. Maybe this person heard a cantorial melody from his father or grandfather, or when he was a little boy they took him to listen to a cantor and one or two melodies stuck in his head, and that is all he knows. This is how he is going to judge a *hazzan* for the entire congregation. The trick is to create a consensus from all those subjective opinions. It is not easy, but for this audition I was prepared. I knew that I would either succeed or fail. I was confident. I thought I could handle the human aspect vis-à-vis the congregation. After all, I was not a novice; I had plenty of congregational experience. I did not think I would fail, and even if I did, I still had a job.

I was asked to conduct *ma-ariv*, the evening service, for those in the congregation. The pews were filled with the synagogue's executives, the full board, several past presidents and a handful of so-called connoisseurs or *mevinim*, the mavens who they called in to listen and add their opinions to the mix. Rabbi Epstein, of course, was there too. I wanted to sit on the *bima*, to be near the pulpit as if it was a regular service rather than a concert. I asked the rabbi if that were possible. "It's all yours," he said. "Do whatever you feel like, whatever you want to sing, whatever you want to announce, or if you don't want to announce, go right ahead. Do as you please. It's yours."

I performed a little extra *hazzanus*, some extra cantorial chants that I would not normally have added to the *ma-ariv* service. At the end of the service I asked those in the sanctuary, "Ladies and gentlemen, what is your pleasure? What would you like to hear?"

This was my first time in the South and I had to control myself, not to laugh as the board members pronounced the names of their favorite prayers with a Southern accent. I was cool as calls came out from the audience. "Cantuh," one lady called in an old drawl, "please chant the *keedoosh*." Another voice came from an old man with a European accent who was one of the *mevinim*. He asked if I would chant the Thirteen Attributes that we do during Festivals, before we take the Torah from the ark. I saw him in the audience and he was an elderly man. From that and from his accent, I knew what he wanted to hear. I sang an interpretation from my childhood, from the old country, and I could see him nodding his head in agreement. I knew I had at least one vote in my favor.

What got the biggest reaction, and had the most potential to sink the audition, was when one man, a doctor who seemed to be knowledgeable in Hebrew, asked me to sing *Kol Nidre*. Without taking time to think about it, I said, "I don't mind singing *Kol Nidre*, but I would not do justice to it, here in June on a Tuesday night. It will not sound the way *Kol Nidre* would sound on a Yom Kippur night. The mood, the atmosphere is just not here." I could hear a buzz move through the room. It was a risky response, but it was honest.

After a few more requests for some songs in English, Yiddish and Hebrew, I had a feeling it was moving along well. They asked me to wait in the sanctuary with some of the other congregants as the committee met in the boardroom. After a little while they called me in. "Tell us something about yourself."

"Well," I said smiling, "how much time do we have? I have a long history. I will try to make it as brief as possible...," and I told them a little about myself, my family, my age, what I accomplished, my schooling and so on. Afterwards they excused me, telling me I could go back to my hotel as they deliberated. When I left the room there were several members outside waiting to greet me, to ask me questions, such as where I was from. They were friendly, telling me that their parents came from Poland or Lithuania or Russia. I started to retain some of their names immediately.

The next morning the phone in my hotel room rang. It was Michael Kraft, the synagogue president. "We'd like to get your wife down here," he said. I was happy because that meant I was halfway there. It was Fourth of July weekend and very difficult to get a flight, but we finally did and Betty arrived. We were taken out, wined and dined, in a show of real Southern hospitality. I was pleased with their reaction, but at the same time a little confused. It was like day and night to me, being in this part of the country. It was, at times, like being in a different country. Was this America? I was never exposed to the Southern way, to their approach, to the way they handled things, and the conservative way of life and slower pace. These people were very deliberate.

I had met the congregation's president, Michael Kraft, at his home while he was recuperating from a heart attack. He was a really refined individual, a real *shul mensch*. He and his wife Ray had Betty and me over to their house for dinner and we were talking. "If I were the president of this congregation," I said to him, "I would not hire a cantor unless I hear him on a Saturday. To hear me in the middle of the week, and listen to me sing a few pieces, is like hearing me out of context. If I were an officer or a board member I would insist that before I made a final decision, I want to listen to the cantor at a regular service, to see how he works with the rabbi, how he harmonizes with everything going on, on the pulpit." He liked the idea. Right then and there he decided to keep me for the weekend and invited me to do the services Friday night and Saturday morning.

We continued talking, when out of the blue Ray asked, "Do you happen to know Rosa Loeb?" I almost fell off my chair.

"Do I know her?" I said. "She is my accompanist in Cleveland."

"She's my first cousin," came the response.

I knew right then that a telephone call was going to be made to Cleveland, and I felt bad because not a soul there knew where I was and what I was doing. I was sure that now the whole city would find out. I did not give Ahavath Achim any names to call because the audition was supposed to be confidential, until I could notify the congregation in Cleveland, and except for this incident which was really not the synagogue's fault, they respected it and did not jeopardize it.

Meanwhile, I had the audition coming up that weekend and notices were sent out immediately to the entire congregation to come and listen. There was quite a crowd. When I met with Rabbi Epstein before the Friday night services, he told me, "This is your *Shabbat*. Do whatever you want."

So I did the services and by Sunday night I came to an agreement with the board about salary. They asked me if I could work the High Holidays, only two months away. I said, "I'm sorry I won't be able to do that. I cannot leave my congregation without a *hazzan*. They are very good to me and I owe this to them." The board did not argue with me about it, and agreed to allow me to start after the holidays.

Less than a week after we returned to Cleveland, Rosa Loeb called and invited us to dinner. I turned to Betty and said, "I think the word is out." Sure enough, Rosa told us that her cousin called her and she wanted us to know that she gave me a good reference and that she was sorry to see us leave. I told her I felt the same way. Then I heard from a doctor in the congregation who said he heard I was leaving, and of course there were others who knew.

Betty took the boys and left Cleveland at the end of August 1965 so they could start school in Atlanta. I arrived after the holidays and on October 29, 1965, I took the pulpit at Ahavath Achim for the first time as cantor of the congregation.

CHAPTER
28

ATLANTA

When Rabbi Harry Epstein told me during the auditions that it was my pulpit, my service and my *Shabbat*, I thought that he was just giving me some freedom to show off my skills to the congregation. It was not until the first time that I stepped on a *bima* as the new cantor that I realized Rabbi Epstein was telling me that I would always be "on my own." This was a new thing to me. It was a new environment.

At the pulpit a rabbi and cantor have certain duties and responsibilities that include a mutual respect and understanding between them. The rabbi is the spiritual leader of the congregation; the cantor does his job according to the rabbi's wishes as part of the congregation. A rabbi like Rabbi Epstein leads the congregation in a way so there is no misunderstanding or confusion between the cantor, the congregation and him. The tradition and integrity of the pulpit are maintained only when there are no clashes between the rabbi and cantor during services. I could not come in and say, "I'm going to change the whole thing. I don't believe in this particular part of the service." That does not work.

When Rabbi Epstein said to me, "You're on your own," he was telling me that I was free to create my own relationship with the congregation, personally and professionally. Compared to Atlanta, Cleveland was very chummy, everyone calling the rabbi and cantor by their first name. But in Atlanta, it seemed that there was an invisible fence between Rabbi Epstein and the rest of the congregation. By extension, I was on the clergy side of that fence. In the beginning I thought that maybe it was supposed to be that way, but as time progressed I realized that "you're on your own" meant I could break down that fence if I wanted, not drastically but a little at a time. I succeeded in doing that not by bringing anything new but just by bringing my personality and myself. I gave of myself as much as I possibly could while working within the framework of the traditions established by the congregation. At the same time, I went beyond what was required so the congregation would see my personality and not just "Cantor Goodfriend who stands above us on the *bima*." I became accessible to people, and by finding a group of friends within the *shul*, Betty and I became part of a large family of a congregation with nearly two thousand families.

A congregation the size of Ahavath Achim needed true leadership, and that is what Michael Kraft [ל″ז] brought to his position as president of the congregation. Being a professional cantor for sixteen years, I had been around congregations and their officers and I could tell how special he was. Michael was born and raised in Rome, a rural town in northwest Georgia, and still spoke Yiddish as fluently as he spoke English. In the brief time I knew him, we spoke frequently about services and tradition. He was a traditionalist and so am I. He was a man who liked to *daven* every day, and who understood the dynamics of a relationship between a rabbi and cantor. He wanted to know my feelings and aspirations, and I wanted to hear his view.

Unfortunately, the only time Michael heard me sing was on a tape I gave him for Chanukah. I went to visit him at his house the first day of my first Chanukah in Atlanta, and helped him light candles. He was still recuperating from the heart attack he had over the summer and never made it into *shul* to hear me perform. He died two days later. Harry Lane Siegel became the next president and his help to my family and me was invaluable.

When Betty came to Atlanta before the holidays, she knew we had to start anew. We had to create our own environment. Even though it was difficult for her — taking care of the boys and organizing a home — she had done it before, and being a cantor's wife she knew how to handle herself in the congregation without me. Betty knew that to become part of the community we had to create a new group of friends. It was not long before she made contact with some of her *landsleit*, other Lithuanian people who were in the ghetto and camps with her. By the time I arrived after the holidays, there was already groundwork laid to become part of the survivor community. They were people who spoke the same language, with whom we could exchange and express a little bit of home.

But the Organization of Survivors was in splinters: the group's coffers were empty and there was a lot of infighting. People did not talk to each other because of minor grievances and personal misunderstandings to the point of envy and even hatred. One survivor would say, "I'm not getting involved in an organization with that woman," and another would say, "I won't get involved with any group my friend will not be in," and petty things like that, which are a part of many organizations. It was shocking to me to see that the few survivors who were in Atlanta would not cooperate as a unified organization. As individuals the survivors were quite financially successful, but perhaps because of the scars of their pasts, rather than coming together as other survivor communities had, they had an inherent mistrust of each other, and that is something that never has been rectified. But despite their difficulties, in early 1965 they dedicated a very stirring Holocaust monument in a local cemetery so they would have a place to say Kaddish on Yom Hashoah.

Little by little, I involved myself with them and tried to help. They called on me because they knew about my experience in Cleveland's survivor community and because I was the *hazzan* of the "big *shul*" (Ahavath Achim was the largest synagogue in the Southeast) and I was one of them. Their confidence in me made it possible for me to be involved, despite the organization's problems.

To get involved with other parts of life in the community was not too difficult. My first public appearance in Atlanta was on behalf of Israel Bonds, a charity I had done a lot for in Cleveland. Betty and I were also very active in the Jewish National Fund in Cleveland. It was our first love. When we asked around we found out that Hadassah ran the JNF in Atlanta. They filled their annual quota to JNF in January by holding card games and collecting the proceeds and the blue *pushkees* people had in their homes. In one month they would collect twenty-five hundred or three thousand dollars and that would be it for JNF for the entire year. That was very small for a community like Atlanta, so Betty and I decided to open a Jewish National Fund office. We had quite a difficult time getting it started because many in the community felt that it was already being handled so there was no need for another organization. "We are not taking away from any organization's effort or work," we argued. "This is to compliment them. We would like to help coordinate it. There is no reason why Atlanta, Georgia, should only contribute twenty-five hundred dollars."

Within six months of us initiating the project, JNF sent us a *shaliach*, a representative, and we organized the first meeting in our house. We contacted the leaders of all the local Zionist organizations including the Zionist Organization of America, Hadassah, Labor Zionists and Pioneer Women, and they all met in our house to organize a JNF in Atlanta. Because of all we were able to accomplish for the JNF, Betty and I were honored in 1980 by the establishment of the Isaac and Betty Goodfriend Playground in the American Bicentennial Park on the outskirts of Jerusalem.

I have to say that it is not normal for a cantor to be so involved in community organizations; it is up to the individual. Some synagogues may oppose too much involvement if it jeopardizes a rabbi or cantor's obligations, but my first loyalty was always to the synagogue. Still, if somebody wants to take the time to contribute to community organizations, then it is only a question of working a little harder. My personal feeling is that life is too short and it is a sin to waste time when there is so much to be done. If I can personally contribute to a cause I believe in, then I will do it. I will do it because it is important. That is why I got involved in the Zionist movement and became president of the Zionist Organization of America. I want to get across to both the Jewish and non-Jewish world that Zionism did not disappear when Israel became a state. It is something as alive today as it ever was because it is essential to Jewish survival.

People need someone to lead them, to move them to get involved and to inspire them to work together. Ecumenically, if I cannot build a community that is united, then very little can be done. I try to be a model for that kind of involvement. How do I sell involvement to others? I organize. How does anything happen, any new idea? We were able to open up a JNF office by showing people our commitment to Zionism and how important it is to Jews everywhere. Even Hitler could not have been successful without an ability to move people. It only takes a few people to move a concept forward. I moved things forward, and once they know you, you get pulled in to different things.

Getting up for work and coming home after nine or ten hours only to stick to the four corners of the house is not for me. That is a lonely life. I am not only part of the Jewish community, but I have an obligation to do what I can for all my neighbors, Jews and non-Jews included. There are concerts and recitals, symphony events and operas, all contributing not only to the community as a whole, but also to my personal quality of life. I participate in it as an aficionado and a performer, as an organizer and a supporter. Whether it is the Hebrew Academy or the opera or the Cantors' Assembly (where I served in an executive capacity for a number of years), if I excelled I usually overexcelled, overextended and overexerted myself. This is who I am and I would not have it any other way.

Our involvement in the Atlanta community proved to be the realization of the hopes and dreams we had since we stepped off the boat in Halifax in 1952. We felt fulfilled spiritually and culturally, beyond the simple satisfaction I felt in Cleveland. It was a new plateau of community and involvement. I was so involved with the congregation that after I had announced my retirement to the synagogue's board in 1993, the congregation persuaded me to stay on for another two years. Even though I retired from being a full-time cantor in 1995, I am still active in many organizations, and willing to give of myself to the community. I continue to participate in the annual Martin Luther King Jr. Day activities at the church where he preached. I am on the national board of American Friends for Yad Vashem, the famous Holocaust museum in Jerusalem, and I was appointed by the governor of Georgia to the state's Holocaust Commission.

I have spoken at schools often, mostly public schools, about the Holocaust. Children do not know what happened. The history books do not go into it. I was invited to speak about my experiences, experiences that were part of me, are part of me and will be a part of me as long as I live. That is why I was active in the United States Holocaust Memorial Council and in creating the United States Holocaust Museum in Washington, D.C. That activity came out of my involvement in politics that really began when I was a child in Poland.

CHAPTER
29

THE *MIKVAH*
POLITICIAN

Politics in my life goes back many, many years. Before we knew about political science, or even that politics was a science, we talked about political powers, the politics of countries and their relationship to each other, and political ideologies. I was exposed through my own interest at an early age, reading books in the ghetto about the Russian Revolution. In my childhood we used to call these discussions "*mikvah* politics." When I was young, I was naïve enough to believe that the generals on the front lines were doing exactly that, only with a globe or map and some of their "elders." It gave us hope that the war was going to end, because these "*mikvah* politicians" had been around since the First World War and they had to have the right reasoning and philosophy.

As mythical as the conclusions of the *mikvah* politicians of my childhood turned out to be, they pointed out one thing: everything we do is politics. There is politics between a husband and wife, between parents and children, and of course at the workplace. There are more politics in a synagogue than any place you can imagine. Politics is a game, and not always the nicest game, but I try to play it according to my own convictions. It is not enough to come forward and say, "I support this candidate because I like him." Liking him is not important — I have to know the issues and what this person stands for. Does he think along the same lines as I would if I were in his place? Only then do I say to myself, "A candidate of this sort is worth supporting." Supporting means not only financial support, but moral support as well. I say, "I believe in you. You, I trust. You can represent me because you think along the lines that will be good for people." It has to be better, not the way it is, but better.

Politics and progress are tied together, because politics is taking a look at the latest events and talking about how it will affect a particular situation. I watched my television when we put the first man in a rocket and launched him into space; I remember the first jet and what an achievement that was. We live in a tremendously interesting time of history and technology. It all has an effect on politics. Survivors are, in many ways, the continuation of the *mikvah* politicians. We read the paper; we follow events and keep up with the world situation. We love to talk politics, and that includes adding our own interpretations and our own feelings. It is a natural thing for people who were nearly destroyed because of the madness of world events. The creation of the State of Israel, after coming out of hell, after coming out of the dead and rising from the dry bones of which our prophets speak — though cultural and religious — has a tremendous effect on politics. The Zionist movement, and my involvement in it, is political. I have to know what exactly is going on in the world and be my own *mikvah* politician. I listen to what the president is saying about our country and foreign affairs and Social Security because it all affects me.

When I was a child and World War Two was just starting, I wore a Civil Defense armband and a gas mask and helped build trenches to protect my mother and my family. Even when no bombs fell at the height of the Cold War, people were building bomb shelters because they were affected. Politics is a part of life, and some get so involved it becomes their life.

I am a voter. Ever since I became eligible to vote, I have voted in every election. Sometimes I drew my own conclusions based on my experience with a candidate, and sometimes I listened to why others supported a candidate. A friend tells me who he is supporting and why, and I say, "If this man believes in him, then maybe there is something there. Let me look into it." And I jump on the bandwagon. This is how I became involved with Andrew Young's run for Congress from my district. I did not go canvassing for him, but I put a bumper sticker on my car and when my friends asked me whom I supported, I told them "Andy Young," and then I told them why. Like any kind of organizing, it was easy to talk about something I believed in.

I had been involved in many things with Jimmy Carter while he was governor of Georgia. The Jewish National Fund had a function in the Governor's Mansion, and when he appointed the first Jewish woman to the State Pharmaceutical Board I was invited to the swearing-in ceremony. We shared the podium when Hadassah had its national convention in Atlanta. I also knew some of the key people involved in his campaign for president, including Gerald Rafshoon and Stuart Eizenstat. When he announced in 1974 that he was going to run for president in 1976, nobody knew he was going to win. I said to myself, "I'm going to work because I believe. I believe in him because of my personal experience of him and because of the others who are getting involved. If these people are for him, then he must have something good." I knew the people involved to have 100 percent integrity, and I knew they would not be mixed up in anything phony. That is how it began, and what followed were trips to different cities, a lot of speeches and radio appearances to Jews and non-Jews alike. Mostly, though, I was sent to Ohio to reach out to the Jewish community there.

My congregation in Atlanta was very understanding and did not object. The fact was that most of the congregation was for Jimmy Carter, so there was no conflict philosophically or with regard to my time — though it was a revelation to some of them that a cantor could be politically involved. I made sure that my work on the campaign did not conflict with my job as cantor of Ahavath Achim. I did not go away for weeks at a time; I usually went for a day at a time, often coming back the same day. It was a hard schedule, but I was doing something I believed in. I believed in the man who was running for the office. I was convinced, and if I was convinced, I was compelled to sell my conviction to others. I was interested in selling Jimmy Carter on his merits. Besides, I had the support of Betty and the children, who were grown young men by this time and very excited about my involvement in the campaign.

One morning I was told that I had to write a speech for Ruth Stapleton, Carter's sister, to deliver to five congregations in the Baltimore Jewish community. She needed it like yesterday because she was giving the speech that very night. I sat down and wrote it, and when I read the papers the next day I saw she used the entire speech verbatim. That was very satisfying.

I also wrote telegrams to different organizations that requested a note from candidate Carter. Calls came in from groups across the country asking, "We are honoring one of our members. Please see that we get a telegram from Governor Carter." Sometimes they asked for more than just a telegram, "We would like to invite candidate Carter to speak at our function." Sometimes he was available and sometimes he was not. When he was not, I had to pass the same answer to the people who made the request that I heard from the superiors. "We are so sorry," I would tell the organization on the phone, "but Governor Carter has another engagement that evening, and as much as he would like to, he cannot be at both affairs the same night." That is what I did when I was in the campaign office.

When I traveled, it was a different story. I was able to speak publicly about the candidate I believed in. I came to Cleveland, Ohio, once to speak on a Jewish morning radio talk show. I had only twenty-four hours notice. The station had been promoting "a guest from the Carter campaign" for the past day. Before we went on the air, the host said, "Many people called in who heard your name and remembered you. They had so many questions." He gave me a run-through of some of the things people wanted to know.

As the show progressed, he said to me, "I had a request from some people who wanted to hear you sing a song in Yiddish." I did not sing for them; instead, I campaigned in Yiddish. As for the song, I made a promise that I would come back after Governor Carter won the primary season. "I promise you I will come back and sing," I told the radio audience.

The host said, "This is a promise?"

"Yes, it is," I answered.

Sure enough, after the primaries I was sent to Cleveland for two days on a schedule that had me spending a half of every hour speaking to a different group. The other half-hour was spent going from place to place. One of the stops that day was with a senior citizens group from the Jewish Community Center. I campaigned with them a bit, but they were waiting for the song. "Alright," I said to my captive audience of about 250, "I'm going to sing a song. I usually do not count notes, but I spent all night last night counting the notes in this song. There are 2,374 notes, and if you want to hear me sing, for every note I want a vote." That cracked them up! It was the first time I used that spiel, but I used it many times after that on the campaign trail.

All this traveling, all to get a man elected president, made me realize what a serious responsibility I had taken on. When the campaign kicked into high gear after the convention, I took stock of what I was doing. "Oh boy," I said to myself, "you're putting your name on the line. Do you know what you are doing? People trust you. If anything goes wrong, God forbid, they'll have your head.

"But you've reached a point of no return now," my thoughts reassured me. "This is it. You've got to push and put the pressure on. If you back out now, you spoil the whole thing. This is politics and this is campaigning and this is selling."

With that, any moments of unsureness I felt became moments of reassurance. This was evident whenever I spoke before a group of people who knew me, for that was where I had the most risk and felt the most responsible. But I knew I was doing the right thing. I knew it. If I did not feel that certainty, I never would have gone out. That was my reassurance. I used to preface my remarks with, "I'm not here today because you know me. I'm here because I'm convinced. I'm not going to force you to vote for one candidate or the other. I am here to state the facts. I'm going to state the facts about the other candidate and the facts about my candidate. You make the decision."

When campaigning to those groups, no matter how well I knew them, the discussions were not simply friendly conversations. The questions came popping out, not to "Cantor" or "Isaac," but to "Mr. Speaker," as in "Mr. Speaker, you mentioned this," or "Mr. Speaker, how will the governor handle that?" It was all about the candidate's policies and issues. Of course I had all the information and I knew all the answers, but this drove home to me that when they saw me they did not see Isaac Goodfriend; they saw Jimmy Carter.

It bothered some people when I called on them for support. I knew rabbis and cantors in every community in the country, and some said I had no business supporting a Southern Baptist. They would have preferred a

Northerner, like a Kennedy. They did not give their support, either over the phone or at any of my public appearances on Carter's behalf. I did not hold it against them. It is a free country with a democratic process. They did not challenge me publicly, but a few made some private comments to me.

As part of the campaign, I appeared before Jews and non-Jews. One event I remember was at a senior citizens home that had a mix of people from different faiths. The afternoon called for a representative of President Ford's campaign to be there also, and there was a moderator. The rules gave us five minutes each to make our presentations, and then answer questions from the audience. If the question came to me, then the Republican would get a two-minute rebuttal, and vice versa. It was supposed to start at two o'clock. At 2:15 the Republican was not there, so I said to the moderator, "I'm sorry, but my time is limited. Either I go on or we forget about it. I insist that you let me speak to the people; it's not my fault the other man did not show up. I can state my facts."

The moderator went to the chairman of the event and discussed it with him, and they agreed to let me speak to the elderly folks and others gathered at the home. I gave my five-minute presentation, then opened the floor to questions. An eighty-five-year-old woman raised her frail arm. "Mr. Goodfriend, Candidate Carter is a Baptist, isn't he?" I nodded, and she continued, "Well, I am a Methodist. Can you tell me, if he is elected president, would he just promote the Baptist ideology or will he honor all the other religions as well?"

I immediately saw the question as an opportunity to portray him as a human being, in human terms. "Our country is not based on certain religious affiliations," I began. "When he is running for president of the United States, he is running for all the people of the United States. I don't believe that Governor Carter is going to discriminate against one religion over another. If he would, then he is not worthy to run for president, and I would not support him."

She stood up and looked around the room. "Ladies and gentlemen," she announced, "I think I just made up my mind."

I smiled and said, "God bless you. Would you like to come with me to the next speaking engagement?"

"Yes," she replied, laughing, "if you'll carry me!"

It was a good feeling. How deeply I had gotten involved in Carter's presidential campaign was unexpected. The turn of events happened so fast, and one thing came after the other so that I did not have enough time to reflect on the way it affected me personally. If I did, it would have been as an afterthought: "Here is a boy from a town in Poland who saw death twenty times a day and gave up on everything; here he is now helping to elect a president of the United States. Am I crazy or is the world crazy? Is it true or is it just another one of my dreams?"

I became carried away by the campaigning. I did not understand how powerful the feeling was at the time. It meant quite a lot to be involved from the beginning with the men who ran the campaign, such as Stu Eizenstat, who was in charge of domestic affairs and the economy, Jerry Rafshoon, who was the media man, and of course Ham Jordan, Jody Powell, Bobby Lipshutz and the rest of the staff.

What meant the most to me was that I accomplished what I set out to do: to talk about the candidate. I did it like I do many things — wholeheartedly and sincerely — because I believe in them. I thought he was the right man to be the president. "What a feeling this is," I said to myself, "and what a great achievement. What else can a person do? How much more can I ask for in this life?" Little did I realize what kind of power the president of the United States has. I did not know what it meant to know the president. When I campaigned, I did not do it for any reward or expectation of anything. I did not know what happens at the end if you help elect a president. I was a novice. It did not occur to me that the normal way in politics is to pay back certain favors to make people happy. I did not think about getting anything like a post in the White House. I did not deserve that. There were people more capable of political appointments than I. It was a fantasy that never entered my mind. Being rewarded for doing something I believed in did not occur to me, that is, until the party on election night.

Jimmy Carter's election night party was held in the main exhibition room of the World Congress Center in Atlanta, near the Omni Hotel. It was November 3, 1976. I was in the VIP room at the hotel, and every half-hour or so we went down to the big room to find out the latest tallies. The press room was buzzing with people from all over the world. It was very exciting. The atmosphere around the inner circle was festive from the beginning of the evening. "Of course he's going to make it," Jerry Rafshoon said. "He's going to be our next president." He was sure beyond a doubt and his excitement was reflected by the rest of the people. Still, they all knew that we had to wait for the final results before we could make an announcement. It was to be a very long night.

Early in the evening I was sitting in the VIP room and Charlie Harris walked in. Charlie was a very close friend of Carter's from way back. He owned a department store in Ocilla, Georgia, not far from Plains. He came up to me and we talked about the campaign and about how rewarding all the hard work had been. Then, out of the clear blue, he asked me a question I could not have anticipated. "How would you like to sing 'The Star Spangled Banner' at the inauguration?" Just like that.

I was shocked. "I would love to if he wins," I said. It was still early, not yet ten o'clock, and I was not even thinking past the governor's victory. "I would love to. It would be the greatest honor."

"Consider it done. I'm going to the governor's room now, and we'll discuss it," and he left the room without another word.

At about four in the morning the last state came in for us. It was Mississippi and it put us over the top in electoral votes. It was a very close election. Despite the hour, thousands of people filled the big hall in anticipation of Governor Carter's announcement. Everybody who had anything to do with the campaign was pushing to get on the stage. There was laughing and crying, happiness and lots of tears. As the state troopers blocked off a path to the stage to allow the president-elect to enter, Jerry Rafshoon stood next to me applauding and cheering. Suddenly, he saw his mother standing a few feet away and he grabbed her and hugged her and cried, "Mama! We made it! We made it! Thank God we made it." They were crying on each other's shoulders and I started to cry. It was very moving to realize that after working for almost three years, we had really accomplished something. This was not just making a good deal or doing good business. We helped elect a president. It really hit me then, and I realized that we had elected not just a president of the United States, but a president of the "free world." I was consumed with enthusiasm over his victory. I worked for him, I gave him the Jewish vote in

Ohio, maybe even the whole state, and he won!

The next day I went to the headquarters at Colony Square to see what was going on. They were organizing a transition team, and people were filling out applications to be part of the team and the new administration. These people were not just workers — they were really involved. Politics can suck you in like a vacuum and once in, the excitement is as contagious as a virus. I think it is the most exciting thing a person can do. It is a powerful feeling, but it is not the search for power that is rewarding for me. I never thought of, nor was I interested in, being part of government in that way and I did not fill out an application. I neither wanted nor expected a job in Washington. I already had a job, and simply involved myself in the campaign as a gesture of my commitment to Jimmy Carter. I was not interested in the politicking that I was starting to see with people competing for the attention of those in charge of the new administration.

My prime political concern came out of the *mikvah* politics of the old country. Through all the hand mapping and arguments of the old Jews in the *mikvah,* there was always only one consideration: would it be good for the Jewish people? My commitment to the Carter campaign was because I knew that he would be good for Israel, first and foremost, and of course good for the country. We needed someone to lift this country up from its political ills, especially after Watergate and Vietnam. We were not trusted in the world. Jimmy Carter has qualities I admire — rare virtues that are hard to find in human beings. He is the most humble person I have ever met. That alone meant to me that he would be good for the country because he was not out for his own gain; he was for the success of the country. It was a domino effect for me, that if he is good for the country, and the United States is good for Israel, then he would be good for Israel and subsequently the Jewish people. I felt that his humility could bring about a rebirth of the old democracy in America, the one envisioned by the Declaration of Independence and the Constitution.

Naturally I was available to the team for anything I could help them with, but my main concern now was the outcome of my conversation with Charlie Harris. It was later in November when I got a telephone call one Friday afternoon from Bob Lipshutz. He said, "Isaac, I can notify you that you are going to sing 'The Star Spangled Banner' at the inauguration.

It is still unofficial, but you will be notified."

I had some minor surgery earlier that week and I was still recuperating. I wanted to dance or jump or scream. I could not dance or jump because it hurt so much, so I screamed to Betty, "Guess what!" Tears were streaming down my face when I told her. It touched me so. I called a few friends and told them. Early the following week I received a letter stamped "The Congress of the United States." It was from Senator Howard Cannon of Nevada, who was the chairman of the Joint Committee on Inaugural Ceremonies. I opened the letter and read the first line:

Dear Cantor Goodfriend,

On behalf of the Joint Congressional Committee on Inaugural Ceremonies, it is our honor to invite you to sing the National Anthem at the Inauguration of President-elect Jimmy Carter and Vice-President-elect Walter F. Mondale....

I could not continue. I broke down and cried like a baby. There were so many things, so many thoughts flooding in: "Me? Why me? It's a dream. I must be dreaming." I was overwhelmed with emotion. I was not even thinking about the singing, the practicing or the preparing; the doing of it was the farthest thing from my mind. I took a deep breath and said to myself, "Alright. You've shed your tears. You're happy. Now pull yourself together and do what needs to be done."

The first thing I did was telephone my children to share the news with them. Perry was in Israel, Enoch in Miami and Mark was in Houston. Everybody was so excited. Then the events took on a life of their own. Within a couple of days I was getting calls from radio and television stations, from UPI and AP, from the *Washington Post* and the *New York Times*, and of course from the Jewish Telegraph Agency. They all wanted a little background on me, to know who I was to be the first cantor ever to sing at an inauguration. I became a celebrity overnight.

What did not occur to me at first was that I was to be the only Jewish person participating in the inaugural ceremony itself. In the past rabbis had sometimes been asked to participate by giving either the invocation or the benediction, but this time I was the sole Jewish representative. I received hundreds of letters from all over the world commending me and congratulating me. Still, there were some that felt a cantor singing the National Anthem does not represent the Jewish community. There were even editorial letters from rabbis in the Atlanta papers saying that my participation was not right and did not represent them as American Jews. They felt that it did not indicate any kind of religious inclusion on the part of President-elect Carter. Well, people will say what they have to say. It did not bother me. Besides, I had plenty of supporters to fight that battle so I did not have to. Most understood that it was an honor bestowed "at the request of the President-elect," as the letter said. To my supporters, it was the finest gesture Jimmy Carter could have made to a man who had worked hard for him. I realized he was thanking me for what I did for the campaign. After all, would he really have looked for a cantor to sing "The Star Spangled Banner" regardless? Of course not. It was rewarding. It was a sign of appreciation.

Looking back on my life, what else is there for me to appreciate? I am a Holocaust survivor. It will always be a part of my life. I was born in a little *shtetl* in Eastern Europe. I lost my home. I lost my parents. I lost my brothers and sisters. I am a man who somehow managed to build a bridge between two distinct lives: the ashes from whence I came and the heights to which I soared. I achieved the greatest honors a man with my life can achieve. If a cantor can reach a professional zenith within the confines of the liturgy and music of Jewish culture, then I did not do too badly. If he is able to reach a personal zenith, a high point as a person, from which you never come down, a point reached without money and wealth but with commitment and conviction, then I feel I have reached the top. The inauguration ceremony is the highlight of my life. Twenty-five years later, I am still the cantor who was invited to sing at Jimmy Carter's inauguration. It is part of American history, part of something my children and grandchildren can look at and be proud of.

Still, there is a limit to where I can go as a survivor. I am not talking about my profession or my achievements. I am talking about where life ends, for whatever a man achieves, his life is sure to end. So I say to myself, "What have I done? What have I accomplished? Yes, I've achieved something historic, but what kind of legacy am I really leaving my children, my family, my community?" And it comes back. The fog of accomplishment lifts and the memories come flooding back, of a time when everything was dark and everything was bleak and when we said that there was no way out. How many times was I exposed to death? How many? There was the time the Germans chased my friend and me with the motorcycle, put us against a wall and put a gun to our heads. There was the incident when I broke down the chimney and nearly got sent away to the Gestapo. There was the Russian major in Piotrokow after the war who would have shot me as a spy, had the old woman not been walking by. Who was watching over me when I jumped the fence and six guards walked by and did not look up to see me? Who was it that had the Polish girl smile at me and say, "Go with Godspeed?" My life could have ended sixty years ago and that would have been the end of any legacy. I would have become another number, a part of a martyred multitude of six million. Am I special? I do not consider myself special.

But God gave me a chance; He gave me life. He gave me another sixty or seventy years, and this is who I am. I have achieved one thing, and that is I am finally at peace with myself because I did what I was supposed to do. I do not know if somebody in my place would have done the same things I did. My legacy was thrust upon me through evolving episodes and historic events. I have done something and I can call it an accomplishment. Whether it was my commitment to Zionism as an active president of the Zionist Organization of America in Atlanta, or my work on the Presidential Commission on the Holocaust and the establishing of the United States Holocaust Memorial Museum, or even my time in the spotlight as the cantor who sang the National Anthem at Jimmy Carter's inauguration, I lived life the way I knew, the way I felt was right. I feel satisfied that I am leaving a legacy for my children and for the Jewish people.

I involved myself in many organizations because I feel that every group adds a little bit of culture to the community. There are people who say that a community can be over-organized. In my opinion, these are people who are sick and tired of working. If you set a goal for yourself and say, "Well, I'm going to work for this organization. I believe in it and I am going to commit myself," then of course that commits you to the organization. That leads you to get involved with other organizations. That is the way it was for me.

It is true that at times my commitment to do things for others — that I thought no one else would do — took me away from my family, but they know better than I did what drives me to commit myself to these things. They remember the stories I have told them of my father and my mother and a way of life that blew away with the ashes of the Holocaust. Now my children are doing things that we should have done when the war ended, but we could not. They have met with other children of survivors and organized, picking up the pieces and helping to put the events in historical perspective. That is what they feel must be done in order to understand the impact and importance of this difficult and painful legacy. For me, I realize now how short life is and how much there is left to accomplish. I have to talk fast, and quickly tell future generations while I still have the breath to do so.

EPILOGUE

Whenever I have the opportunity to speak about my experiences during the war, I always describe those events as a bad dream, as a confusing nightmare that never goes away. It will never end as long as I live. After I left Poland in 1945, I vowed never to return. Yet, I found myself violating this promise when I traveled to Poland in 1979 during a fact-finding mission to Eastern Europe as part of the United States Holocaust Commission, under the leadership of the chairman, Elie Weisel. It was the first time I had been there since the end of the war.

As our plane began its descent into Warsaw, I felt I was descending into the infinite, to the bottom of the inferno. Memories were piling upon memories, forming a cluster of entangled webs representing my past. Winding its way through my thoughts was an odd question, "Who of my family will welcome me at this airport? Who will be impatiently waiting at the other end of Polish customs to greet me?" The answer was no one. The people I spoke to thirty-seven years earlier and the voices I still thought of every day were now barely echoes.

Stepping off the plane, with the clouds, the drizzle and the fog creeping toward me from the horizon, I felt as if I were creating another dream. Each raindrop encouraged me in my dream making. When I saw the face of Benjamin Meed, a survivor of Warsaw and advisor to the commission, a friendly face in this fog, I was puzzled. What was he doing in this God-forsaken country, where the soil is soaked with the blood of our dear ones? Or is it he who will greet me in the name of the Jews who should be there, the ones whose echoes I can hardly recall? For that moment, my mind stopped functioning. "Oh God," I began to pray, "Please give me the strength as you have in the past, so that I may continue with my thoughts and with a clear mind absorb what has been happening around me." I saw the faces of the other members of the commission but not quite clearly. I kept flashing back to the more familiar faces that belonged in this country, in this place.

It was not until we walked up the steps to the Warsaw Ghetto Memorial that I realized we were being stared at by the stern faces on this impressive monument. They seemed to say, "We are glad that you did not forget us. We are glad to greet you. Sorry! We are the only remnant of this once-vibrant Jewish community. Keep telling the world! Don't be silent! Don't be ashamed! We did what was necessary to bring honor and dignity to our people during total annihilation. If you wish, you can call us the modern Maccabees, the Bar Kochbas, the Masadas."

I wanted to scream but nothing came out. Even the one word "why" could not come out of my mouth. I guess because there are so many why's: Why am I here? Why was my fate different than theirs? Or, is it because they sacrificed their lives that I am alive? If so, then there is no reason for me to recite the *Kayl Mole Rachamim*, the liturgical dirge that remembers the souls who have gone; a different prayer, a song of praise and exultation that pays tribute to our heroes may have been more appropriate. But tradition bids that we remember our martyrs, never to forget what the Amalekites, both old and in modern times, did to our people. So, with a head bowed in reverence, I recited the memorial prayer on Polish soil in front of the monument's bronze witnesses, their kind eyes indicating their approval.

I will always remember that moment, when every word of the prayer had so many meanings — so different than the usual interpretations of this common funeral prayer. With every word my concentration moved to another thought, with each phrase my mind cascaded down a chain of memories. During the Mourners' Kaddish that followed, I suddenly heard the voice of the great scholar Reb Levi Yitzchak of Berditchev as he called God to a challenge in his great work, the *Din Torah*, "Let us all cry out, 'What do you have against your people? We shall not move from this place until you promise to watch over us.'" And the Kaddish droned on: *yisgadal v'yiskadash shimei robbah....*

At Mila 18, the last stronghold of the Jews during the Warsaw Ghetto Uprising, a lonely stone on a mound marked the place where Jewish fighters fought their last battle to glorify and sanctify the eternity of our people. I heard a song come out of my throat:

"I came to you Warsaw from a faraway place;
Numb and sad, I am standing here.
I have traveled by sea and by air
To find my father and my mother somewhere.
Alas, to my dismay, I have found no one here."

With the ceremonies complete, I was about to venture on a journey that I had waited thirty-five years to take — to return to Piotrokow and visit Stanislaw Wypych, Marcinkowskis' nephew, who had saved me. I did not dare to go alone, so I invited five people to come with me. As the taxi passed the old familiar cities such as Tomaszow and Rava, each place brought back memories of the family that used to live there. Now these towns are only names. There is no more family; there are no more Jews.

As we approached Piotrokow, I started to have the same feelings as I did when arriving in Warsaw — there would be no one there to greet me. In Piotrokow, though, I was surrounded with the familiar. The streets were the same — they had the same names — yet they were not the same. We turned on to the *Yidden gass*, where the ghetto fence once wound. I closed my eyes and asked the cab driver to make a right turn. I asked him if it was the Peretz Gass. "Yes," he said, "it is." Then I asked him to go very slowly, and still with my eyes closed I said, "You will come to an open square called Plac Zamkovy."

"Yes," he said, "here we are." I asked God to give me the strength to be able to withstand the rush of emotion I was feeling. I opened my eyes and there it was: my grandparents' house that for a time had been my home, too. I carefully scanned the outside. It was the same gate, the same balcony where I sat as a child and played. It was the place where the sound of learning always permeated the walls and spilled onto the quiet streets outside. Even now I could hear the same sounds in my ears — a passage of Talmud, a portion of Torah. I wanted so much for my dreaming to continue, for the flood of memories to somehow be real, as if nothing had happened. There I am, waiting my turn to be tested by my grandfather on what I have learned. It was then that I remembered the last time I heard from my grandfather, when he was in the synagogue with my mother and baby brother and sister, waiting to die with the rest of the 162 who were murdered.

I left the cab and walked through the courtyard of the apartment building toward the old *shul*. It looked the same from the outside. The Communists had turned it into a library. I must have been mad to even think of going in. I gathered my courage and entered. The washbasin was not there, and neither were the traditional prayers on the wall. The doors to the old sanctuary were bricked over. I rushed through the corridors trying in vain to find the entrance, my heart beating faster every second. Every door I opened was an office, staffed by the bewildered faces of the people who worked in the library. I was afraid to ask, "Where is the sanctuary?" They would not know. They would not understand what I was asking. I climbed the stairs to the balcony, to what used to be the *veiber shul*, the part of the sanctuary where the women sat. I was standing in the reading room of the library. The librarian asked us to sit down and read something, but my eyes were on the ceiling that once held the beautiful symbols of the twelve tribes, now covered over with cheap, white paint. As I tried to trace the old design in the ceiling, I heard again the sounds of the *hazzan*, Reb Baruch Kamenetsky, with his beautiful choir. But there was only an empty ceiling and a quiet library. I had to leave — I had to find the people who were not there, who were supposed to be at the airport, in the house, at the *shul*. So I went to the cemetery.

The last time I had been in the Piotrokow cemetery was when my father died in June 1941. I never had a chance to put up a tombstone. With that in mind, I moved toward the cemetery gates. I was not walking — I was being carried by unknown forces that taunted me, "Is this where Jacob wrestled with the Angel?" they asked me. "I dare you to find the graves of your loved ones in this place."

"But," I said, "they are all my loved ones — every one of them. We lived and suffered together as one; we belong together."

I looked up and found myself standing at the mass grave of the 162 martyrs who died at the synagogue. Placing my hand on the grave, I was speechless. Even in trying to pray, nothing came out of my mouth. Yet there was so much I wanted to say. After all, I owed them thirty-seven years of prayers, thirty-seven *yahrtzeits*, for the years when I never visited their graves. All I could manage to say was, "Please forgive me, for so many things. I feel guilty. I did not do enough. It is too late for revenge, but I promise, as long as I am alive on this earth, I will try in my humble way to work for a better world and better understanding between people. I swear that I will keep on reminding the world that what happened to you shall not ever happen again." Then, as I stood there reciting the Kaddish, I emphasized each word for a member of my family I had lost. I ran out of words.

With the sun setting, I went to visit the family that had saved me. When I saw Stanislaw, I embraced him. My initial reaction was one of gratitude to a man who had risked his own life to save me. "Hold me tighter," he said, and we communicated through silence and memories and tears. My apprehensions subsided in his embrace.

We sat and reminisced. In his plain, wise and unsophisticated way, my rescuer said something that will always be with me. "You say I saved nine Jewish lives. You are wrong. Maybe thirty, forty or even fifty. You all have families now, children and grandchildren. I am not saying that for honor or recognition of what I did. I did it because of human decency. We, the Polish people, could have saved more Jews if we had more concern for our fellow men. We are all God's children."

GLOSSARY

Aliya (ah-LEE-yah) n. — the honor of being called up to recite the blessings during segments of the Torah reading whenever it is read at a prayer service; immigration to Palestine or Israel

Balehbus (BA-le-BUSS) n. — a responsible man who creates a comfortable home for his family and his guests

Baale-bussteh (BA-le BUS-te) n. — a caring and responsible homemaker, wife and mother who creates a comfortable home for her family and her guests

Ba'al Tefila (BA-al teh-FEE-la) n. — one who leads a prayer service

Cheder (KHAY-dir) n. — the traditional beginning religious classroom for religious Jews in Eastern Europe

Chometz (KHAW-mayts) n. — anything containing a leavening or rising agent that is forbidden to eat during Passover

Chumash (KHU-mash) n. — the Five Books of Moses

Farblunjen (fahr-BLUN-jen) adj.; *Farblunjet* adv. — lit. lost; used to describe those who have lost their way in Judaism

Goy, Goyim (Goy, GOY-yeem) n. — gentile, gentiles

Gribbenes (GRI-benes) n. — a delicacy of small pieces of onions and chicken or goose skin fried in chicken fat until well done

Kaddish (KAH-dish) n. — an old Aramaic prayer of praise for God which appears in various forms in the Jewish liturgy; commonly refers to the form of the prayer used by mourners

Kavana (ka-VAW-neh) n. — the deeply personal meaning with which a prayer is said or a deed is conducted that brings one closer to God

Kiddush (KI-dish) n. — prayer said over wine during Sabbath and holidays

Landsmen, Landsleit (LAHNDS-men, LAND-slait) n. — countryman, countrymen; can also refer to people from the same town

Maccabees (MAK-uh-beez) n. — the leading band of a Judean revolt over the Assyrians

Macher (MAH-kher) n. — derogatory term for a big shot who used people for personal gain

Maftir (MAF-teer) n. — the final aliya for the last section of the weekly Torah portion

Mayven, Mevinim (MAY-vin, meh-VEE-neem) n. — expert, experts; lit. those who understand

Mechitsa (meh-KHEE-tsa) n. — a divider, usually a curtain or wall that separates men from women during religious services

Midos (MEE-dos) n. — virtues, as qualities of a belief system

Mikvah (MIK-vah) n. — a ritual bath

Minyan (MIN-yen) n. — a group of at least ten men over Bar Mitzvah age necessary to complete the liturgy of Jewish prayer services

Nigun, Nigunim (NI-goon, ni-GOO-neem) n. — wordless melody or melodies, usually sung a capella

Orchim (OR-kheem) n. — guests, often used when referring to those invited for a Sabbath or festival meal

Pesach (PEH-sakh) n. — Passover

Pogrom (paw-GRUM) n. — a racially motivated violent attack by one group of people on another

Purim (POO-rim) n. — the holiday celebrating the accounts in the Book of Esther

Peyes (PAY-us) n. — the side locks or curls worn by orthodox and ultra-orthodox Jews

Shabbesdig (SHA-bis-dig) adj. — worthy of the Sabbath; having the qualities associated with the holy Sabbath

Sheitl (SHAY-t'l) n. — a wig worn by married, religious Jewish women to cover up their hair out of modesty

Shirayim (shee-RA-yim) n. — those morsels of food blessed by the rebbe after he has tasted the food; leftovers

Shiva (SHI-va) n. — the week-long mourning period following the death of a close family member

Shloshim (SHLOE-sheem) n. — the thirty-day mourning rituals after a person has passed

Shtetl (SHTET-il) n. — any one of hundreds of small Jewish towns prevalent in Eastern Europe in the last three hundred years of the second millennium

Shtiebel (SHTEE-bil) n. — a small house of prayer, or the small congregation that makes up such a house

Shul (shool) n. — a synagogue or any Jewish house of prayer

Siddur (SI-der) n. — prayer book

Tallis (TAH-lis) n. — a Jewish prayer shawl

Tefillin (teh-FIL-in) n. — leather boxes, containing certain declarations of faith, worn by Jewish men on their arms and foreheads; also called phylacteries

Tish zitser (TISH ZI-tser) n. — lit. table sitter; one who has the honor of sitting at a Hasidic rebbe's table for meals

Tsoris (TSAW-riss) n. — problems; troubles; aggravation

Tzedakah (tse-DAW-ke) n. — charity

Tzitzis (TSI-tsis) n. — a four-cornered, fringed tunic worn by religious boys and men according to Biblical law; literally the fringes themselves, which also appear on the corners of a tallis

Yartzeit (YAR-tseit) n. — the anniversary of a death, when certain prayers are said

Yontif (YUN-tif) n. — literally a "good day," meaning any Jewish holiday

Z'miros (zeh-MEE-ros) n. — traditional Sabbath table songs

ACKNOWLEDGMENTS

The stories I retell here were, for the most part, recorded in a series of interviews I did in 1979 and 1980 with my dear friend, Kaethe Solomon, as the interviewer. I am deeply indebted to her for her friendship and encouragement, and to another friend, Phyllis Arnold, who took on the task of transcribing the more than fifty hours of tape. Without them, these stories would be only memories.

In addition to the contributions of Kaethe and Phyllis to this project, I want to thank my son Perry for his untiring assistance in bringing this book to fruition, and I thank my wife Betty and my children for their support. I am especially indebted to my friends Gilbert and Lee Bachman for their generosity in making sure this book was published. I deeply appreciate their assistance. Finally, you would not be reading this book without the genuine efforts of Barbara Kaufman, Tysie Whitman and the staff at Longstreet Press. Above all, I thank the Almighty for keeping me alive and enabling me to share my story.